Efficiency, Equality and Public Policy

Also by Yew-Kwang Ng

INCREASING RETURNS AND ECONOMIC ANALYSIS (*editor with K. Arrow and X. Yang*)

MESOECONOMICS: A MICRO–MACRO ANALYSIS

SOCIAL WELFARE AND ECONOMIC POLICY

SPECIALIZATION AND ECONOMIC ORGANIZATION (*with X. Yang*)

WELFARE ECONOMICS

Efficiency, Equality and Public Policy

With a Case for Higher Public Spending

Yew-Kwang Ng
Professor of Economics
Monash University
Victoria
Australia

First published in Great Britain 2000 by
MACMILLAN PRESS LTD
Houndmills, Basingstoke, Hampshire RG21 6XS and London
Companies and representatives throughout the world

A catalogue record for this book is available from the British Library.

ISBN 0–333–67165–1

First published in the United States of America 2000 by
ST. MARTIN'S PRESS, INC.,
Scholarly and Reference Division,
175 Fifth Avenue, New York, N.Y. 10010

ISBN 0–312–23208–X

Library of Congress Cataloging-in-Publication Data
Ng, Yew-Kwang.
Efficiency, equality and public policy : with a case for higher public spending /
Yew-Kwang Ng.
p.   cm.
Includes bibliographical references and index.
ISBN 0–312–23208–X
1. Policy sciences. 2. Economic policy. 3. Expenditures, Public—Decision mak-
ing. I. Title.
H97 .N5   2000
338.9—dc21
                                                                99–056733

This book is printed on paper suitable for recycling and made from fully managed and sustained
forest sources.

10   9   8   7   6   5   4   3   2   1
09   08   07   06   05   04   03   02   01   00

Printed and bound in Great Britain by
Antony Rowe Ltd, Chippenham, Wiltshire

To
Siang, Aline, Eve, and Tess

Contents

Preface

This book addresses some important and fundamental problems of public policy, arriving at remarkable and controversial conclusions. For example, it is argued that pure efficiency ('a dollar is a dollar') should rule in any specific issues, leaving the objective of equality to the general tax/transfer system. While redistribution through the tax/transfer system may generate substantial disincentive effects, doing so through specific measures like taxing/subsidising goods consumed disproportionately by the rich/poor also has the same degree of disincentive effects in accordance to its redistributive effects. In addition, the latter measure has additional distortive effects and hence is inferior. I arrived at this principle of 'a dollar is a dollar' in my attempt to prove it wrong. A strong case for higher public spending, especially on research and environmental protection is also made. Despite some inefficiency in public spending, higher public spending is likely to be more welfare-improving than private spending. In countries that are no longer poor, further increases in private consumption fail to increase happiness. The small consumption effect may be more than offset by the negative environment disruption effect. People still engage in the rat race for making more money mainly due to competition and the related relative-income effects. Subjective well-being and objective quality-of-life indicators correlate more with the increase in knowledge at the global level than with income per capita. Public spending on research and environmental protection undertaken by national governments is much lower than optimal, partly because of the global and long-term nature of these items. (A more detailed introduction and summary is contained in Chapter 1.)

Elizabeth Kwok wordprocessed this book and purged the manuscript of many mistakes and inconsistencies. Her patience and efficiency are gratefully acknowledged. Tina Bell, Kate Orchard and other students in my Welfare Economics class made useful presentational suggestions.

1
Introduction

1.1 A dollar is a dollar: a simple solution to the big efficiency–equality tradeoff

As emphasised in the title of Okun's (1975) book, efficiency versus equality is the big tradeoff in public policy. It is probably the most important problem in the foundation of public economic policy. It appears in almost all fields of public economic policy. Yet, according to my argument explained in this book, it should basically only be confined to one area of public policy – the general tax/transfer system – though it remains an important problem. In all other areas, efficiency (the principle of 'a dollar is a dollar') should be allowed exclusive reign. This provides the most efficient method of achieving whatever degree of equality is aimed at, or whatever value of tradeoff allowed for. If accepted, my proposal leads to a tremendous simplification in the formulation of public policy in general and in cost–benefit analysis in particular. Thus, no economist, at least no economist concerned with policy issues, can afford to ignore this argument.

Before tackling the big efficiency–equality tradeoff, even more basic issues on the appropriate ultimate objectives of public policy are first discussed, as outlined in Section 1.3.

1.2 A partial resurrection of the old 'new welfare economics'?

The old welfare economists (represented by Pigou, 1912/1932) assumed cardinal utility and interpersonal comparability of utility. The 'new' welfare economists tried to dispense with both, but the attempt proved unsuccessful (Suzumura, 1997). For example, the debate on compensa-

1

tion tests or welfare criteria in the 1940s and 1950s ended with the ambivalent attitude towards the Little (1949, 1957) criterion. Though I strongly defended (in Ng, 1979/1983, Chapter 3) the acceptability of Little's criterion (compensation test plus a distributional proviso), it gives no answers to many cases and its distributional part requires interpersonal comparison of cardinal utility. Thus, in its attempt to get rid of cardinal utility and interpersonal comparison, the new welfare economics failed.

In this book, I argue that interpersonal comparison of cardinal utility is necessary for making social choice. However, my proposal for tackling the efficiency–equality tradeoff by treating a dollar as a dollar whomsoever it goes to at every specific issue, leaving the pursuit of equality to the general tax/transfer system means that cardinal utility and interpersonal comparison are not needed except in determining the optimal tradeoff between efficiency and equality in the general tax/transfer system. Thus, in this sense, the objective of new welfare economics in doing away with cardinal utility and interpersonal comparison may be said to be largely (but not completely) met in our proposal.

1.3 Introductory summary

An economic problem is typically the maximisation of the relevant objective subject to certain constraints. This is true both for an individual economic actor (consumer, worker, firm) as well as for the whole society or the government. However, for the former, the relevant objective is usually less controversial; the individual actor can decide whatever objective she wants to maximise, though her decision may be affected by legal, moral and social factors. For the case of the society, what the objective should be is a heavily debated (not only by economists but also by philosophers, political scientists, politicians, religious leaders, and persons in the street) but apparently unsettled issue.

The first objective of this book is to provide a compelling argument that the ultimate social objective should be the maximisation of the unweighted sum of individual cardinal utilities. (Here, we have largely abstracted away complications of non-human sentients, national boundaries, and variable sets of people, problems which I have dealt with in Ng, 1983, 1989a, 1995.) Chapter 2 argues that the beliefs of (apparently) the majority of economists on the sufficiency of ordinal utilities and the impossibility of interpersonal utility comparison are certainly mistaken. Chapter 3 argues that the social objective or social welfare should depend ultimately only on individual utilities (welfarism). Chapter 4 argues that, where individual utility (representing her preference) and individual welfare (representing her happiness) differ, happiness should be the ultimate concern. (Where I continue to use 'utility', it is partly due to its more popular usage, partly to the presumption of no divergence, and partly to distinguish it from 'social welfare' more clearly.) Chapter 5 argues that social welfare should be an unweighted sum of individual cardinal utilities/welfares (utilitarianism). Rational individualistic egalitarianism alone is sufficient to yield utilitarianism. Harsanyi's (1953, 1955) arguments for utilitarianism are defended against their recent critics and utilitarianism is defended against the criticism that it ignores process fairness.

While interpersonal comparison of cardinal utilities is necessary for social choice, it is in practice very difficult to obtain these utility indices and to compare them interpersonally. A simple method to largely solve this dilemma is proposed in Chapter 6. Basically, the willingness to pay is used to reveal individual intensities of preference and the unweighted sum of these figures ('a dollar is a dollar') is used as the criterion in order to achieve efficiency, leaving the objective of equality to be tackled in the general tax/transfer system where interpersonal comparison of cardinal utility is still needed to achieve a rough trade-off (between efficiency and equality). This achieves a tremendous simplification in the formulation of public economic policy in general and in cost–benefit analysis in particular. This principle of 'a dollar is a dollar' is consistent with the utilitarian objective but utilitarianism is not necessary for the principle. This principle can be based just on the normal Pareto principle. If my argument is correct, anyone accepting the Pareto principle must accept the principle of 'a dollar is a dollar'. This rules out specific purely equality-oriented policies such as the use of distributional weights in cost–benefit analysis, subsidies/taxes on goods consumed mainly by the poor/rich, the first-come-first-served method for car parking spaces to provide 'equal access' in city-centre parking, etc. However, it does not rule out measures based on efficiency considerations such as external effects, second-best factors, etc. For example, subsidies on education and health care may be justified on the grounds of external benefits but not on the ground of equality. It is not in favour of more or less equality. Rather, for any degree of equality aimed at, it is more efficient (in the Pareto sense) to achieve it by adopting the principle of 'a dollar is a dollar' and using the appropriate degree of progressivity in the tax/transfer system.

The basic argument for 'a dollar is a dollar' is this. The objective of equality is more efficiently achieved by the general tax/transfer system since specific purely equality-oriented policies impose additional inefficiency by distorting specific choices. It is true that the general tax/ transfer system also involves inefficiency in the form of disincentive effects. However, specific purely equality-oriented policies also possess the same disincentive effects (in addition to the specific distortive effects). Rational individuals take account not only of the tax rates but also the degree of preferential treatment in the expenditure system (including the specific purely equality-oriented policies). For the same degree of equality in real income (utility) achieved, the same degree of disincentive effects applies whether it is achieved by tax/transfer alone or complemented by specific equality-oriented policies. Thus, transferring some of the equality-oriented methods to specific efficiency-inconsistent policies does not reduce the overall degree of disincentive effect, it just adds on the unnecessary distortive costs. It is thus inferior.

My argument in favour of 'a dollar is a dollar' may be regarded as extremely right-wing. However, I can prove that the conclusion was derived by logic, not by ideology. I reached that conclusion starting out from a somewhat left-wing presumption in favour of the poor (I was a strong and active communist supporter as a teenager), while attempting to prove 'a dollar is a dollar' wrong due to the diminishing marginal utility of income, in my lunch-time disagreement with my colleague, Professor Ross Parish. Moreover, 'a dollar is a dollar' is not quite 'right-wing' in comparison to the apparently more outrageous argument made in Chapter 6 (Section 6.3) that economists, *as a group*, should be in favour of a reverse weighting system (counting a dollar to the poor as worth less than a dollar to the rich). That they have not done so is explained by their ignorance of the relevant argument for 'a dollar is a dollar'.

Chapter 7, the last chapter of Part I, argues that the boundary of economics (where dollars rule), especially with politics (where 'one person one vote' applies), is mainly sustained by the general insufficient understanding of economics. With the more widespread understanding of economics, the sphere of economics should gradually expand, as it was in the past.

1.4 A case for higher public spending

Part II discusses the appropriate size of government spending, an issue regarded as *the* central problem in public finance by Feldstein (1997). Contrary to the current world-wide trend towards privatisation and the attempt to reduce or to limit the growth in the size of government, a strong case for higher public spending is made. Both happiness surveys and quality-of-life indicators (discussed in Section 8.5) suggest that higher (real and per capita) incomes are not as important to welfare as the general advance in knowledge at the world level. The latter depends more on government spending, especially on higher education and research, than on private consumption. While absolute incomes are unimportant, relative incomes remain important (if not increasingly so), making people, the rich and the poor alike, still engage in the rat race for making more money. Together with the significant environmental disruptive effects of most consumption and production, this may result in welfare-reducing growth. At higher levels of income, it is likely that a higher proportion of the GNP should be used for public spending to achieve efficiency, as environmental quality and most public goods are not inferior goods. However, the importance of relative-income effects biases people in favour of private spending, making the traditional estimate of the optimal size of public spending an underestimate. Together with the global public goods and long-term nature of environmental quality and most basic research, this makes public spending by myopic national governments well below the optimal level. On top of this, the existence of other taxes with negative excess burdens (or even burden-free taxes, e.g. on diamond goods – goods valued for their values rather than their intrinsic consumption effects) makes the true cost of public spending much less than commonly believed by economists. In addition, Chapter 9 discusses the important argument by Kaplow (1996). Since at least the time of Pigou (1928), virtually all economists (myself included before I read Kaplow) accept the view that the benefits of public goods should exceed their direct costs by an amount sufficient to outweigh the excess burden or distortionary costs of taxation. Kaplow argues that it is optimal to supply a public good whenever the benefit–cost ratio exceeds one. While Kaplow's argument has to be subject to some qualifications, he is basically correct. Large excess burdens may exist on the revenue side but are largely offset by the negative excess burdens or distributional gains on the spending side.

1.5 The misguided consensus

As noted by Amartya Sen (1979, p.537), Wassily Leontief has summarised succinctly the normative properties 'on which something like a general consensus of opinion seems to exist' in the formal discussion of public economic policies:

> In the discussion of public economic policies – the normative character of the problem has been clearly and generally recognized. There the mathematical approach has crystallized the analysis around the axiomatic formulation of the (desirable or conventional) properties of the 'social welfare function'. Social utility is usually postulated as a function of the ordinally described personal utility levels attained by each of the individual members for the society in question.
>
> The only other property on which something like a general consensus of opinion seems to exist is that 'the social welfare is increased whenever at least one of the individual utilities on which it depends is raised while none is reduced'.
>
> Leontief, 1966, p.27

The second property is of course the (strong) *Pareto principle*. The first property is further factorised by Sen into the following three distinct parts:

> (1) *Welfarism*
> Social welfare is a function of personal utility levels, so that any two social states must be ranked entirely on the basis of personal utilities in the respective states (irrespective of the non-utility features of the states).
> (2) *Ordinalism*
> Only the ordinal properties of the individual utility functions are to be used in social welfare judgements.
> (3) *Non-comparable Utilities*
> The social welfare ranking must be independent of the way the utilities of different individuals compare with each other.
>
> Sen, 1979, p.538

Sen then launched a vigorous attack on these four conditions. As usually happens between friends, I agree partly with Sen but disagree with him on the other half of his argument. Thus I wish to defend welfarism and the Pareto principle but to question ordinalism and non-comparability. In fact, the Pareto principle and welfarism are very close to each other. No one accepting welfarism wants social welfare to be decreasing instead of increasing in individual utilities. Thus, with this requirement on positivity, welfarism implies the Pareto principle. On the other hand, the Pareto principle also implies welfarism. If individual utilities are not the only elements affecting social welfare, then someone better off with no one worse off cannot be a sufficient condition for an increase in social welfare, since other factors (unless lexicographically less important than individual utilities) affecting social welfare could decrease substantially to offset this. Thus, ignoring factors less important than 0.000 . . . 1 util, our defence of welfarism in Chapter 3 is also a defence of the Pareto principle.

While ordinalism is sufficient (and hence preferable to cardinalism on the ground of Occam's razor) for the theory of consumer demand, it is certainly insufficient for social choice (Chapter 2). Graduating from cardinalism to ordinalism is a significant methodological advance in consumer theory. Economists, in emphasising this advance, have taught their students to reject cardinalism even in social choice. This is the fallacy of misplaced abstraction (Ng, 1979/1983, pp.13–15). Denying the use of cardinal utility in areas (social choice, optimal population, valuation of life, choices involving risks) where it is useful is like insisting that a person must shave off his moustache on the ground that it is unnecessary for eating, ignoring the fact the he may want to keep it to increase his sex appeal.

1.6 Three basic problems of social choice/public policy

If we regard issues like strategic behaviour, incentive compatibility, mechanism design as advanced topics, we may identify the following three basic social choice or public policy problems.

I. What types of information are relevant and needed in making social choice?

Most economists accept the Fundamental Value Proposition of Individual Preferences (Bergson, 1938), rejecting the existence of a mythical society or state independent of, or over and above the various individuals composing the society, and thus regard the relevant information as individual preferences. This must also be the case if we accept the widely used Pareto Principle. However, as noted above, Sen (1979) calls this welfarism and attacks it as ignoring principles as no-exploitation, no-torture, etc. In Chapter 3, welfarism is defended as compelling if applied at the fundamental level, viewing moral and legal principles as instruments for the promotion of individual welfares.

Arrow's (1951/1963) theorem established the impossibility of a reasonable social choice based on individual ordinal preferences within a multi-profile (or inter-profile) framework where alternative profiles of individual preferences are considered. Kemp and Ng (1976) and Parks (1976) (generalised by Roberts, 1980) show the same impossibility within the single or intra-profile framework where individual preferences are unchanged. Sen (1970a) shows the impossibility of social choice without interpersonal comparison. It is thus well-established that reasonable social choice requires the interpersonal comparison of individual cardinal utilities. This necessity of interpersonal cardinal utilities is explained in non-technical terms in Chapter 2.

II. How can we obtain the required information?

Following from the solution to the first basic problem, the required information is the interpersonally comparable individual cardinal utilities. The problem of how these may be obtained has been largely ignored by social choice theorists and economists in general. However, I have proposed the use of a maximal indifference (akin to Edgeworth's concept of a just perceptible increment of pleasure) as an interpersonally comparable unit of utility and discussed ways of practical measurement (Ng, 1975a, 1996a). I have also shown that the cardinal utility index obtained by using the Neumann–Morgenstern expected utility method is in fact the subjective utility index of the neoclassical economists and hence is a suitable ingredient for normative social choice (Ng, 1984a). Contributions from non-social choice theorists may also help. (See, e.g. van Praag, 1968, 1991; Veenhoven, 1984, 1993.) Nevertheless, a lot more work should be done to answer this second basic question.

III. Which form of social welfare function (SWF) should be adopted?

Even assuming that we agree that the relevant information is interpersonal comparable cardinal utilities and somehow have obtained them, there is still the problem of how these data are to be aggregated to form the social preference or to define the social welfare index. Should the SWF be an unweighted sum of these interpersonally comparable individual cardinal utilities (defined as utilitarianism) or a product or some other form? This third basic problem is answered in Chapter 5 where it is argued that compelling axioms force us to accept utilitarianism. Apparently compelling objections to utilitarianism are shown to be unacceptable.

1.7 Some specific points made

Some other specific points argued in this book include the following:

- More research should be done to perfect the methods of electrical and other forms of brain stimulation (known for nearly half a century) to make them safe for common use to achieve a quantum leap in welfare. (See Appendix A.)
- Higher public spending may be needed if only to raise the remuneration of those working in the public sector to attract top talents back from the private sector. (See Section 8.8.)
- Non-affective altruism (or malice), or altruism in reason rather than in emotion, not only makes it necessary to use individual welfares instead of utilities as what public policies should ultimately be concerned with (Section 4.1), but may also make the otherwise compelling Pareto principle unacceptable in certain cases. (See Appendix D.)

1.8 A methodological note

(General readers may skip this subsection.)
Most of the arguments made in this book are positive. (Substantial normative arguments are also made in Chapters 3 to 5.) However, many specific points made also involve normative judgments, concerning what should be done. For example, the case in favour of higher public spending on research and environmental protection is clearly prescriptive. However, the gulf between positive analysis and normative prescription is not that big if we accept the following convention, as I do for this book and most of my other writings. Whenever some prescriptive/normative statement is made, e.g. public spending should be increased, it means that the prescribed action (e.g. higher public spending under whatever specified conditions) will increase social welfare which is an increasing function of individual utilities/welfares. Usually, this is sufficient (especially in view of the principle of 'a dollar is a dollar'; see Chapter 6). (Where a specific functional form is needed, then the unweighted sum is used, as amply argued for in Chapter 5.) With this convention, an apparently prescriptive statement (X should be done) is made equivalent to a more positive one (X will increase social welfare or X will increase the sum of individual utilities.) Whether it is desirable to increase social welfare so conceived remains a normative issue. (Arguments in its favour are offered in Chapters 3 to 5.) On the cardinal measurability and interpersonal comparability of individ-

ual utilities/welfares, see Chapter 2. With this convention, it means that one may differ with my prescriptive/normative statements due to disagreement with my positive analysis and/or to disagreement with my concept of social welfare. However, with this convention, I cannot be accused of confusing positive analysis with normative judgments. It is elementary (Hume's law) that any prescription must be based on some normative judgments.

It is true that, due to the difficulties of measuring and comparing individual utilities (substantially lessened however by the principle of 'a dollar is a dollar'), many prescriptive statements are not just supported by the above convention and some positive analysis, but also by some subjective judgments of fact. However, as I argued in Ng (1972), economists are more qualified in making those subjective judgments of fact (which are usually confused with value judgements proper) that are closely related to their field of study, than non-economists, though not with respect to value judgments proper. Recognising the distinction between value judgments proper and subjective judgments of fact thus substantially increases the role of economists in policy recommendation.

1.9 What this book is not about

Generally speaking, this book is concerned with the more general issues of public policy at the more fundamental level. Thus, it is concerned with what public policy should ultimately aim at rather than with secondary principles and specific issues. It is concerned with the ultimate ethical foundation of public policy rather than with issues at the practical or political levels. While it discusses the problem of public spending and names some specific areas (research and environmental protection), it is still mainly concerned with the more general and fundamental issues than with specific items and complications of implementation and political feasibility. This does not mean that such issues are regarded as unimportant; rather, they are beyond the scope of this book and also largely beyond the expertise of the author. While issues of feasibility and practical difficulties have to be faced at the stage of actual policy decisions, the issue of basic objectives and fundamental principles remains important and relevant even at the implementation level.

This book avoids unnecessary formalism and technical analysis. Virtually no mathematics is used except in some appendices. While by no means against the use of rigorous mathematical techniques (as I have used them myself), I believe that their use has become excessive and is unnecessary in many cases. Two examples related to the theme here may be given. It is compelling, at the ultimate level, that the desirability of a social state depends only on all its relevant variables or characteristics (rather than that of another social state), due to the exhaustive nature of 'all relevant variables' and the mutually exclusive nature of social states. This makes the pure element of independence a compelling condition. Then, analysis is sufficient by using the concept of a social welfare function (with the social welfare of any social state depending only on variables at that social state) instead of that of a social welfare functional (with the social welfare of any social state depending on the variables of all social states). Though it is formally more general to conduct the analysis in terms of a social welfare functional and then impose the compelling condition of independence, this makes the analysis unnecessarily more complicated and less accessible to people unfamiliar with the complicated technical framework. As another example, when stripped of its technical facade, the essence of the (valid) argument by Roemer (1986, 1996) that resource egalitarianism implies welfare egalitarianism may be seen in a simple diagram (see Appendix B). Thus presented, the rationale for the validity of the argument, the ethical unacceptability of both resource egalitarianism and welfare egalitarianism are all clear. However, I am sympathetic towards Roemer (and others) for their presentation of arguments in complicated mathematics; it is increasingly difficult to publish academic papers *not* using complicated mathematics. If Roemer's argument were originally presented in the transparent form of a simple diagram, it would almost certainly have been rejected by the *Quarterly Journal of Economics*. When formalism has progressed to such a level, a reconsideration is in order. (For a critique of formalism in modern economics, see Blaug, 1998; for a discussion, see Backhouse, 1998; Chick, 1998; Krugman, 1998 and Weintraub, 1998.)

Part I

The Foundation of Public Economic Policy

2
The Necessity of Interpersonal Cardinal Utility

2.1 An intuitive explanation using a parent's choice

Suppose you are a parent having to make certain decisions affecting the well-being of the whole family. Assume that no one else (including animals) other than your family members will be affected by your decisions. You do not hate any of the members and you care about all members. Thus, you believe that your decisions should depend on their (including your own, being a family member yourself) utilities. You also agree that if any one member is made better off with no member made worse off, it is a better situation. In other words, you accept the Pareto principle. This is sufficient for our presupposition. Some readers may object that the Pareto principle may not be sufficient here because, for example, one may want one's children to have the right moral principles and training, and be willing to sacrifice the utility of some members in exchange. In my view, this is due to the favourable effects of the right principles and training on one's future well-being and/or on that of other individuals. I believe most parents accept this. Either including such favourable effects in the calculation or abstracting from these complications here, the Pareto principle should be acceptable to most people. In any case, this issue is discussed in Chapter 3.

In one trivial set of cases, interpersonal (i.e. between family members here) comparison of cardinal utility is not needed for your choice. This is when your decisions always affect the well-being of all your family member in the same direction. If you have only one decision of choosing between x and y and all members are better off in x than in y, then it is clear that you should choose x. Here, adherence to the Pareto principle solves your problem of family choice.

In most cases, conflicts arise in the sense that the choice of one alternative over the other makes some members better off but some other members worse off. It is such cases of conflict that make the problem of social choice of substance and interesting. For simplicity, assume that you and your spouse are always indifferent over the relevant alternatives and hence you choose purely in accordance to the preferences of the children. There is another trivial case where interpersonal comparison of cardinal utility is not needed. If one of the children is your favoured child such that you let him/her choose, ignoring the preference of other children, then your family choice problem is solved by the dictatorial choice of this favoured child. (This is ruled out by Arrow's condition of non-dictatorship.)

You might adopt the simple rule that, for divisible choices, always divide equally between all the children and for indivisible choices, always toss a coin to decide. This may 'work' and appears 'fair'. However, it violates the weak Pareto principle (which says that if all individuals prefer x to y, the society or the family should prefer x to y). For simplicity, take the case of only two children, Jan and Kelvin, and only one divisible good, money, to be allocated. The principle involved is applicable to general cases.

Suppose Jan prefers hot weather if she has enough money ($75) to enable her to go surfing but would rather have cold weather with less money than enduring the heat without surfing. On the other hand, Kelvin prefers cold weather if he has enough money ($75) to go skiing, but would rather have hot weather with less money than watching the snow without being able to ski. Now consider the following four alternatives H1, H2, C1, C2, each pair corresponding to two different distributions of the given $100 in two alternative weather conditions:

H1 = (Jan has $75, Kelvin has $25, Hot weather)
H2 = (Jan has $50, Kelvin has $50, Hot weather)
C1 = (Jan has $25, Kelvin has $75, Cold weather)
C2 = (Jan has $50, Kelvin has $50, Cold weather)

The preference patterns of Jan and Kelvin described above may be illustrated in Figure 2.1 which readers may wish to use for reference. The rule of dividing money equally between Jan and Kelvin means that H2 is (socially) preferred to H1 and C2 is preferred to C1. However, both Jan and Kelvin prefer C1 to H2 and both also prefer H1 to C2. Thus, combining the egalitarian division rule with the weak Pareto principle,

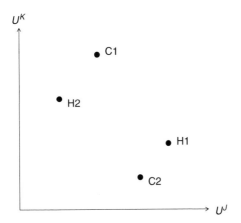

Figure 2.1

we have the following preference cycle: C1 preferred to H2 (weak Pareto), H2 preferred to H1 (egalitarian rule), H1 preferred to C2 (weak Pareto), and C2 preferred to C1 (egalitarian rule). This means that the use of the egalitarian rule violates the weak Pareto principle. This violation may be given the following intuitive explanation.

The preference patterns of Jan and Kelvin mean that money is more important to Jan if the weather is hot, and more important to Kelvin if the weather is cold. Thus, a Pareto-consistent or utility-efficient method of dividing the $100 is to give more money to Jan if the weather is hot and more to Kelvin if the weather is cold, rather than equal division irrespective of the weather. Subject to practical difficulties, a good parent should find out the different needs of the children under different situations and hence be able to satisfy their needs better, rather than just adopt some rigid rules such as equal division or random choice (coin tossing). However, to learn about the different needs requires the interpersonal comparison of cardinal utilities.

2.2 Economists' misplaced hostility against cardinal utility

When I first studied Arrow's impossibility theorem, I quickly attributed the difficulty to the lack of cardinal utilities. (See Ng, 1971. Later, when

I studied Sen, 1970a and DeMeyer and Plott, 1971, I realised the necessity of interpersonal comparison as well.) However, after the ordinalism
revolution in consumer theory, economists are very hostile to cardinal
utilities. A recent textbook example is Varian. (A non-textbook example
is Kolm, 1993.)

> But how do we tell if a person likes one bundle twice as much as
> another? How could you even tell if you like one bundle twice as
> much as another? One could propose various definitions for this kind
> of assignment: I like one bundle twice as much as another if I am
> willing to run twice as far to get it, or to wait twice as long, or to
> gamble for it at twice the odds. . . . Although each of them is a poss-
> ible interpretation of what it means to want one thing twice as much
> as another, none of them appears to be an especially compelling
> interpretation.
>
> Varian, 1993, pp.57–8

There is in fact an interpretation that is especially compelling. This is
whatever the individual concerned values ultimately. If we abstract
away effects on other individuals and sentients, what I ultimately value
is my net happiness (i.e. enjoyment minus suffering, including the sen-
suous as well as the spiritual). On the grounds of evolutionary biology,
daily experience, and interviews, I have reasons to believe that I am not
an exception here but rather quite representative. Since, for myself, it
is ultimately net happiness that I want, it has an especially compelling
interpretation (for cardinal utility).

For most of my sleeping time and much of my time awake, I
am neither enjoying (feeling good) nor suffering (feeling bad). My
happiness is zero over those periods. When I am sick, hurt (bodily
or emotionally), sad, etc. my happiness is negative and the extent
of the negative happiness may differ depending on the intensity of
the pain. When I enjoy myself either sensuously or mentally, my happiness is positive, with again different degrees, as shown in Figure 2.2.
My net happiness (over any period) is the area above the line of
neutrality minus that below. Thus, despite different types of well-being
(poetry versus pushpin), the overall happiness is one-dimensional.
(See also Joseph and Lewis, 1998 on the unidimensionality of happiness. While indirect, external, and long-term effects on oneself and
others complicate measurement, they do not affect the unidimensionality. On a recent discussion of the concept of well-being, see Qizilbash,
1998.)

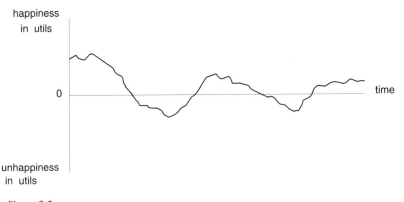

Figure 2.2

I want money but not for its own sake, only to obtain, ultimately, happiness. Thus, I have diminishing marginal happiness of money. For big variations, my willingness to pay twice as much does not indicate twice as much happiness or utility. (The two are the same if we abstract away ignorance, concern for others, and irrational preference. This is so with my definition of irrational preference as preferring something that decreases one's own happiness or welfare, neither due to ignorance nor to a concern for the welfare of others. Utility here is taken as representing preference which can be cardinal. See Chapter 4 for details.) However, as I want happiness for its own sake, if bundle *A* (or anything else) gives me twice as much happiness as bundle *B*, it is perfectly sensible, natural, and informative to say that I prefer (reminding the abstraction of ignorance, etc.) bundle *A* twice as much as bundle *B*.

Even if we re-introduce factors other than personal happiness in the preference function, I have no difficulty (except for imperfect information to be discussed presently) in comparing the intensities of my preference for different pairs of alternatives. Thus, if I take into account the income or welfare levels of others, there is no problem in allowing for that. For the simple case where both my and the only other person's welfare are functions of the log of own income, my preference or utility function could be the log of my income plus alpha times the log of the other person's income, where alpha is a positive number slightly larger than zero. I could also allow for alpha itself to be a function of the income or welfare level of others. It is true that I often have difficulties knowing the intensity of my preference for an alternative over another. This is due to the lack of information (or lack of perfect memory for past events) as to how my and other people's welfare values will be under different alternatives. Given this lack of information, I even have difficulties knowing whether I prefer *A* to *B* or vice versa. Thus, not only are the intensities of preference or cardinal utility made unclear but the ordinal preference or ranking itself is also made unclear. If you put two close enough quantities of water into two containers of different shape, I may have difficulty judging which container has more water. But that does not mean that the volume of water is not a cardinally measurable quantity!

I have also no difficulty saying that my welfare level is positive, zero, or negative. When I am neither enjoying nor suffering, my welfare is zero. Thus, the value of my welfare is a fully cardinal quantity unique up to a proportionate transformation. I am also sure that I am not bestowed by God or evolution to have this special ability of perceiving the full cardinality (both intensity and the origin) of both my welfare and preference levels. In fact, from my daily experience, observation, and conversation, I know that all people (including ordinalist economists) have this ability, except that economists heavily brain-washed by ordinalism deny it despite actually possessing it. This denial is quite incredible. If your preference is really purely ordinal, you can only say that you prefer your present situation (*A*) to that plus an ant bite (*B*) and also prefer the latter to being bodily thrown into a pool of sulphuric acid (*C*). You cannot say that your preference of *A* over *B* is less than your preference of *B* over *C*. Can you believe that? (See also Ng, 1997).

I attempted to show the bias of economists against cardinal utility, at least in comparison to the general public, in a small survey. While the result may be said to confirm my expectation, it is not as clear-cut as I expected. The questionnaire asks four questions.

Question A: 1. Compared to the corresponding period yesterday, my net happiness (i.e. happiness minus unhappiness) for today so far is higher/lower/about the same; 2. by 0%/1–10%/11–30%/31–100%/over 100%.

Question B: 1. Think of a person (other than yourself) whose happiness/unhappiness you know best, and for a period you know best. In comparison to that of a corresponding period for yourself that you can easily compare, is her/his happiness over that period higher/lower/about the same; 2. by 0%//1–10%/11–30%/31–100%/over 100%.

For all questions, respondents are also provided with boxes marked 'cannot answer' and 'this question is meaningless'. I had expected far more economists to regard Question A2 as either unanswerable or meaningless than the general public. The difference is much smaller than I expected. The sample size is 49 for the general public (from shopping and entertainment centres) and 52 for economists, consisting of participants of an econometrics conference (31) and a social choice conference (21). For the general public, 16.3% (8 out of 49) answered either 'cannot answer' or 'meaningless' for Question A2. If we group all economists together, 32% (16 out of 50; 2 did not answer) ticked 'cannot answer' or 'meaningless'. While this is certainly a significant difference, the difference is not as remarkable as I expected. I expected more than half to tick so. On hindsight, it may be said that, the majority of economists still retain the commonsense that happiness is cardinally measurable, despite their professional training to the contrary. I also expected the group from the social choice conference to be more sympathetic to cardinal measurability than the group from the econometrics conference. But there is no significant difference (7 out of 21 and 9 out of 29 respectively).

For the general public, 14.3% (7 out of 49) and 18.75% (9 out of 48) answered either 'cannot answer' or 'meaningless' to Question B1 and B2 respectively. The corresponding figures for economists are 40.4% (21 out of 52) and 51.1% (23 out of 45; 7 did not answer) respectively. Again, there are no significant differences between the two sup-groups of economists. Less than 10% of any group answered 'cannot answer' or 'meaningless' to Question A1.

2.3 The impossibility of social choice based on ordinal utilities

Samuelson (1967, 1977), following Little (1952), rejects the relevance of Arrow's theorem to economics. Essentially, they argue that Arrow's impossibility theorem was proved by requiring some reasonable conditions over alternative sets of individual preferences. While this may be relevant for politics, they argue that it is not relevant for welfare economics. For the latter, we need a SWF for a given set of individual preferences. If the set of individual preferences changes, we have another SWF. By not requiring any consistency or reasonable conditions between the different SWF's corresponding to different sets of individual preferences, Arrow's impossibility result does not apply. Honestly, I am not persuaded by this line of reasoning. As individual preferences change, the social ordering or social choice may change. But why should the rule used to aggregate individual preferences into social choice change? Nevertheless, for my purpose here, I would rather have readers agreeing with Little and Samuelson, as this would increase the importance of the following result that I was involved in proving.

Kemp and Ng (1976) and Parks (1976) show that, even operating within the same set of individual preferences or holding individual preferences unchanged (the so-called single-profile or intra-profile framework), impossibility results may still be proved using compelling conditions, if we have only individual ordinal preferences to base on. This impossibility result was quickly generalised (Hammond, 1976; Pollak, 1979 and Roberts, 1980), establishing the existence of a corresponding (impossibility or possibility) proposition in the single-profile framework for every proposition in the multi-profile or inter-profile (i.e. the original Arrowian) framework. This should seal the fate of ordinalism but Samuelson objected.

Samuelson (1977) argues that an axiom (Anonymity Plus Orderings Only) used by Kemp and Ng is objectionable. Since no one objects to anonymity, the real issue concerns ordinalism. For the general social choice problem, I myself regard ordinalism as unreasonable. However, since the point here is about whether ordinalism is a sufficient basis for the single-profile social choice, the axiom is a natural condition to impose. If Samuelson objects to this axiom, he should not continue to insist on the sufficiency of ordinalism.

Some years after the Kemp–Ng–Samuelson debate, I discussed the problem with Arrow. He said that, if Samuelson insisted on ordinalism, he had to give up independence. I replied that independence is compelling. Later, I realised that independence is really implied in the Bergson–Samuelson tradition of writing social welfare at any social state x as a function of individual utilities at x only. This tradition is all right if we have interpersonally comparable cardinal utilities. However, Samuelson insists that the individual utility indices are only ordinal. This is the crux of the impossibility. (See Appendix E for more detailed argument.)

Despite the necessity of interpersonal comparison of cardinal utilities, the need to make such difficult comparisons may be minimised (but not avoided completely) by using the willingness to pay to reflect the cardinal intensities of preferences. (See Chapter 6.)

3
Welfarism

Welfarism is the belief/principle that social welfare depends (positively) only on individual welfare (or utility) levels. (Abstracting away the differences between utility and welfare, on which see Chapter 4. Questions of animal welfare and national boundary are also ignored.) Most people (including Sen) accept that individual welfares matter but many want to add other desiderata. While one may use any number of secondary instrumental principles, one can only have a single ultimate objective. Given a sufficiently wide domain of choice and sufficient differences in individual preferences, a conflict must arise with multiple ultimate objectives/principles, as exemplified by Sen's (1970b) impossibility of a Paretian liberal. (See also Ng, 1982 on the impossibility of a Paretian X where X is any other principle.)

Partly for its own interest and partly for expositional colour, the issue of the acceptability of welfarism is first discussed in Section 3.1 with reference to my debate with Sen. Two separate arguments for welfarism are then presented in Section 3.2 and Section 3.3.

3.1 The Sen–Ng debate on welfarism: an appraisal

As noted in Section 1.4, Sen (1979) strongly criticises welfarism. Welfarism may be criticised on two different levels. First, owing to lack of complete information about individual welfares, we may wish to base our social decision on the objective information about the various social states or alternatives. On this point, I am in complete agreement with Sen, provided he agrees that this is not an argument against welfarism as such but is rather a consideration of the ways to achieve our objective (even if welfarist) in the absence of perfect information.

For example, suppose we agree (for argument's sake) that we should maximise the SWF of the sum or the product or some other quasi-concave function of individual welfares. If we also have complete information about individual welfares in various social states, what we need to do is just to compare these various sums or products, etc. of individual welfares. However, usually we cannot do just this owing to the lack of information. If we also believe in diminishing marginal welfare of income and similar capacity to enjoy income (or that this capacity is not strongly positively correlated with income and we do not know who has high or low capacity; see Lerner, 1944 and Sen, 1973b), then a certain policy may be regarded as desirable if it increases the incomes of the poor and reduces those of the rich without reducing total income. Then, a consideration that affects our social decision appears to be that of income equality or some similar consideration, among others. Our SWF appears to be a function not only of individual welfares but also of some objective indicators such as the equality of income distribution of social states.[1] But it is clear that we use such objective indicators only as indirect measures or estimates of individual welfares. Thus, far from being a rejection of welfarism, the use of such objective indicators serves to achieve our welfarist objective. Such principles as 'giving priority to the interests of the poor over the interests of the rich' need not be non-welfarist if it is derived from a welfarist SWF plus certain other assumptions such as diminishing marginal welfare of income.

Sen's objection to welfarism is, however, much more fundamental since he 'criticizes welfarism even when utility information is as complete as it can conceivably be' (Sen, 1979, p.547), even with completely cardinal, unique and interpersonally comparable individual welfare indices (which we shall be using here). Basically, Sen believes that we may wish to place value on such principles as liberty, non-exploitation, no-torture, etc. over and above or besides their contribution in promoting individual welfares. Thus, even if two social states are exactly the same with respect to individual welfares, we may prefer the one that adheres to these principles to the one that violates them. For illustration, Sen (1979, p.547) provides the following examples (Sen remains very critical of welfarism along the similar line in his 1997 paper):

Consider a set of three social states, *x*, *y* and *z*, with the following interpersonally comparable cardinal welfare numbers for a two-person community:

	x	*y*	*z*
Person 1's welfare	4	7	7
Person 2's welfare	10	8	8

In *x*, person 2 is eating a great deal of food while person 1 is hungry. In *y*, person 1 consumes a bit more of the given food supply. While 2 is made worse off (in comparison to *x*), 1 is made better off by a larger amount and the sum of welfare becomes larger (with diminishing marginal welfare). It is clear that *y* must be judged to be better than *x* by utilitarianism, and also by virtually all the criteria that have been proposed using data on individual welfares. Let us take *y* to be socially better than *x*.

Consider now *z*. Here person 1 is still as hungry as in *y*, and person 2 is also eating just as much. However, person 1, who is a sadist, is now permitted to torture 2, who – alas – is not a masochist. So person 2 does suffer, but resilient as he is, his suffering is less than the utility gain of the wild-eyed 1. The utility numbers in *z* being exactly the same as in *y*, welfarism requires that if *y* is preferred to *x*, then so must be *z*. But *y* is socially preferred to *x*. So *z* is preferred to *x* as well, thanks to welfarism.

Sen, 1979, pp.547–8

In a footnote, Sen adds: 'It is assumed that there are no indirect consequences of torture, e.g. in attitude formation. These indirect effects do not change the nature of the difficulty, even though they can be properly accommodated only in a much more complex analysis.'

The above argument of Sen against welfarism appears very persuasive. However, it seems to me whether one has to reject welfarism on the grounds of such moral principles as no-torture depends on whether one believes in these principles as his basic value judgements. 'A value judgement can be called "basic" to a person, if the judgement is supposed to apply under all conceivable circumstances, and it is "non-basic" otherwise' (Sen, 1970, p.59).[2] Those whose belief in no-torture is more basic than welfarism must withdraw their commitment to welfarism in circumstances like *z*. But one, like myself, may also believe in no-torture not as a basic value judgement but as derived from a welfarist SWF because one may believe that in practically all circumstances, torture leads, directly and indirectly, to more harm than good. However, most people believe that it is wrong to inflict harm on others even if the pleasure of doing so exceeds the direct and indirect sufferings caused. Thus, it is very tempting to reject welfarism (and utilitarianism, a specific form of welfarism, in particular) at the immediate intuitive level. But as argued by Hare (1976), the rejection of utilitarianism at the immediate intuitive level is consistent with the support for utilitarianism at a deeper 'critical' level.

One may accept a welfarist SWF as their most basic value judgment. It is, however, difficult to do a precise welfare calculation for every decision made. Thus, it is generally desirable to adopt certain rules such as honesty, liberalism, non-exploitation, no-torture, etc. which generally contribute to the promotion of social welfare as defined by the welfarist SWF. In time, these rules become moral principles and tend to be valued for their own sake even to the extent of persuading people to reject the original welfarist SWF. But in my view, this is confusing the more basic value with less basic values. This is like insisting on telling a cruel, dishonest invading army the truth in order to stick to the principles of honesty. However, I am not advocating giving up these moral principles lightly owing to the enormous long-run implications through attitude formation.

Some people may wish to regard certain principles such as freedom from torture as being based on, say, human rights independent of or over and above welfare considerations. However, if one presses oneself hard enough with the question, 'Why human rights?', I believe that one will most likely come up with a welfarist answer. I enjoy walking. But this enjoyment is based on the violation of the 'rights' of stones, sands, etc. for freedom from being stepped upon. So why don't stones have 'stone rights'? Why do we hear about 'human rights', 'animal rights', etc. but not 'stone rights'? An obvious answer is that stones do not feel pleasure and pain. But this is clearly a welfarist answer. It is possible that certain basic human rights are so definitely conducive to the improvement of welfare and the violation of them on the grounds of short-run welfare (or non-welfare) considerations so likely to produce effects very unfavourable to long-run welfare, that the insistence on these human rights on a political or practical level without regard to any welfare consideration becomes defensible. But this does not negate the belief that, on a deeper philosophical level, these rights are ultimately derived from welfare considerations.

Sen believes however that:

> any serious theory of human or civil rights will bring in other [than sentient] aspects of people which also differentiate them from stones. The respect and concern that one person owes another can hardly be seen as a function only of the latter's capacity for pleasure. Indeed,

even after a person dies and obviously has no further capacity for pleasure or pain, right-based considerations *vis-à-vis* him do not all cease to apply, e.g. they are relevant in disposing of his body, or in defending him against vilification.

Sen, 1981, p.534

In my view, such post-mortems 'rights' can be explained by the preferences of living individuals and the effects on future behaviour. For example, living persons may want to show respect for people in general and specific individuals in particular by having proper burial in general and national burial for heroes that, in addition, may encourage heroic behaviour. It is true that people differ from stones in many other aspects. For example, stones and even animals cannot exercise such rights as voting in elections. But I am referring to the more elementary rights of freedom from being unnecessarily hurt (which I believe should apply to all sentients). Moreover, if there exist non-sentient objects (super-machines?) that can 'exercise' certain rights (e.g. voting) operationally, I would treat them no more favourably than stones.

While I maintain my basic defence of welfarism given in Ng (1981a), I am happy to make the following three concessions to Sen. First, though I find welfarism a perfectly defensible principle as an ultimate value judgement, it does not mean that those who attack welfarism must thus be wrong in any logical or scientific sense. Since this concerns questions of basic value beliefs, perfectly rational and logical persons may differ ultimately. On the other hand, this does not mean that such questions cannot be logically discussed or that the discussion is useless. One may logically show which axioms (including some normative ones) imply certain normative principles or which normative principles imply some desirable or undesirable outcomes. In the process, one may persuade opponents to abandon their initial value judgements which they mistakenly believe to be basic but turn out to be non-basic upon critical analysis. (See the appendix of Ng, 1981b, on the use of axiomatic value theories.)

Secondly, I think Sen is right in believing that the consensus of economists on welfarism is 'based on not examining explicitly the problems of conflict that can and do arise' (Sen, 1981, p.532). If economists were to seriously consider issues raised by Sen, a significant proportion, if not a majority, of them would probably reject welfarism. This concession is made partly due to the fact that moral philosophers, who have pondered over such issues over a long time, are notoriously divided in their views with respect to utilitarianism in particular and to consequentialism in general (for example, see Smart and Williams, 1973). 'Ng's own view of the matter should not be confused with a claim that a consensus does exist on this question' (Sen, 1981, p.532), though I may attempt to persuade economists to stick to welfarism, and for the defectors to re-embrace welfarism after a more 'critical' examination.

The third concession I wish to make is based on practical considerations including the lack of complete information about individual welfares mentioned above. Partly because of this lack of information and partly because of the cost of making a detailed welfarist calculation for each decision, it is sensible to adopt some principles, procedures, etc. that are generally consistent with the ultimate welfarist objective. (The relevance of arguments, e.g. Suzumura, 1999, on the importance of the appropriate procedures should be seen in this light. They are relevant and important and yet do not affect the validity of welfarism at the ultimate level. See also Section 5.5 which argues that utilitarianism is consistent with process fairness.) In time, these principles are valued for their own sake and these secondary or derived values have to be reckoned with even by a pure welfarist (who may however try at the same time to persuade people not to value non-basic principles over and above their instrumental values so that we can avoid being the slaves of certain 'moral principles' which are no longer conducive to social welfare due to new circumstances). Therefore, while I continue to adhere to a pure welfarist objective at the basic philosophical or 'critical' level, I am quite willing to concede that, at the practical day-to-day (or even year-to-year, decade-to-decade) basis, characteristic of most economic and social decisions, non-welfarist (from the short-term viewpoint) principles have to be reckoned with. At least in this sense, then, Sen's objection to a purely welfarist calculation is important.[3]

After making these concessions to Sen, I am sure I will not jeopardise my friendship with him by adding a caution against his following conclusion: 'Arrow's impossibility theorem can be seen as resulting largely from combining 'welfarism' (ruling out the use of non-utility information) with remarkably poor utility information (especially because of the avoidance of interpersonal comparisons)' (Sen, 1979, p.554). I agree whole-heartedly that the poor utility information (non-cardinalism and non-comparability) is of paramount importance in producing the impossibility result (see Chapter 2). I also agree that the introduction of non-welfarist principles may help social choice in particular instances. However, without richer utility information, the rejection of welfarism itself does not provide a satisfactory solution to the paradox of social choice, as shown in Chapter 2 above. (For more rigorous demonstration of the inadequacy of ordinalism even with non-welfarist principles, see Ng, 1982, 1985.)

3.2 Another argument for welfarism

Welfarism (including, of course, utilitarianism) subsumes consequentialism – the belief that the moral goodness of an action depends only on its consequences. However, it is possible to divorce welfarism from consequentialism, as discussed below. (For an argument on consequentialism, see Hammond, 1996.)

A main objection to consequentialism is that the motive behind an action should not be completely ignored in assessing the moral goodness of an action. Two different reasons for this belief may be distinguished. First, good motives and their encouragement may contribute to good consequences in the long run. But this is not inconsistent with consequentialism provided a long-run, complete view is taken (Radford, 1988). Secondly, some people may regard good motives as good in themselves irrespective of their consequences. Person A attempted out of altruism to save someone dying at a great cost to himself. However, due to ignorance, he used a wrong method which hastened the death. Person B maliciously tried to kill someone just for fun. However, due to some unlikely occurrences, some benefits were effected. Most people feel that A is good and B is bad rather than the other way round. This is partly because we know that A/B is likely to do many other good/bad deeds most of which would lead to good/bad consequences. Even abstracting from this factor, most people still believe that motives cannot be completely ignored in assessing moral goodness either of a person or of an action. This objection to consequentialism may be resolved by the following distinction.

Let us apply moral goodness to motives and to consequences separately. We can then say that the motive behind action X is good though its consequences are bad or vice versa. We may then confine welfarism to moral assessment with respect to consequences. Thus revised, welfarism is the belief that what makes anything morally good or bad in terms of its consequences ultimately depends only on its effects on individual utilities. In other words, welfarism rules out non-utility consequences as of ultimate relevance for moral goodness with respect to consequences. Thus defined, welfarism can be seen to be compelling as shown below.

Consider the following value axiom.

A1. *In a world with no conscious beings, nothing is of any moral consequence*

Here, a 'world' is defined as a four-dimensional totality, encompassing all space and all times and of course all beings and events therein to eternity. Thus a world with no conscious beings means no conscious beings even in the future. Possible goodness such as in the conservation of resources or natural beauties for possible future beings to appreciate does not therefore arise. Since there is nothing conscious in such a world to perceive anything, it seems extremely reasonable, if not compelling, to say that nothing is of any moral consequence.

From A1, it does not take a huge step to accept A2.

A2. *In a world with no sentients, nothing is of any moral consequence*

Here, a sentient is defined as a being that is capable of being happy or miserable. Thus, a sentient must be a conscious being but a conscious being need not be a sentient. For example, one can logically imagine beings that can perceive lights or even see and feel (the existence of) things without being able to feel subjective pleasure and pain. In fact, many lower forms of animals in our world are likely to actually fit this description. It is likely that the ability to perceive evolved earlier than the ability to feel rewards and punishment, because the latter ability serves no purpose without the former.[4] However, while these animals eventually evolve into sentients in our world, they shall never do so in a world satisfying the precondition of A2.

Suppose that our world W_0 is transformed into W_1 by changing all sentients (including ourselves) into non-sentient conscious beings (to eternity). According to A2, nothing is of any moral consequence in W_1. However, we (i.e. human beings after being made non-sentient but still conscious) may still regard some acts (such as lying) as immoral though without the feeling of moral compulsion (otherwise we would still be sentients). But this must surely be due to our memory of affairs in our present world. Let us transform our present world W_0 into W_1 by not only changing all sentients into non-sentient conscious beings but also eliminating their memories of affairs in W_0. Would lying still be regarded as immoral in W_1? Many people (including, say, Arthur) may reply in the affirmative and believe themselves to have such a moral view in W_1. To see that such a view is untenable, consider a different world W_2 which is similar to ours in most aspects (it even has a counterpart of each and every individual in our world) except that lying in W_2 does not cause any real hardship, mistrust, or any other undesirable effects. Rather they lie to add colours to their life. People that seldom lie are regarded as rather dull. Lying in W_2 is like telling a joke in W_0. Everyone in W_2 regards lying as morally good. Now, let us transform W_2 into W_3 by making all sentients into non-sentient conscious beings and eliminate all their memories of affairs in W_2. Moreover, make some minor changes if necessary such as to make W_3 exactly the same as W_1 in every aspect. If we ask the counterpart of Arthur in W_2 (call him Arthur$_2$) what he thinks or would think of the moral standing of lying in W_3, he will probably say that lying is still morally good even in W_3. But by construction W_3 is identical to W_1. How could the same thing (lying) in the same world (W_1 or W_3) be both morally bad and good at the same time? Such absurdity can be avoided by accepting A2.

The acceptance of A2 seems to compel the acceptance of A3.

A3.   *In a world with sentients, what is of moral consequence is ultimately due to the effects on the feelings of happiness or unhappiness of the sentients in that world.*

If what is of moral consequence is not ultimately due to the effects on the feelings of happiness or unhappiness of sentients (or sentient feelings for short), then something may be of moral consequence even without in any way, directly or indirectly, affecting sentient feelings. If this is true, something should also be of possible moral consequence in a world with non-sentient conscious beings since there is no morally relevant difference between the two. But this violates A2. Hence we must also accept A3. Using utility to represent sentient feelings, A3 is welfarism. Ultimately, what is morally good or bad depends only on the effects on individual utilities:

$$w = w(u^1, u^2, \dots, u^n)$$

3.3 Rational individualism implies welfarism

In this section, it is argued that the requirements of rational individualism, appropriately defined, already imply welfarism. As we are concerned with the appropriate form of social welfare functions (i.e. with what the society should ultimately maximise), it is natural to take the existence of a SWF as given. Also, as we are dealing with the general principle applicable to all potential situations, the assumption of universal domain (which allows for all logically possible patterns/combinations of individual preferences/welfares) is warranted. These assumptions are not really needed for the substance of the following arguments, but only to rule out cases like: If the number of social alternatives and/or the diversity of individual preferences are severely restricted, e.g. if there is only one alternative or if everyone has the same preference/welfare levels, then our substantive axioms below will have no scope to 'bite' and one may argue that all (or all Paretian) social welfare functions satisfy our substantive axioms in a trivial sense. This is, of course, not substantive. Those who want completeness may take it that we are assuming:

Axiom 0. *A social welfare function exists and the domain of social alternatives and individual welfare levels are not restricted.*

In fact, we do not need the full force of this axiom. As it is purely a non-substantive issue, we will not include this axiom in the following discussion. It may also be noted that, in the absence of either cardinal utilities/welfares or their interpersonal comparison, no reasonable SWF is possible, even if we operate with a fixed set of individual preferences/welfares. (Kemp and Ng, 1976 and Parks, 1976 establish the impossibility without cardinality; Sen, 1970a establishes the impossibility without interpersonal comparison.) Thus, for the question on the appropriate *form* of SWF, we have to operate with the existence of interpersonal comparable cardinal utility/welfare. (See Chapter 2.) We now turn to the substantive axioms.

Axiom 1. Rational individualism: *Where no other sentients outside a given society are affected, what the society should ultimately maximise should depend positively on what individuals in the society rationally and knowledgeably want for themselves ultimately.*

This axiom may be broken into the following four components.

1a. Individualism: *The society consists of individuals and does not exist independently of individuals. Thus, what the society wants should depend on what individuals in the society want; what the society should pursue ultimately should depend on what individuals in the society ultimately want.*

1b. Positive dependence (the Pareto principle): *The dependence of social choice on individual values should be positive other than negative.*

1c. Proviso on others: *Just as my pursuit of my welfare is subject to certain constraints to avoid causing great harm to you, on my neighbours, on animals, etc. a society's maximisation is subject to a similar proviso.*

However, since the appropriate constraints and/or tradeoff is beyond the scope here, this proviso is just noted without discussing its detailed implications, by confining to choices where no other sentients are affected. Due to this confinement, any disagreement on this proviso has no effect on our arguments. For example, suppose someone disagrees that animal welfare should enter this proviso. This does not affect our arguments which are concerned only with choices where animal welfare is not affected. Another might believe that we should not have this whole proviso at all. This only means that our conclusions would then apply without subjecting to 'no effects on others'.

1d. Rationalism: *The individual preferences that should be used in determining the social preferences should be those that are free from correctable ignorance, irrationality, and non-affective altruism or malice.*

This consists of three components.

1d1. Informed preferences: To a certain extent, individual preferences may be distorted by ignorance, imperfect foresight, or misinformation. Many of these are not correctable as the society is similarly ignorant. Others are correctable. The fluoridation of water is partly justified on this ground. Harsanyi (1997) has convincingly argued for the use of informed preferences over actual preferences. (See Chapter 4.)

1d2. Exclusion of non-affective altruism: *Non-affective altruism is the pure concern (or malice if the concern is negative) for the welfare of others (which need not be confined to human only) independent of or over and above the effect on one's own welfare.*

I may donate money to the poor because I feel happier seeing them in a less deprived condition (affective altruism) or because my donation will increase my status in the community (not real altruism). However, if my welfare loss in the money donated is larger than my welfare gain through the above and all other effects and yet I prefer the donation, non-affective altruism is involved. Non-affective altruistic preferences should be excluded from social choice because the welfare of each person (including that of the poor) should already be fully concerned with on its own right in the relevant social welfare function. Including non-affective altruistic preferences will lead to multiple counting. This, together with a more detailed distinction of affective versus non-affective altruism, the existence of the latter, and the unacceptability of the Pareto principle in terms of preferences in the presence of non-affective altruism are contained in Section 4.1 and Appendix D.

1d3. Rationality: *Social choice should be based on individual preferences that are not distorted by irrationality.*

The preference of an individual is defined to be irrational if they prefer A to B while their welfare will be higher at B than at A and if their preference is due neither to ignorance nor non-affective altruism.[5] This definition makes ignorance, non-affective altruism, and irrationality three exhaustive reasons for the divergence between the preference and the welfare of an individual. Section 4.2 in the next chapter explains causes of irrational preferences and argues why they should be excluded.

Due to the above considerations (and that of Section 4.2), I believe that most reasonable people realising our confinement to the ultimate level including all indirect and long-term effects would agree after critical examination that Rational Individualism is compelling.

Definition 1. Welfarism: *Where no others are affected, what a society should maximise should be a function of (i.e. depend on) individual welfares of members of that society, i.e.*

$$W = W(w^1, w^2, \ldots, w^I)$$

where W = social welfare, w^i = welfare of individual i, I = number of individuals in the society.

Proposition 1. Rational individualism implies ('positive') welfarism

Proof: Where no others are affected, Individualism requires the society to pursue what individuals in the society ultimately want. An individual may ultimately want: 1. their own welfare, 2. the welfare of others, 3. any other things. Factor 2 is excluded by Axiom 1d2. Factor 3 could be due either to ignorance or irrationality which are respectively excluded by Axiom 1d1 and 1d3. This leaves only the welfare of the individual. Thus, Rational Individualism implies Welfarism. Axiom 1b further requires the welfarist social welfare function to be 'positive' in the sense of satisfying the Pareto principle, i.e. $\partial W/\partial w^i > 0$ for all individuals. *Q.E.D.*

In Chapter 4, it is argued that, where individual welfares (representing their happiness) differ from their utilities (representing their preferences), social choices/public policies should ultimately be based on individual welfares. Chapter 5 goes further than welfarism to argue in favour of utilitarianism (social welfare should be an unweighted sum of individual welfares). For a philosophical defence of welfarism, see Sumner (1996). (However, Sumner uses a somewhat different concept of welfare. Though he rejects the objective conceptions of welfare, he also rejects the state-of-mind concept used here. Rather, he has a mixture of state-of-mind and state-of-world concept of welfare as 'authentic happiness' or informed and autonomous happiness, somewhat similar to Harsanyi's 'informed preference' discussed in Chapter 4.)

4
Utility, Informed Preference, or Happiness[1]

Even accepting welfarism (argued to be compelling at the ultimate level in Chapter 3), there is still the issue as to what the individual welfares in the welfarist social welfare function should represent. In particular, should the welfare of individuals be their (net) happiness as I define welfare, or should it be their utility (representing their preferences) as most economists seem to be assuming? Recently, Harsanyi (1997) argues, among other things, that in welfare economics and normative public policy, what are important are people's *informed preferences*, rather than either their *actual preferences* (as emphasised by modern economists) or their *happiness* (as emphasised by early utilitarians). The main purpose of this chapter is to argue that pursuing Harsanyi's argument that allows him to move from actual to informed preferences to its logical conclusion forces us to accept happiness as the ultimately important thing. The early utilitarians were right after all! Since I personally approve of Harsanyi's basic argument, I regard myself as a follower who has become more Catholic than the Pope. (On the importance of distinguishing between preference and happiness, or between 'decision utility' and 'experienced utility', see Kahneman *et al.*, 1997.)

It is not denied that, in practice, the practical difficulties and undesirable side effects of the *procedure* of using happiness instead of preferences have to be taken into account. Thus, even if we ultimately wish to maximise the aggregate happiness of people, it may be best in practice to maximise their aggregate preferences in most instances. This important consideration will be largely ignored in this chapter.

The use of individual happiness instead of preference for social choice may seem (especially to economists) to make the problem more difficult since happiness appears more difficult to discover. However, it also makes the problem less intractable as happiness is more cardinally measurable and interpersonally comparable than preference. (See Ng, 1996a on a practical method of measuring happiness cardinally and interpersonally comparably.) Also, the use of happiness instead of preference creates some difficult problems like evaluation in the presence of preference changes (on the prevalence of which see Bowles, 1998) tractable. Holding the welfare of others unchanged, whatever changes in my preference, what I am ultimately concerned with is my happiness which is cardinally measurable, inter-preference-pattern comparable, and as concrete as my morning jam. All ultimate evaluation may thus be made in terms of happiness.

4.1 Non-affective altruism: the pure concern for the welfare of others

A person's actual preferences are 'indicated by his choice behaviour and by his verbal statements'. His informed preferences are 'defined as the hypothetical preferences he would have if he had all the relevant information and had made full use of this information' (Harsanyi, 1997, p.133). In addition, to qualify as informed preferences, 'our preferences should be genuine preferences rather than spurious ones' (p.134). There are various classes of spurious preferences including compulsive behaviour and self-deception.

Now, let us compare Harsanyi's distinction outlined above with my distinction between happiness (or welfare, defined to be the same) and (actual) preference (Ng, 1979/1983; 1989b). (From now, 'actual' will be dropped unless when emphasis is needed while 'informed' will be kept throughout.) The preference of individuals may differ from their welfare due to either one or more of the following exhaustive reasons: 1. ignorance or imperfect foresight; 2. a concern for the welfare of others (the definition of 'others' could be broad enough to include animal welfare); and 3. irrational preferences. The last is defined to be any divergence from welfare other than due to the first two factors. (This definition makes the tripartite classification exhaustive, though some readers may query the use of terminology.)

Comparing the above two schemes of distinction, it is clear that there should be a complete agreement where the divergence is due to ignorance, imperfect foresight, or misinformation. If a person's preference of medical treatment A over B is based on misinformation, the actual superiority of B over A seems uncontroversial. For this type of divergence, economists' preference for using actual preferences may still be sustained on the practical grounds of: 1. the difficulties of discovering the informed preferences and 2. the possible unfavourable side-effects of diverging from the actual preferences of people. Where these two considerations are not important and/or the degree of ignorance is more important, then it is uncontroversial that welfare or informed preferences should prevail over actual preferences, as witnessed by the prevalence and widespread support of fluoridation of water and prohibition of hard drugs.

To a large extent, the spurious preferences of Harsanyi corresponds with my concept of irrationality. (I will return to discuss some possible differences later.) Thus, whether informed preference or welfare should be used for social evaluation depends mainly on how the divergence between preference (actual or informed) and welfare due to a concern for the welfare of others (non-affective altruism/malice) should be dealt with. I wish to argue strongly that such a concern should be ignored in social evaluation. In other words, social evaluation should take account of happiness or individual welfare rather than preferences (actual or informed). This is so for the simple reason that otherwise double or rather multiple counting will be involved. (Harsanyi allows for 'truly altruistic actions' which seems to correspond to my 'concern for the welfare of others' or non-affective altruism; however, he does not discuss the implication of this for the choice of individual welfares versus utilities as the appropriate arguments in the social welfare function. Elsewhere, Harsanyi and others appear to reject all forms of altruism from consideration in social choice on the ground of multiple counting. As argued below, *affective* altruism should not be so excluded.)

For simplicity, consider a society of two individuals. Individual 1 is self-concerning and maximises his own welfare, with utility function $u^1 = w^1$. Individual 2 has a substantial concern for the welfare of individual 1, with utility function $u^2 = w^2 + 0.5w^1$. Also for simplicity (but not essential for the argument), suppose that the relevant social welfare function is utilitarian, maximising the unweighted sum of individual values. The question here is whether the individual values should be individual utilities or individual welfares. Note also that, for this exercise (i.e. summing, and in fact any other reasonable method of aggregating individual utilities or welfares to arrive at social welfare) to be possible, we must have a framework of interpersonally comparable cardinal individual utilities or welfares, as argued in Chapter 2 above. Thus, in Table 4.1, the welfare and utility figures are cardinal and interpersonally comparable.

Table 4.1

Social states	w^1	w^2	u^1	u^2	Σw^i	Σu^i
x	2	7	2	8	9	10
y	6	2	6	5	8	11
z	8	5	8	9	13	17

For the situation depicted, should the society choose x or y for the choice between x and y only (with z not feasible)? If Σw^i is used, x is preferred to y; if Σu^i is used, y is preferred to x. In my view, it is clear that Σw^i should be used and x should be socially preferred to y. In fact, since the individual welfare profile of x is (2, 7) while that of y is (6, 2), in terms of individual welfares, x will be preferred by any social welfare function that is anonymous and increasing in individual welfares. Though x has a lower Σu^i, this is so only because the substantial concern of individual 2 for the welfare of individual 1. If individual 2 were to make the choice herself, she would prefer z (if feasible) to x. Though her welfare is lower at x than at z, her concern for the welfare of individual 1 more than offsets this as w^1 is much higher at z than at x. However, her concern for the welfare of individual 2 is not sufficient for her to prefer x to y. For social choice, the use of Σw^i already takes full account of w^1, i.e. w^1 is already treated at a par with w^2. Thus, there is no further need to take account of the concern of individual 2 for w^1. To do so would involve the double counting (multiple counting in the case of many non-self-concerning individuals) of the welfare of individual 1. In using Σu^i, w^1 is counted fully (i.e. with the weight of unity) under u^1, and then counted again at the weight of 0.5 under u^2. It is thus counted 1.5 times, while w^2 is counted only once.

It may be thought that, since w^1 enters u^2 at the weight of 0.5 while w^2 does not enter u^1, it may be right to count w^1 1.5 times while counting w^2 only once. This is inappropriate. Consider the concrete example of parental choice. Usually, parents have sufficient concern for the welfare of their children such that the society does not find it necessary to interfere and just let parents choose for the whole family. (There are also reasons of the practical difficulties and side-effects of interference which we shall ignore for simplicity.) However, to tackle some special cases of gross parental negligence, there are appropriate legislations.

Nevertheless, even ideally, such legislation should only aim to ensure that the welfare of children are taken fully (i.e. at a par with that of the parents) into account, not that the welfare of children should be more important than that of the parents. To do the latter would be making the mistake of correcting a mistake excessively.

A reason why some people may prefer using Σu^i rather than Σw^i (or other functions of individual utilities rather than individual welfares) is due to a failure to distinguish 'minding' from 'concerning'. A self-minding person is one whose welfare (or happiness) is not affected by the welfare levels of others. A person may feel bad knowing that there are people suffering in Africa. This is a 'minding' effect or affective altruism. A self-concerning person is one whose utility (or preference) is not affected by the welfare levels of others, except possibly through their effects on his/her own welfare (i.e. through the 'minding' effect). A person may choose x over y even if her welfare is lower at x than at y *because* the welfare levels of others are higher at y than at x. This is a 'concerning' effect or non-affective altruism. A self-centring person is one who is both self-minding and self-concerning.

In functional forms and ignoring ignorance, we may write the utility of a rational person as:

$$u^i = u^i(w^1, w^2, \ldots, w^I)$$

where u = utility, w = welfare, and a superscript indicates the person concerned, and I = the number of individuals concerned.[2] And:

$$w^i = w^i(a,b,c,\ldots,w^1,w^2,\ldots,w^{i-1},w^{i+1},\ldots,w^I)$$

where a, b, c, . . . are some variables such as consumption that enter the welfare function but are not the focus here. The 'minding' effect is $\partial w^i/\partial w^j$, $j \neq i$ and the 'concerning' effect is the direct effect of w^j on u^i without going through $\partial w^i/\partial w^j$.

It is true that these two effects are usually intertwined. If a person is concerned with the welfare of another person, she is also likely to be non-self-minding towards his welfare. (The reverse may also be true though with less force, as the minding effect is usually stronger and more prevalent than the concerning effect.) Thus, parents are typically happy knowing that their children are happy (minding effect) *and* also willing to choose something against their welfare for the welfare of their children (concerning effect). It is true that they will feel good knowing that they are sacrificing for their children and that the welfare of their children increases, but if this is not sufficient to offset their welfare loss due to other factors (such as a lower level of consumption, less leisure, worse health), the concerning effect is involved over and above the minding effect.

As the minding effect actually affects the welfare level, it is already taken fully into account in the social decision in accordance to Σw^i, as it should be. For the concerning effect, the welfare of the concerning person is not affected, but her preference is affected by her concern for the welfare of others. However, in using, say, the unweighted sum of individual values, the welfare of others is already taken fully into account, i.e. is already fully 'concerned' with. Hence, there is no further need to take the concern of this person for the welfare of others into account.

The existence of non-affective altruism (the concerning effect) may be doubted (especially by economists, as mentioned to me on several occasions). This attitude has some advantages as many instances of apparent altruism are consistent with self interest due to the influence of social pressure, obligations, fame-seeking, future rewards, and the like. (For a collection of papers on the economics of altruism, see Zamagni, 1995. See also Bagwell and Bernheim, 1996 and Harbaugh, 1998 on the status or prestige motive for making charitable contributions; Clark, 1998; Eshel *et al.*, 1998; Laitner and Juster, 1996 and Rose-Ackerman, 1996 for evidence and economic theories regarding altruism; Lunati, 1997 on some ethical aspects; and Mulligan, 1997 on parental altruism towards children. Altonji *et al.*, 1997 show that a dollar increase in parental income plus a dollar decrease in the child's income only lead to a \$0.13 increase in transfer, contrary to the altruistic model. However, this is so only for a specific altruistic model, not necessarily so for some more general one.)

It may be argued that, if Ms 2 is willing to choose z over x in consideration of the welfare of Mr 1, she must be happier with z than with x. So, u^i and w^i must always go together such that the situation depicted in Table 4.1 where u^2 and w^2 conflict each other with respect to the pair (x, z) cannot logically arise. In other words, only 'minding' is possible; 'concerning' is not possible. This argument is incorrect. As conceded above, the two effects usually intertwine with each other, and 'minding' is more prevalent than 'concerning'. Many apparently 'concerning' effects may actually be 'minding' effects upon closer examination. However, some truly pure 'concerning' effects are possible. To see this, consider the following purely hypothetical construction which nevertheless illustrates the point most dramatically:

Suppose that you are commanded by the all-powerful Devil to press either button A or B within 2 seconds. You know with certainty that the following outcomes will happen depending on which button you press.

A: You will go to 'Bliss' with your happiness level at 1,000 trillion units. (Those who prefer concreteness may imagine a health-enhancing island with all the material supplies you want plus 100 abiding partners of your dream.) All others on earth will go to Hell with happiness level at *minus* 1,000 trillion units each.

B: You will go to 'Bliss Minus' with your happiness level at 999 trillion units. (The same as above but with 99 partners.) All others will go to 'Niceland' with happiness level at 100 trillion units each.

C: If you do not press any button within the 2 seconds, you *and* all others will go to Hell.

There will be no communication between Bliss, Niceland, Hell, etc. You will lose all memory of the present world once you press either button or fail to press within the 2 seconds. So you will not have any guilt feelings in Bliss or Bliss Minus. Within the 2 seconds, you will be too preoccupied with pressing the right button that your welfare will be zero whichever button you press. (It is too brief to experience any significant amount of welfare anyway.)

Thus, by construction, your welfare will be higher with A than with B. However, most people would choose B. (I would have not the slightest hesitation at all in choosing B, even if Bliss Minus involves only 500 trillion units of happiness.) The choice of B over A exhibits non-affective altruism, though it may not be a very strong one. If you still prefer A, change the happiness level of Bliss Minus into 999.999999 trillion units. If you still prefer A, then you may really be perfectly self-concerning. But how could you condemn all others to Hell for a tiny fractional increase in your own welfare?

Now consider more realistic choices. It is true that, as parents, we usually feel happy doing something for our children (or other loved ones) such as sacrificing our time, effort, money. Thus, the importance of the 'minding' effect is uncontroversial. However, are we willing to make such sacrifices *only if* our loss in welfare due to the sacrificed time, effort, or money is more than made up by our warm-glow feeling of helping our children? If the loss is not fully made up but yet the welfare of our children will be significantly increased at a moderate or even small net loss to our own welfare, will not at least some of us be willing to do that?

If we have a true concern (over and above the 'minding' effect) for the welfare of our children, can we not have a similar (though lesser in degree) concern for our siblings, our relatives, our friends, our fellow countrymen/women, the whole humankind, and eventually all sentients? (For some evidence for true altruism, see Hoffman, 1981 and Monroe, 1996.)

To further support the distinction between preference and happiness, it may be noted that neuro- and behavioural scientists (e.g. Berridge, 1996) found that wanting (related to preference) and liking (related to happiness) arise from two different neural systems, and therefore preference may not be synonymous with happiness.

Moreover, our behaviour and preferences are affected by our biologically determined inclinations. Natural selection results in the maximisation of inclusive fitness (Hamilton, 1964; Wilson, 1975). Fitness here is the ability of an organism to survive and transmit its genes to the next generation. Inclusive fitness consists of the individual's own fitness plus her effects on the fitness of genetically related neighbours. Thus, an individual may be expected to be altruistic towards her close relatives, especially her own children. In addition, Trivers' (1971) model of reciprocal altruism shows that natural selection had to favour some degree of altruism even between non-related individuals provided that there is a significant chance of role reversal, as may be expected for social species, including *homo sapiens*.

We care about our children/relatives because they carry/share our genes. Sometimes one (or one's spouse) may wonder why one is so willing to help one's siblings (or other relatives) whom one does not really love much, not knowing that perhaps the genetically determined subconscious inclination may play a role. Thus, the existence of some non-self-centring effects is a biological necessity. However, whether the biologically determined non-self-centring effects manifest mainly/only in the 'minding' or the 'concerning' effects remains to be explored. Of course, we are much more influenced by nurture than other animals and also have a higher, if not exclusive, sense of morality. It may be conjectured that, the more important is the influence of nurture and the more important is the sense of morality, the more likely is it for the true concerning effect to be present and significant.

From the above discussion, it may be concluded that true concern (i.e. on top of or over and above the 'minding' effect) for the welfare of others does exist. Moreover, when preferences (actual or informed) differ from welfare due to a concern for the welfare of others, it should be the individual welfare rather than the utility values that enter the social welfare function.

While Harsanyi does not discuss the appropriate treatment of altruistic preferences in his 1997 paper, he discusses it elsewhere (Harsanyi, 1995, p.325). He suggests that all 'external' preferences, even if altruistic, should be excluded in social welfare consideration, presumably based on similar reasoning as our argument above. Here, external preferences are 'preferences for assignment of goods and opportunities to others' (Dworkin, 1977). The belief in the need to exclude altruism (or its opposite, malice) is also held by a number of other authors discussing the issue (e.g. Hammond, 1987/1995). My point here is that these authors do not distinguish between affective (i.e. the minding effect) and non-affective (the concerning effect) altruism and seem to suggest that they should all be disregarded. As argued above, while non-affective altruism should be excluded to avoid multiple counting, affective altruism should be included.

To see the reasonableness of including the minding effect, consider the hypothetical example that either S or M has to die and a lot is drawn to decide who has to die. Suppose that the two are equally old, capable, etc. except that S is single with no close friends and M has many close relatives who love her very much and will suffer a lot from her death. Then, other things being equal, most people will hope that the lot will turn out to let M survive rather than the other way round. The death of M will cause more suffering. Counting this suffering does not involve double counting. The minding effect should be treated differently from the concerning effect. If I feel sad or happy for a certain event, such feelings should certainly count in assessing the social desirability of that event. On the other hand, if I have some non-affective concern for the welfare of others, such a pure concern should not be counted if the welfare of these others are already fully accounted for in the social welfare function.

How could we say that the sorrow of a mother from the death of her child should be disregarded as it is 'external' preference? It could cause more suffering on her than starvation! Perhaps Dworkin would reply that the death of a child would adversely affect the opportunities of the mother, and hence the mother's preference here is not wholly external. However, for any definition of opportunities (unless it is defined to coincide with welfare), one can revise the example such that the preference is external as defined by Dworkin (i.e. regarding the assignment of goods and opportunities to others) and yet the person concerned (who has the external preferences) genuinely suffers a lot subjectively. Such external preferences should not be ignored. (However, we may have to disregard many external preferences even when they genuinely affect people's welfare, on grounds of practical difficulties and undesirable side effects; but this problem has been abstracted away in this chapter.)

The recognition that affective/non-affective altruistic preferences should be included/excluded in social choice has practical implications. For example, this is related to the issue on the extent to which gifts should be taxed or subsidised. (There are of course other considerations related to the tax/subsidy of gifts; see Kaplow, 1998. On the possible unacceptability of the Pareto principle due to the presence of non-affective altruism, see Appendix D.)

4.2 Irrational preferences

As mentioned above, Harsanyi regards 'spurious' preferences as not real preferences and hence should not be used for normative purposes. He gives two examples of spurious preferences. One is 'compulsive behaviour' where, for example, 'some neurotics wash their hands far too many times a day for no obvious reason. Their behaviour may be to some extent voluntary and to that extent a result of their own *preferences* to act in this way. But at a deeper level, it is obviously a result of a more or less irresistible *inner compulsion*, very much *contrary* to their true preferences' (p.135). This may be regarded as some degree of psychological sickness due perhaps to some subconscious need to wash away some guilt or 'dirtiness'. Such spurious preferences should not be treated on a par as normal preferences. Thus, curing such sickness should be regarded as an improvement but we do not want to change a person's normal preference of, say, apples over pears. However, before the sickness is cured, we may still want to 'respect' his preference as, for example, denying him the water to wash his hands may make him feel very uncomfortable. But why is curing his compulsive behaviour good while denying him water bad? In my view, this is due to different effects on his (and perhaps also on others') happiness. Thus, again, happiness is more fundamental than preferences.

The second example of spurious preferences is 'self-deception':

> Some people pretend to have, and may in the end even convince themselves that they have, some preferences they think to be fashionable and sophisticated – even though their real preferences may

be quite different, or even though after a point they may not really know themselves what their real preferences are. Devotees of various esoteric art forms of questionable aesthetic value often form coteries that seem to display this kind of behaviour.

Harsanyi, 1997, p.135.

I do not know much about these esoteric art forms but it could be debatable to call the preferences of their devotees self-deception.

Harsanyi believes that informed preferences, by definition, will always be based on all the relevant information, so that they will always be in agreement with our real interests. However, it is debatable that people's preferences must always coincide with their interests if they are fully informed. The meaning of 'interests' here is vague. If it means whatever people prefer under full information, then it coincides with informed preference tautologically but the terminology of 'interest' is misleading. If it means welfare, happiness, or something similar, then it is not true that people's preferences when fully informed always coincide with their interest, for at least two reasons. First, there is non-affective altruism (and possibly also malice), as discussed in the last section. Secondly, biological and psychological motivational factors may affect preference or behaviour in ways not fully consistent with welfare, as argued below.

There are a number of causes that may make preferences differ from happiness other than ignorance and a concern for the welfare of others, hence irrational according to my definition. There are at least three sources of irrational preferences:

- Natural selection programmes us to maximise our biological (survival and reproductive) fitness which may be different from our welfare.
- *Homo sapiens*, the most intelligent species on earth, is still not perfectly rational as rationality is costly to programme.
- Side-effects (largely unavoidable) of generally good moral education and upbringing.

The first source is not difficult to see. We are a biological species that has evolved through many generations to survive natural selection. (Otherwise I/you wouldn't be here to write/read this book.) Natural selection works through the preservation of those attributes (created by random mutation) that are beneficial to the survival of the organism and the reproduction of offspring. In most lower species, their behavioural patterns are completely determined by genetic programmes and their interaction with specific environmental conditions. However, when the environment became more complex (largely due to the evolution of more species and more complex species), the fitness enhancing responses became more difficult to programme in advance. When consciousness evolved to make choices, an important advantage is gained by delegating some responses to be decided at the specific moment. Individuals of species of such capability decides on 'fight or flight' by sizing up the specific situation instead of relying on a fixed response triggered by a given stimulus. However, when consciousness has evolved to guide choices, such conscious choices have to be generally consistent with fitness for consciousness to survive natural selection (Ng, 1995). God (or natural selection) solved this problem by endowing the conscious species with a reward/penalty centre (or centres). Thus, activities consistent with fitness, such as eating nutritious food when hungry or mating with fertile members of the opposite sex, are rewarded with pleasure and those harmful to fitness, such as injuries to the body, are penalised with pain. (This makes the flexible species also 'rational' as defined in Ng, 1996b which shows that complex niches favour rational species which make the environment more complex, leading to a virtuous cycle that accelerated the rate of evolution, partly explaining the dramatic speed of evolution based mainly on random mutation and natural selection, a speed doubted by creationists. Note that a more 'rational' species refers to a species with less fixed behavioural patterns; hence that 'rationality' differs from the concept of 'rationality' used in this chapter.) Due to this, there is a high degree of consistency between fitness and welfare. However, the consistency is not perfect.

On top of the *ex-post* rewards and penalties, we are also endowed with inner drives to satisfy the fitness-enhancing functions like mating. On the whole, these powerful temptations and drives work in the right direction, making us do things that both enhance our biological fitness and psychological welfare. However, since evolution is largely fitness-maximisation and the welfare-enhancing aspect is only indirectly to enhance fitness, some divergence between our behaviour and our welfare is unavoidable, as our behaviour is not completely determined by rational calculation but also partly by the programmed inclination, including drives. For example, traits that incline individuals to produce a number of offspring larger than that dictated by welfare maximisation may be selected (Ng, 1995). Thus, we are not only born with reproductive capabilities that we may rationally use to increase our welfare and fitness together but we also possess biological *drives* that incline us to behave or prefer activities not fully consistent with our welfare, at least in many occasions.

As an example, adolescent girls and boys often engage in careless sexual acts propelled by their sexual drives and tempted by sexual pleasure even at high risk to their long-term welfare, such as having unwanted pregnancies and contracting AIDS. While this is partly due to ignorance, the role of biological drives cannot be denied.

Consider a specific example. Suppose that a person agrees that, for choices involving risks, the correct thing to do is to maximise expected welfare (assuming no effects on the welfare of others) and also actually do so for most choices. However, for choices concerning seeking sexual activities, he chooses x over y though his expected welfare is lower with x than with y and that he knows this to be the case. Here, x may involve having sex with an obliging partner of his dream or having sex with many partners without clear knowledge (this knowledge is assumed to be not feasible to obtain and hence not relevant) about her/their infectability of AIDS. His (expected) welfare-reducing choice of x may be due to the biological inclination to seek many sexual encounters. He knows that doing so has a non-insignificant chance of contracting AIDS and hence is welfare-reducing. He has all the relevant feasible information and yet chooses (due to the powerful sex drive) x that he knows to be of lower expected welfare. (This is not really a hypothetical example. I am confident that, out of 100 average adult males, at least 10 have actually made such choices. If one wants more solid evidence, one may look at the frequency of prostitution and extra-marital sex despite the danger of sexually transmitted diseases including AIDS.) Should we call this preference informed as the person has all the relevant feasible information, or not informed because it is not in agreement with his real interests? (See Elster, 1998 for a survey of the role of our various emotions in our behaviour and welfare, especially in relation to economic analysis.)

For another example, traits that incline individuals to be excessively in fear of death may also be selected. Undergoing enormous hardship for a long time may enable one to bring one's children to survivable ages and perhaps also further chances of passing on one's genes. However, the life-time welfare may well be very negative.

Though we are the most intelligent and most rational species on earth, we are still not perfectly rational. This is so because rationality is costly to programme. For example, an important aspect of rationality requires the individual not only to take account of current costs and benefits but also those in the future (with appropriate discount for the uncertainty on their realisation for costs and benefits in welfare terms, or a discount at market interest rate for monetary costs). However, the ability to purposefully take account of future costs/benefits appears to be very rudimentary, if it exists at all, for most species. The storage of food by ants and the burial of nuts by squirrels are hard-wired instincts, not deliberate choices. If calculated choices are made by animals, they are largely confined to sizing up the current situation to decide the best move at the moment, like fight or flight. The ability to anticipate rewards in the fairly distant future requires much more 'reason', 'imagination', and 'telescopic faculty' than normally cost-effective to programme in most other species. However, we know that we are endowed with some such faculty. (This is not to say that we are not also partly driven by what Keynes called 'the animal spirit'.) Nevertheless, since this advanced faculty is almost completely absent in most other species, it is natural to expect that it is not fully developed even in our own species. Moreover, different members of our species may be endowed with different degrees of such faculty. The existence of a significant proportion of our species that do not possess a full telescopic faculty is thus not surprising.

Many people tend to take inadequate care for the future or have excessive discount rates. This is widely noted, including by economists. For example, Pigou (1929, p.25) called it the 'faulty telescopic faculty', Ramsey (1928, p.543) called it the 'weakness of imagination' about the future, Harrod (1948, p.40) regarded it as the 'conquest of reason by passion'. A discount on future consumption, income, and any other monetary values is rational as a dollar now can be transformed into more than a dollar in the future. A discount on future utility may still be rational if the realisation of the future utility is uncertain. (For healthy people, this uncertainty is usually very small.) Discounting the future for more than these acceptable reasons is probably irrational. A manifestation of this irrationality is the insufficient amount of savings for old age, necessitating compulsory and heavily subsidised superannuation schemes. I came across an extreme example of such under-saving during a survey regarding how much more people would be willing to save if the rates of interest were higher (Ng, 1992a). The question implicitly assumed that everyone did some saving, as the answers were in terms of how many percentages more one would save. One subject declared that he did not save anything. I then asked him to change the answers to be chosen from 'saving 20 per cent more' into 'saving $20 more per month', etc. He still said that he could not be induced to save anything even at annual interest rates of hundreds of per cent. It was only when I said, 'If a dollar saved now could become a million dollar next year, would you save?' that he admitted he would save then. I was careful enough to find out that this healthy-looking young man was not expecting early death from a terminal disease or the like.

Related to both the above causes of irrational preference but bordering on ignorance is the tendency of people (and animals) to choose mainly in accordance to current utilities, ignoring the effects on the utilities of future choices, and to underestimate the effects of current pleasures/pains in decreasing/increasing future enjoyment through the adaptation effects. For example, most people believe that winning a big sum of money will bring them great happiness and are thus willing to spend a lot of money buying lottery tickets at unfavourable odds. However, psychologists find out that lottery winners are typically not happier than non-winner controls. (See Brickman *et al.*, 1978; Herrnstein and Prelec, 1992.)

Most people regard our own species as the only one that has morality. I am agnostic on this. (I cannot rule out some rudimentary sense of morality in, say, the chimp.) However, I accept that the sense of morality evolved very late in the phylogenetic scale. The inborn feelings for morality probably helped our survival by enhancing cooperation in our species which relies less on hard-wired fixed response patterns. Our sense of morality is not only inborn, we are brought up and educated, and we also learn and teach others, to behave morally, to value justice, etc. This is extremely important in the smooth functioning of the society and in improving human relationships. Morality is not only important for the welfare of the individual but also for others. If anything, I believe that modern education is deficient in the moral aspect. However, the inborn and learned strong sense of morality also, at least occasionally, make us do and prefer things consistent with our moral principles but contrary to our welfare. If an individual acts against his own welfare in order to observe certain moral principles, this need not be irrational. First, his sacrifice may benefit others. Secondly, he may *feel* bad in violating principles he values. Thirdly, violating moral principles may have long-term undesirable effects both for him and for others, including weakening the degree of morality. Fourthly, his choice may be due to ignorance. However, if an individual knowingly sacrifices so much welfare not made up by all of the above considerations put together, he is irrational according to my definition.

An example of welfare-reducing moral principle that had been observed for a long time with disastrous consequences is the scruple (in ancient China in particular) that a woman has to stick to a single husband even after the early death of the husband. Statues were erected to extol the virtue of not marrying again, observing the widowhood for decades from youth to death. Enormous family and social pressures were put on widows, with or without children, not to marry again, simply because it is not virtuous to marry again. Most people agree now that such blind insistence on moral virtue is irrational and indeed morally wrong. Shouldn't those who insist on whatever moral principles now irrespective of or independent of their welfare implications take some lessons from this example? (It may be thought that draconian anti-welfare moral principles, such as the no-remarriage commandment, no longer exist today, especially in the West. However, consider the principle 'life is sacrosanct' and the related strict anti-euthanasia legislation and the artificial prolonging of hopeless lives in pain by modern machines. The amount of unnecessary suffering is still enormous.)

The above causes of irrational preference show that, due either to imperfection in our endowed faculty, the biological bias in favour of reproductive fitness, or certain side-effects of morality, we may do things not quite consistent with our welfare. The issue here is that, for normative purposes, should we use welfare or actual preferences/behaviour. It seems clear that, where individual irrational preferences are due to the bias of biological drives or to imperfect telescopic faculty, social choices should try to exclude such irrational preferences and be based on individual welfares instead. An old Chinese dictum says, 'Out of the three unfilial acts, not having offspring is the greatest.' However, for the human species as a whole, we are certainly not getting smaller in population size. Moreover, a long-run social welfare function accounting for the welfare of future generations should account for that. If we go for biological fitness, we will prefer unlimited procreation even if that means that we will all be suffering to a smaller population with a higher aggregate welfare. *We* are the feeling selves that care ultimately about our welfare (positive minus negative affective feelings). *We* are not them, the unfeeling genes that, through random mutation and natural selection, programmed us to maximise fitness. Unlike other species who are almost completely controlled by their genes and the environment, we have learned to change our fate by using such measures as birth control. For normative issues, it is *our* welfare, rather than the selected random dictates of the unfeeling genes, that should count.

For irrational preferences due to rigid adherence to out-dated moral principles, it may be more controversial. In fact, some people may be against calling such preferences irrational. However, before the evolution or development of morality and the like, we (perhaps still in the form of apes) had no moral or other principles, no concept of commitments and justice, etc. Self-interest dominated totally, though this does not exclude genetically endowed 'altruism' for the maximisation of inclusive fitness. As we evolved and relied more and more on our high intelligence and social interaction for survival, the instinct for moral feelings also evolved which helped our survival by enhancing cooperation. This was enhanced by learning the importance of such moral practices as honesty in improving our struggle against nature (including wild animals) and against competing human groups. No one can deny that the initial evolution/development of morality must be purely instrumental (in enhancing either our welfare or our surviving and propagation fitness) as there existed no morality to begin with. We then learned and taught our children and students to value moral principles, etc. first as a way to increase the degree of adherence to these principles and hence our welfare. Eventually, some, if not most, people came to value these principles in themselves by learning and probably also by instinct. (The evolution of such commitment enhancing devices as blushing can be fitness-enhancing; see Frank, 1987.) Failing to see the ultimate values is a kind of illusion fostered by learning (I dare not say indoctrination) and perhaps genetics. However, I personally have great moral respect for people with such illusions. They most probably make better citizens, friends and colleagues. But illusions they are nevertheless, at least at the ultimate analytical or critical level. While on the whole positive (in maintaining the moral standards), such illusions do have some costs in delaying the rejection of certain outdated moral principles and in contributing to the wide disagreement in normative discussion.

For those who agree with Harsanyi in rejecting spurious preferences for normative purposes, it seems likely that irrational preferences due to biological drives and imperfections and psychological conditioning should similarly be rejected. However, there is a class of preferences ('*autonomous* desire *not* based on hedonistic considerations') that may be classified as irrational using my definition but insisted by Harsanyi to be respectable, as discussed in the next section.

4.3 Autonomous desires

Instances of autonomous desires not based on hedonistic considerations given by Harsanyi (1997, pp.132–3) includes: altruistic desires, desires for accomplishments, our natural desire to satisfy our curiosity. I allow for altruistic desires to be rational as a concern for the welfare of others. This has been discussed in Section 4.1 above.

I quite agree that some of our desires are not based on hedonistic considerations. However, I believe that the satisfaction of desires or preferences as such has no intrinsic normative value; it is the effects on happiness that is ultimately valuable. Otherwise, why are spurious preferences not normatively important?

We do have a *natural* desire to satisfy our curiosity. We are probably both born and brought up to be so. As our species manages successfully to survive mainly based on its superior intelligence and knowledge, curiosity has a fitness-enhancing effect. Hence, we are also rewarded in satisfying our curiosity by feeling very good. And the increased knowledge contributes to future success. Thus, the satisfaction of this desire is generally consistent with our welfare. However, there are cases where the satisfaction of our curiosity actually makes us worse off. If a person sees a box in her office, she will naturally open it to have a look. If a colleague prevents her from doing so by seizing the box away from her, she will be made a little unhappy. However, if the box contains a poisonous snake, she will be very grateful to her colleague. It may be said that, in this case, it is only the uninformed preference that is violated, not the informed one. But suppose the box contains a photograph of her mother being raped by a soldier. Then, even after being informed of that, she may still be unable to overcome her curiosity and will open it to have a look. If this disturbs her a lot, she will be made much worse off than by the seizing away of the box from her. Suppose that there are no benefits, directly or indirectly, of so looking at the photograph, to her or to others and that there are no side-effects of seizing the box away from her. Most people will agree that, in this case, seizing away the box from her is the right thing to do. If I were her, I would be most grateful for that. The satisfaction of my (even if informed) preferences as such has no normative significance for me; it is important only because, in most cases, it makes me (and/or others) happier, directly or indirectly.

Now consider the desire for accomplishment. This may also have some genetic basis and may be related to the accumulation instinct possessed by many animal species. However, it is clear that this desire is also affected by social and educational influences. We are not only born and taught, but we also learn, to want to do useful things. Parents teach and influence their children to be so for the good of themselves, their children, and perhaps also of others. Having a desire to achieve is generally good for the welfare of ourselves and of others. However, good qualities may also be detrimental occasionally. Wise people try to avoid this but not all people are perfectly wise. An extreme example of the lack of wisdom is the saying 'If I cannot be famous for my good deeds,

I will still try to be notorious for my bad ones.' Once a person has a strong desire to achieve, the satisfaction of the desire will make him happy. However, he may be willing to undertake so much hardship that far exceeds the happy feeling of achievement. This may still not be irrational if his accomplishments greatly increase the welfare of others. However, most of us have on some occasions been trying to fulfil our desire for accomplishment (or for revenge) in such a way and to an extent that decreases our own welfare without increasing that of others. If this is not just due to ignorance, it is irrational according to my definition. Though this definition may be debatable, we may achieve some agreement by noting that there are different degrees of irrationality. In any case, I do not find that there is any intrinsic normative significance in having the desire for accomplishment fulfilled, except for the welfare effects of such fulfilment, including the indirect ones through the accomplished deeds. Other autonomous desires (such as preferring a less happy 'real-world' life to one of being attached to a pleasure machine) may be similarly analysed.

Now, consider a concrete real example. As reported in *Ming Pao Daily* (a reliable leading daily in Hong Kong) on 23 March 1997 (p.A11), a man in Tienjin was sent to a hospital after fainting while cycling. Further investigations revealed that he decided to buy a cellular mobile phone costing more than $9,000, despite having a monthly salary of only about $600 and a life saving of only $5,000 (all in Chinese dollars). He thus cut down on all his expenses including food. After more than four months of semi-fasting, he managed to buy the cellular mobile phone with a loan of another $2,000 from relatives. The phone was not for any business or other essential use. Rather, he used it to show off to his friends, cycling from one house to another, ending up in the hospital. Maybe he was ignorant of the possibility of fainting. However, even if he did not faint, I do not think that the happiness he would obtain from showing off his phone would be more than his welfare loss from spending more than $9,000, including making himself rather unhealthy from semi-fasting. His desire to have the phone, whether autonomous or not, is likely to be irrational.

4.4 Why is happiness fundamental?

Why do I regard the satisfaction of preferences, desires, etc. as such not of normative significance while happiness is? Why is happiness fundamental while other things important, ultimately speaking, only to the extent that they directly or indirectly contribute to happiness? The simple answer is that happiness/unhappiness is good/bad in itself and no other thing is so in itself.

There are many things we want: money, job security, status, freedom, etc. However, we do not want them for themselves, but to make us more happy or less unhappy. But we want happiness for itself. It is true that, being happy may also have some instrumental values such as making us healthier and/or more successful in our jobs. However, being healthier or being more successful in jobs are, ultimately speaking, only valuable (in the normative sense) by contributing to happiness directly or indirectly. Happiness is itself valuable without having to contribute to anything else. If my happiness does not make any other sentient less happy, it is valuable. I do not have to argue with philosophers for thousands of years to establish this since I can directly perceive the enjoyable/painful feelings and know that they are intrinsically good/bad in themselves. But for extreme philosophical solipsists, no one will object to my presumption that other normal individuals have the same capacity for such enjoyment/suffering. (To be less controversial, let us ignore animal welfare here.) Their enjoyment and suffering are intrinsically good/bad to themselves.

To see that happiness is more fundamental than preference, consider advanced computers in the 21st or 22nd century that have preferences but no affective subjective feelings. Clearly their preferences should not count morally. If it is replied that only human (informed) preferences should count, not machine preferences, then consider animals now and advanced computers in the 25th century that do have subjective affective feelings, i.e. they have pain, joy, etc. then most morally sensitive persons will agree that their welfare should also count. Thus, clearly welfare is more important and fundamental than preferences, informed or not, ultimately speaking.

If we follow (as I largely do) Harsanyi in rejecting actual and opting for informed preferences, it is difficult not to go all the way to happiness, in contrast to preferences, as what is ultimately normatively valuable. This is particularly so if we realise that much of our actual and informed preferences and/or our actual behaviour are shaped by our genes to increase our biological fitness which may be at variance with our actual welfare. As pointed out above, it is our welfare that is normatively valuable rather than the dictates of the unfeeling genes formed by random mutation and natural selection. Lastly, as we can all naturally *feel* that enjoyment/suffering is intrinsically good/bad but cannot naturally feel the same for anything else that may be held to be intrinsically good/bad, the burden of argument rests with those who want to replace/supplement happiness by/with something else as ultimately good/bad.

At the risk of repetition, the argument for recognising happiness as ultimately the valuable thing at the fundamental moral philosophical level does not rule out the importance of insisting on such useful principles as honesty, freedom, democracy, law and order, justice, human rights, etc. at the practical, political, or day-to-day level. However, recognising the real ultimate objective will help us in making decisions on more fundamental issues like the trade-off of the useful principles especially when they are in conflict with each other, the long-term choices of the appropriate institutions and principles to promote. The existence of an objective more fundamental than preference also allows us to analyse more fruitfully changes in preferences which have left economists largely voiceless. As economists assume given preferences and take preferences as the ultimate objective, they are largely at a loss when preferences changes. This partly explains their insistence on stable preferences and try to explain most, if not all, of the changes in terms of changes in constraints, especially incomes and prices. They have indeed been very successful in many of these explanations. However, true changes in preferences are also quite prevalent in the real world (see Bowles, 1998). The use of happiness gives us the appropriate criterion to judge the desirability of changes or policies in the presence of preference changes. (On the cardinal measurement and interpersonal comparison of happiness, see Ng, 1996a and Chapter 2 above.)

5
Utilitarianism

Utilitarianism is the belief that the ultimate objective of the society should be the maximisation of the unweighted sum of individual welfares (or utilities, ignoring the differences between the two; in the presence of such differences, it is argued in Chapter 4 that welfares should be the one to use). A utilitarian SWF is the unweighted sum of individual welfares. If we do not confuse non-ultimate considerations with basic values, it seems natural that the right ultimate objective for the society should be the unweighted sum of individual welfares, and was taken to be so by all classical utilitarians. (The difference between preference and welfare, discussed in Chapter 4, is largely ignored in this chapter.) Many modern philosophers and economists are sceptical. However, arguments for the compellingness of utilitarianism are overwhelming. In my view, utilitarianism has never been adequately shown to be unacceptable, if the correct 'ultimate' view is taken. (And if we are confining utilitarianism to the society rather than to the individual level; see Goodin, 1995 for an argument that utilitarianism makes more sense as a public than as a private moral philosophy.)

5.1 Compelling arguments for utilitarianism

Apart from the basic requirements that social welfare is a function of individual utilities only (welfarism, defended in Chapter 3) and that social welfare increases with individual utilities (the Pareto principle, which is uncontroversial, given welfarism), the utilitarian SWF entails three increasingly precise requirements:

1. *Separability*
   That the (social) weight attached to any individual utility is inde-

pendent of the utility levels of other individuals. (This is called separability because it means that SWF is then a separable function of individual utilities.)

2. *Linearity*

That the weight attached to any individual utility is a constant (i.e. unchanged), making social welfare a weighted sum of individual utilities and increases linearly with each individual utility. This is a more precise requirement than separability because the latter allows the weight on any individual to be dependent on the utility level of that individual.

3. *Unweighted sum*

That social welfare is the unweighted sum of individual utilities.

Compelling arguments supporting the above three steps toward the full utilitarian SWF are presented below. (Only the direct substantive justifications are included. Utilitarian results based on informational restrictions, e.g. D'Aspremont and Gevers, 1977 and Maskin, 1978, are not discussed.)

1. *Separability – Fleming (1952) and Sugden and Weale (1979)*

Fleming establishes separability, i.e. $W = \Sigma f^i(W^i)$ from a very reasonable set of axioms: the existence of a SWF,[1] the Pareto principle, and the 'Elimination of Indifferent Individuals' (strong version). For some problems, the existence of a SWF (which presupposes a social ordering) may be a strong assumption to make. But this axiom imposes no restriction at all on the question of which SWF we should adopt. Taking also the Pareto principle as acceptable, let us thus concentrate on the crucial 'Elimination of Indifferent Individuals' (Fleming's Postulate E).

Postulate E (*Elimination of Indifferent Individuals*): Given at least three individuals, suppose that both individuals *i* and *j* are indifferent between *x* and *x'* and also indifferent between *y* and *y'* but individual *i* prefers *x* (or *x'*) to *y* (or *y'*) and individual *j* prefers *y* (or *y'*) to *x* (or *x'*). (See Figure 5.1.) Suppose also that all other individuals are indifferent between *x* and *y*, and indifferent between *x'* and *y'* (but not necessarily indifferent between *x* and *x'* and between *y* and *y'*). Then social preferences must always go in the same way between *x* and *y* as they do between *x'* and *y'*.

The ethics behind the postulate is the following. In the choice between *x* and *y*, since all other individuals are indifferent, social preference should be decided by the preferences of individuals *i* and *j*.

Suppose the preference of individual *i* of *x* over *y* is judged on some grounds (stronger, worthier, etc.) to outweigh the dispreference of *j* such that *x* is socially preferred to *y*. Then in the choice between *x'* and *y'*, since all other individuals are again indifferent for both *i* and *j*, *x* is indifferent to *x'* and *y* is indifferent to *y'*, so the preference of *i* of *x'* over *y'* must also outweigh the dispreference of *j* to give *x'* socially preferred to *y'*.

The strength and possible objections to the postulate spring from the fact that, while all other individuals are indifferent between *x* and *y* and between *x'* and *y'* they are not necessarily indifferent between *x* (or *y*) and *x'* (or *y'*). Thus some people may want (probably based on some misunderstanding, see below) to base the social judgement as to whether the preference of individual *i* should outweigh the dispreference of *j* on the welfare levels of other individuals. One possible reason for this is that welfare levels are misunderstood to be something else such as income levels. Then, even if individual *i* (and also *j*) has the same income levels between *x* and *x'* and between *y* and *y'*, his welfare change between *x* and *y* may be different from that between *x'* and *y'* if the income levels of other individuals differ and produce external effects on *i* (and also *j*). However, Postulate E does not refer to income levels but holds individual *i* (and *j*) indifferent between *x* and *x'* and between *y* and *y'*, taking everything into account. The objection to Postulate E requires in fact the rejection of individualistic ethics. As Harsanyi (1955) explains, Postulate E is a natural requirement of individualistic ethics.

Fleming's set of axioms ensures that social welfare is a separable function of individual welfares, i.e. $W = \Sigma f^i(W^i)$. For any given set of the f^i functions, we may adopt monotonic transformations making W a sum of the transformed individual welfare indices, as Fleming does. This, however, is not permitted by the cardinal welfare framework. As Fleming himself is emphatic in pointing out, the transformed indices need not bear direct relationship to say a cardinal measure of happiness. Thus, in our interpersonal comparable cardinal welfare framework, we must view Fleming's result as no more than separability.

Another contribution in support of a separable SWF is Sugden and Weale (1979). They adopt a set of very compelling axioms within the individualistic, contractarian framework which implies Fleming's Postulate E and the separability in social welfare function. I find their argument so persuasive that I do not find their following conclusion presumptuous: 'In so far as our argument is valid, therefore, future formulations of welfare economics should include this separability requirement as a matter of course.' I do not believe there is any escape from this separability satisfying the individualistic ethics. Those who prefer a non-separable SWF should have a hard time reconciling with their simultaneous belief (as most of them apparently do) in individualism.

However, separability may easily be regarded as a stronger result than it really is. In fact, within the confine of a separable SWF, enormous flexibility is still possible. For example, if we write $W = \Sigma(W^i)^{1-\alpha}/(1 - \alpha)$ where α is some constant, we have a Paretian and anonymous SWF which is separable. But by varying the value of α, we can accommodate virtually all degrees of 'egalitarianism'. With $\alpha = 0$, we have the Bentham SWF; with $\alpha = 1$, we have the Nash SWF, with α approaching infinity, we approach the maximin SWF. Thus, the result on linearity is an important advance over separability.

2. *Linearity – Harsanyi (1953, 1955)*

Harsanyi shows that $W = \Sigma k^i(W^i)$ (where each k^i is a constant) by assuming that social as well as individual preferences satisfy the set of axioms for expected utility maximisation (Marschak, 1950) and that the society is indifferent between any two prospects which are indifferent to every individual.

3. *Unweighted sum – Harsanyi (1953, 1955) and Ng (1975a, forthcoming, a)*

Harsanyi also has a more intuitive argument based on the impersonal observer approach. Each individual is to indicate 'what social situation he would choose if he did not know what his personal position would be in the new situation chosen (and in any of its alternatives) but rather had an equal chance of obtaining any of the social position existing in this situation,[2] from the highest down to the lowest' (Harsanyi, 1955, p.316). Given this hypothetical choice, it is clear that if the person wants to maximise his expected utility (which can be argued to be the only rational objective; see Ng, 1984a), he would choose the alternative that maximises the sum of individual utilities.

That an individual may have difficulties judging the utility levels of other individuals only concerns the practical difficulties of obtaining the interpersonally comparable individual utility indices. If we have these utility indices, Harsanyi's argument means that we should use the sum of utilities as the appropriate social objective rather than any other form.

Another case for utilitarianism is advanced in Ng (1975a). This is based mainly on the following postulate:

Weak Majority Preference Criterion (WMP): For any two alternatives (or social states) x and y, if no individual prefers y to x and (1) if n, the number of individuals, is even, at least $n/2$ individuals prefer x to y; (2) if n is odd, at least $(n + 1)/2$ individuals prefer x to y and at least another individual's utility level is not lower in x than in y, then social welfare is higher in x than in y.

As Mueller observes:

> WMP is obviously a combination of both the Pareto principle and the majority rule principle that is at once significantly weaker [hence more acceptable as a *sufficient* condition for a social improvement] than both. In contrast to the Pareto criterion it requires a majority to be better off, rather than just one [individual], to justify a move. And, in contrast to majority rule, it allows the majority to be decisive only against an indifferent minority. In spite of this apparent weakness, the postulate nevertheless proves strong enough to support a Benthamite social welfare function.
>
> Mueller, 1989, p.435

The reason why WMP leads us to the utilitarian SWF is not difficult to see. It requires that individual utility differences sufficient to give rise to preferences of half of the population must be regarded as socially more significant than differences not sufficient to give rise to preferences (or dispreferences) of another half. Since any group of individuals comprising 50 per cent of the population is an acceptable half, this effectively makes a just perceivable increment of utility of any individual equivalent to that of any other individual.

Ng (forthcoming, a) has a different argument for full utilitarianism. Starting from separability as compellingly established by either Fleming (1952) or Sugden and Weale (1979) (see Section 5.1 above), the following condition is added:

Local Cardinal Individualism: *For any four social alternatives, if all individuals apart from any single individual* j *are strictly indifferent between all the four alternatives, then the social welfare difference between a pair of these alternatives is higher than that between another pair if individual* j*'s utility difference between the first pair is higher than that between the second pair.* In symbols, for all a, b, c, d in the set of social alternatives, for any individual j, if $a \; I^i \; b \; I^i \; c \; I^i \; d$ for all $i \neq j$ (where I^i stands for strict indifference by individual i), then:

$Uj(a) - Uj(b) > Uj(c) - Uj(d)$ implies $W(a) - W(b) > W(c) - W(d)$

The compellingness of Local Cardinal Individualism may be explained. Essentially, it says that, where no one else is affected, the cardinal intensity of preferences by any single individual must be respected. Here, everyone else is strictly indifferent (not even any slightest unnoticeable preference or uncertainty or whatever) between all the four alternatives concerned. Only individual j is affected by the choice among these alternatives. If the society is to respect her preferences and if she prefers a to b more strongly than she prefers c to d, the society should also prefer a to b more strongly than c to d. From this reasonable condition of local cardinal individualism and the compelling separability condition, full utilitarianism (unweighted sum) may then be proven.

The fourth case for full utilitarianism is provided in the next section. Following on from the argument in Section 3.3 above that rational individualism implies welfarism, it is shown that rational individualistic egalitarianism (a strengthened version of rational individualism plus a compelling version of egalitarianism) implies utilitarianism.

5.2 Rational individualistic egalitarianism implies utilitarianism

In this section, it is argued that rationality, (a strong version of) individualism and egalitarianism imply utilitarianism. Thus, utilitarianism is not only consistent with but is also demanded by egalitarianism at the most fundamental level of ultimate objectives. Hence, it is also consistent with some concept of 'justice as impartiality' (title of Barry, 1995). Whoever one is, one carries the same welfare weight at the most fundamental level of the ultimate objective of individuals and society – happiness.

In addition to Rational Individualism discussed in Section 3.3, we add the following axioms.

Axiom 2. Egalitarianism: *All individuals should be treated equally in social choice.*

In itself, Egalitarianism does not answer 'equality in what?'. However, together with Rational Individualism (which implies Welfarism as shown in Section 3.3), it means that individual welfares should be treated on an equal footing. However, this still does not imply (welfare) utilitarianism (which maximises the unweighted sum of individual welfares), if 'equal footing' is given only a general interpretation. Thus, 'equal footing' does not rule out giving w^A (the welfare of individual A) a higher weight than that of individual B when $w^B > w^A$, provided w^B is also given a similarly higher weight than w^A when $w^A > w^B$. Egalitarianism does imply anonymity or symmetry in the social welfare function. The Nash SWF, $W = w^A.w^B$ satisfies egalitarianism but the SWF, $W = 2w^A + w^B$ does not.

Axiom 3. Strong Individualism: For any social alternatives x, x', y, y', if all non-(individual)-welfare variables that may affect social welfare are held unchanged over all these alternatives,[3] and if all individual welfares are exactly identical except for any two individuals A and B, (i.e. $w^i(x) = w^i(x') = w^i(y) = w^i(y')$ for all individuals i except A and B); $w^A(x) - w^A(y) = w^A(x') - w^A(y') > 0$; $w^B(y) = w^B(y') > w^B(x) = w^B(x')$; then $W(x) > W(y)$ implies $W(x') > W(y')$.

The welfare levels of all individuals except A and B are exactly identical over all the four alternatives. The welfare levels of A and B are illustrated in Figure 5.1. (Note: for w^A, x' and y' could be at the same level as, or higher than, x and/or y.) The excess of w^A in x over that in y is exactly equal to the excess of w^A in x' over that in y'. This equality is in terms of the welfare level, what the individual and the society rationally value ultimately. If the equality is in terms of income or some other non-ultimate variables, one may say that the excess of \$100 when the income level is 1 million dollars is less important than the same excess

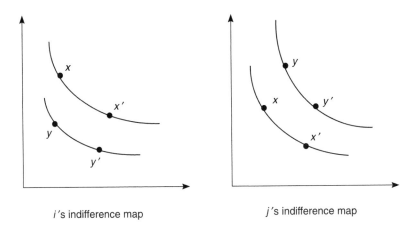

i's indifference map   *j*'s indifference map

Figure 5.1

of \$100 when the income level is only one thousand dollars. However, here the excesses are already in terms of welfare. If there is diminishing marginal welfare of income, the same welfare excess when income is high must already mean larger income excess. The society may also not want to place the same weight on the two excesses or differences if other individuals are differently affected. However, here individual B is affected by exactly the same amount and all other individuals are not affected at all. Thus, there is no individualism-consistent reason not to give the welfare excess $w^A(x) - w^A(y)$ the same social weight as the welfare excess $w^A(x') - w^A(y')$. These are valued to be exactly the same in welfare to individual A. Strong Individualism requires the society to value these two welfare differences also equally. Then, if the society views the welfare difference $w^A(x) - w^A(y)$ as big enough to outweigh the negative welfare difference $w^B(x) - w^B(y)$ to decide $W(x) > W(y)$, it must also regard the welfare difference $w^A(x') - w^A(y')$ as big enough to out-weigh the negative welfare difference $w^B(x') - w^B(y')$, as x and x' gives exactly the same welfare level to B and so do y and y', and all other indi-vidual welfare levels are exactly the same. Thus, although labelled 'strong' to distinguish it from Axiom 1a, Strong Individualism is really compelling.

It might be thought that, despite the fact that $w^A(x) - w^A(y) = w^A(x') - w^A(y')$, the same welfare difference $w^A(x') - w^A(y')$ may be regarded as socially more important than that of $w^A(x) - w^A(y)$ for the following con-sideration. Suppose that person A is poor (in income) at y' and below average at x', rich at y and very rich at x, with other things being the same. While A may regard the increase in income from rich to very rich as of similar welfare significance to her as the increase from poor to below average, others in the society may regard the latter increase as more important. In fact, they may not like A getting very rich as much as they do not like seeing A in poverty. If this is true, as is likely to be the case, it is socially more important to increase A's income from poverty to below average than to increase her income from rich to very rich. However, this does not violate Strong Rational Individualism which holds the welfare levels of all individuals except A and B (which is used for comparison with A) unchanged. In the above consideration, other individuals will have lower welfare levels in y' than x' and lower welfare levels in x than in y.[4] If other individuals all have the same welfare levels, there is no individualism-consistent reason to give the same weight to welfare differences of the same value for the same person.

What if the person herself gives different weights to welfare differ-ences of the same value? Certainty it will then be individualism-consistent to give accordingly different social weights to welfare differences of the same value. However, while one can have diminishing marginal welfare of income (as a unit of income satisfies more urgent needs when the income level is low) or of any other non-ultimate variable, one cannot logically have diminishing marginal welfare of welfare. As non-affective altruism/malice, ignorance, and irrationality have all been excluded by axioms 1d1–1d3 (see Section 3.3), the welfare of the individual concerned is the only thing affecting her preference. It may be thought that one may still have diminishing marginal utility (representing preference) of welfare. However, it can be shown that, provided the welfare levels are measured appropriately, it violates compelling rationality axioms to have diminishing (or increasing) marginal utility of welfare, as shown in the next paragraph. The appropriate cardinalisation of welfare measurement is using the same welfare unit (say, one) to represent a welfare difference of a just perceivable increment of Edgeworth (1881). Edgeworth regarded it as 'a first principle incapable of proof' (pp. 7ff., 60ff.) that such a just perceivable increment is equatable across all pleasures and across all persons. This equatability is shown as a result from some compelling axioms in Ng (1975a). (See Section 5.1 above.)

For simplicity, consider an atemporal framework. (If time is introduced, the just perceptible increment of welfare have to be specified over a just perceptible time duration.) As non-affective altruism/malice, ignorance, and irrationality have all been abstracted away, we may use welfare (representing happiness) and utility (representing preference) interchangeably. The concept of just perceivable increments recognises the fact (consistent with commonsense and well established by psychologists) that human beings are not infinitely sensitive in their capacity to enjoy welfare. Using one to measure the welfare difference of a just perceivable increment,[5] it is not difficult to see that, if two welfare differences of the same value are given different weight, then a perceivable preference will be given a lower weight than an imperceivable one. This is unacceptable. (For more details, see Ng, 1975a, 1984a.)

Definition 2. Strong Rational Individualism requires both Rational Individualism (Axiom 1, Section 3.3) and Strong Individualism (Axiom 2).

Proposition 2. Strong Rational Individualism and Egalitarianism imply Utilitarianism.

Proof: Rational Individualism implies welfarism. Where others are not affected, social welfare is a positive function of and only of individual welfares in the society. (See Section 3.3.) In the specification of Strong Individualism, the case where $w^A(x) = w^A(x')$ and $w^A(y) = w^A(y')$ is not excluded. Since Strong Individualism dictates that $W(x) > W(y)$ implies $W(x') > W(y')$, as long as all individual welfare levels (other than those of A and B) are the same over the four social states x, y, x', y' (i.e. irrespective of being the same at what levels), this means that the relative social evaluation of the welfare levels of A and B does not depend on the welfare levels of other individuals. Since A and B can be any pair of all the individuals, this makes the social evaluation of the welfare level of each individual independent of the welfare levels of other individuals. Hence, the social welfare function is a separable function of individual welfares. Another way of demonstrating this is to note that, for the case where $w^A(x) = w^A(x')$ and $w^A(y) = w^A(y')$, Strong Individualism[6] is equivalent to the axiom 'Independence of Indifferent Individuals' of Fleming (1952) who proves that this axiom, together with the Pareto principle and the existence of a social welfare function, imply that social welfare is a separable function of individual welfares. Since the Pareto principle (Axiom 1b above) and the existence of a social welfare function (Axiom 0 above) are also assumed here, we also have this separability result:

$$W = \sum f^i(w^i)$$

From Strong Individualism, each and every f^i must be linear in w^i. This is so because if any f^i is not linear in w^i, the social welfare significance (effect on W) of some equal welfare differences will be different. Strong Individualism must thus be violated. We must thus have W separable and linear in individual welfares:

$$W = \sum a^i w^i$$

where the a^i are constants. From Egalitarianism, a^i has to be the same for all i. We lose no generality and make no difference in substance in making all a^i equal to one, yielding:

$$W = \sum w^i$$

which is utilitarianism. *Q.E.D*

5.3 A defence of Harsanyi against some recent criticisms

In the last dozen of years, Harsanyi's utilitarianism results have been subject to rather prominent criticisms. Sen (1986, pp. 1122–4) questions the significance of Harsanyi's impersonal observer result on the ground that 'There is no *independent* concept of individual utilities [other than the von Neumann–Morgenstern values] of which social welfare is shown to be the sum, and as such the result asserts a good deal less than classical utilitarianism does' (p.1123). This (or a similar) point is made much clearer and in much stronger terms by Roemer, who asserts that 'Harsanyi's Impartial Observer Theorem has nothing to do with utilitarianism' (Roemer, 1996, p.149). Roemer sustains this strongly worded assertion by arguing that the VNM (von Neumann–Morgenstern) utilities and the fully measurable and comparable utilities needed for social choice need have no relation at all. Where the two sets of utility functions are incompatible with each other, it is easy to show that social decisions in accordance to the sum according to one set will in general differ with the sum in accordance to another set. This criticism of Harsanyi's result is answered by my result (Ng, 1984a) that, using axioms no stronger than those for the expected utility hypothesis, with the recognition of finite sensibility (which is just commonsense and well established by psychologists), the utility function derived by the Neumann–Morgenstern method is the *same* as the subjective utility function of classical utilitarianism and neoclassical economists such as Edgeworth (1881). Given this result, Harsanyi's result does give full support to utilitarianism.

Apart from a few other axioms no stronger than those used by the VNM expected utility hypothesis, I was able to establish the equivalence mainly by the following axiom (which is itself implied by the VNM set of axioms, assuming infinite sensibility, making explicit preference coincide with intrinsic preference):

Axiom A: $\forall r, x, y, z$: (rIx & zPy) implies [$(r, z; 1/2, 1/2)$ $\underline{P}$ $(x, y; 1/2, 1/2)$] where r, x, y, z are alternative outcomes, $(r, z; 1/2, 1/2)$ is the lottery with 50/50 chance of obtaining r and z, $\underline{P}$ is intrinsic preference, I and P are explicit indifference and explicit preference respectively. The need to distinguish intrinsic and explicit preference/indifference is due to the recognition of finite sensibility. If the optimal amount of sugar in your coffee is 1.8, you may not be able to tell a difference between 1.8 and 1.79 and fail to register an explicit preference but 1.8 may be intrinsically preferred to 1.79. (See Ng, 1975a for more details.) This axiom says that the same 50/50 probability mix of obtaining a (explicitly) preferred and an indifferent outcome must be an intrinsically preferred lottery. This is in the spirit of a semiorder that a preference should outweigh an indifference to give at least an intrinsic preference. This is compelling in an atemporal framework where time and future effects have been abstracted away (on which see Section 5.4 below). Axiom A then implies that a maximal indifference (continuous with a marginal preference, or Edgeworth's *minimum sensibile*, or just perceptible increment of pleasure) must be represented by a same positive constant. The VNM utility indices satisfying Axiom A then must be the same as the Edgeworthian cardinal utility indices. It is true that the zero point is left undefined in this. However, for utilitarianism, the zero points do not matter, only utility differences count for making social choice.

Even without using the above rigorous axiomatic justification of the equivalence of the VNM utility and the subjective cardinal utility of the classical utilitarians and neoclassical economists, a commonsense argument may also establish this equivalence. We only need to note that the VNM utility indices do not come from thin air *only* to represent individual choices over lotteries. Rather, each individual *already* has her subjective cardinal utility function to begin with. When I face choices involving risks, I compare the probabilities and the associated *subjective cardinal* utility gains and losses involved before making a choice. Moreover, I choose to maximise, as far as possible, subject to mistakes (which, together with things like regrets, excitement, give rise to various paradoxes and intransitivities; see, e.g. Munier, 1988), my expected subjective cardinal utility. Thus, these subjective cardinal utility functions exist *before* the VNM construction is used. The latter is used to discover the pre-existing individual subjective cardinal utility functions by observing their choices involving risks. The degree of the pre-existent diminishing/increasing marginal (subjective and cardinal) utility (of income or some other objective indices) determines the degree of risk aversion/preference, not the other way round.

What the 'pure representation' economists do is to say that the VNM utility is purely a representation of individual choices involving risks and has nothing to do with the subjective cardinal utility of the same individual. This would be true if individuals did not consult their subjective utility in making choices involving risks. (But then on what basis do they make rational choices involving risks is rather mythical.) There is a sense in which these pure representation economists are right. First, the well-known axioms of the VNM hypothesis does not ensure that individuals do consult their subjective utilities and try to maximise expected subjective utility in making choices involving risks. However, this may be taken as a commonsense requirement for rational choice or, if one wants to be rigorous, Axiom A above may be assumed to ensure this. This then makes Harsanyi's result a full utilitarian one. Secondly, Roemer (1996, p.142) is correct in claiming that the knowledge of all individual VNM preferences or utilities does not give us a meaningful way of making interpersonal comparisons [necessary for any SWF, a utilitarian one in particular]. However, Axiom A and the approach of Edgeworth (1881) and Ng (1975a, 1996a) do give us interpersonal comparability. In Ng (1975a), I argue that a natural way of obtaining interpersonally comparable individual cardinal utility indices is to use a common number (e.g. one) across all individuals to indicate the utility difference of a maximal (non-strict) indifference, recognising that individuals are not infinitely sensitive. (See Section 5.1 above.) In Ng (1996a), I use this method to actually obtain utility indices that are interpersonally comparable, overcoming the non-comparability problem of happiness surveys done by psychologists. There are other ways (some discussed in Section 9 of Ng, 1975a) of obtaining interpersonal comparable utility indices. Thus, even if one does not concede that Harsanyi (1953) is sufficient for utilitarianism, one must admit that Harsanyi (1953) plus Ng (1975a, 1984a, 1996a) are.

Sen also plays down on the significance of the second Harsanyi's (1955) (weighted) utilitarian result, saying that it is primarily a 'representation theorem', not really utilitarianism. Sen has two objections. The first is regarding the choice of individual utility indices. This has already been answered above. The second is that the result is within the single-profile framework with a given set of individual preferences. My defence is twofold. First, as the utilitarian result applies within each single-profile, it really does not matter that it is only a single-profile result. Secondly, Harsanyi's result is easily generalised to the multi-profile framework, as must already be implicit in Roberts (1980) who establishes corresponding results in both frameworks, and as explicitly shown in Mongin (1994).

After a long evaluation of the Harsanyi–Sen debate, Weymark concludes that:

> If utility only has meaning as representation of [ordinal] preference, then Sen is correct in regarding Harsanyi's theorems as social utility representation theorems.... If utility does not simply measure preference, Harsanyi's Impartial Observer Theorem can be interpreted as an axiomatization of utilitarianism provided (i) well-being is cardinally measurable and fully comparable, (ii) each person's well-being, including that of the impartial observer, is measured by a von Neumann–Morgenstern utility function, and (iii) the Principle of Welfare Identity is satisfied.
>
> Weymark, 1991, p.315

This last principle is compelling in the context as it just requires that the impartial observer's ordering of the extended lotteries in which he is individual *i* for certain agrees with individual *i*'s ordering of the simple lotteries. Point (ii) is satisfied given my 1984a result cited above in reference to Sen's objection. Point (i) is compelling to assume for the problem of what form of SWF to take as the existence of any reasonable SWF presumes the existence of interpersonally comparable individual cardinal utilities as argued in Chapter 2. In fact, Weymark (1991, p.299) himself argues that the ordinal concept of utility cannot 'provide an adequate basis for utilitarianism', which can have 'meaning [only] if utility is cardinally measurable and unit comparable' (p.303). Thus, for the problem of the appropriate form of SWF, Harsanyi (or anyone else) must be granted interpersonal cardinal utilities. Thus, despite these queries regarding the relevance of Harsanyi's results to utilitarianism, I believe that Harsanyi (at least after having been strengthened with my arguments) emerges completely unscathed.

A somewhat different objection to Harsanyi's utilitarianism may be considered. Mongin (1988, p.143) asks us to consider a society 'of 100 identical individuals, whose utility functions are egoistical, i.e. depend on the individual's own endowment only. Endowments are distributed once-and-for-all, and one unit of them is taken to be just above the subsistence level'. Would you prefer:

Society *A*:   100 persons get 2 units each
or
Society *B*:   89 persons get 2 units each
1 person gets 1 unit
10 persons get 5 units each
and
Society *C*:   89 persons get 1 unit each
11 persons get 2 units each
or
Society *D*:   90 persons get 1 unit each
10 persons get 5 units each

Mongin has:

little doubt that some ethical observers would choose *A rather than B* and *D rather than C* on the grounds that complete equality should be preferred to any other social solution, but when complete equality is impossible, significant differences in total endowment should tilt the balance towards the best-endowed society. There might even be ethical observers who would choose *B rather than C* and *C rather than D* on the grounds that complete equality is distasteful, but moderate inequality should be preferred to extreme inequality. Of course, none of those ethical observers could consistently be utilitarian.

p.143

I wish to argue that one can have either type of ethical preference and still be a utilitarian, if secondary effects are taken into account. On the other hand, if secondary effects are abstracted away, as apparently intended by Mongin (note his 'once-and-for-all' distribution and the dependence of utility on own endowments only), there is no individualism-consistent grounds for either type of ethical preference.

Mongin's example is the adaptation of a famous Allais paradox to the context of social choice. However, the intended paradox is really there only if there is a confusion of fundamental values with non-ultimate considerations by the ethical observer. Thus, I, a self-proclaimed utilitarian at the fundamental level, prefer society *A* to *B* *and* also prefer *D* to *C*, if the secondary effects of social cohesion in *A* dominates the higher endowment of *B* (valuing the various effects ultimately on individual utilities) and if the higher endowment in *D* dominates the slightly more equality of *C*. However, if the 10 better endowed persons in *B* are able to pursue worthwhile activities contributory to future advance in welfare, I prefer *B* to *A*; if the extreme inequality in *D* results in a polarised society with undesirable secondary effects, I prefer *C* to *D*. Thus, if we take secondary effects into account, none of the ethical preferences mentioned by Mongin need be contrary to utilitarianism, nor is any of them inconsistent. On the other hand, if these secondary effects have been abstracted away (as they should be, otherwise they should be included in the description of the above societies), there is no individualism-consistent grounds for having either of the inconsistent types of ethical preferences mentioned by Mongin. For example, since the utility of each and every individual depends only on her own endowment, none of them finds complete equality distasteful. Then, how could the ethical observer choose 'on the grounds that complete equality is distasteful'? Surely, the hypothetical ethical observer is supposed to choose on behalf of the 100 individuals, not on behalf of herself! She is just a theoretical construct that does not really exist.

5.4 A defence of using just perceptible increments

Edgeworth (1881, pp.7, 60) took it as axiomatic ('a first principle incapable of proof') that a just perceptible increment of pleasure, for all pleasures, are equitable across all individuals. Abstracting from secondary effects as we should and from different time durations (discussed below), I find Edgeworth's axiom compelling. Nevertheless, I derived the axiom as a *result* based mainly on the Weak Majority Preference criterion discussed in Section 5.1. However, the use of just perceptible increments for interpersonal comparison has been strongly objected to, including by Hammond (1991). This objection is taken as so conclusive that a commentator said that the 'method of just perceptible differences is dead, in the eyes of most economists'. If this were true, most economists would be wrong, as the method can be strongly defended below.

The objection by Hammond (see also Arrow, 1963, pp.115–18) is that the method 'tend[s] to favour the sensitive' (pp.216–17). A similar objection I have heard many times at seminars is that the method would give less weights to the incomes of the less sensitive (in enjoying income). This objection is puzzling. A strong (if not the strongest) argument in favour of higher equality is that a dollar to the poor meets more urgent needs or yields higher marginal utilities. Thus, a person is more sensitive to income when poor; each dollar yields more perceptible increments of happiness. So, we should not focus on changes in incomes only. A million dollar increment to the rich may be worth much less than half a million dollar increments to the poor. We should ultimately focus on the subjective units of happiness or utilities. But the method of just perceptible increments in happiness precisely makes us focus on these subjective units rather than the objective amounts of incomes or whatever. To shift focus from the purely objective amounts of production, income, etc. to the subjective utilities and using marginal analysis is an important advance of the neoclassical economists. How ironic if we were to retreat back to the naive income fetishism!

It is true that income inequality may generate certain undesirable effects such as less social cohesion, more crimes, etc. This means that individual welfares in the future will be reduced by inequality now. A long-run SWF will take account of that. Thus, this alleged problem arises only because of the confusion of fundamental values with non-ultimate considerations or because of the confusion of the ultimate objective with the constraints (intertemporal utility feasibility in particular).

Will the application of the utilitarian SWF lead to a very unequal distribution of income? Apart from incentive effects, it is doubtful that differences in sensibility will lead to a great inequality of income. Psychological studies in pain sensation show that the pain thresholds are very close for different individuals (e.g. averaging 230 ± 10 mc./sec./cm² standard variation), as are the number of just noticeable differences (Hardy *et al.*, 1952, pp.88, 157). If there are more differences in the capacity to enjoy income, these are probably due to 'learning by doing', and a long-run SWF allowing for all relevant effects will take account of that. If some inequality still persists after taking all effects into account, I cannot see why this is not an optimal distribution if it maximises aggregate welfare (especially within the scope of this chapter starting from welfarism; for a defence of welfarism, see Chapter 3). Consider the much-cherished principle, 'From each according to his ability; to each according to his needs' (which I personally approve of, assuming no disincentive effect). Why doesn't it read, 'An equal amount of work from each; an equal amount of income to each?'. If a weak person is tired by four hours of work, it is better for a strong person to work longer to relieve him/her. Similarly, if a less-sensitive person does not enjoy the extra income much, it is better that a more sensitive person receives more of it. What prevents us from seeing such a simple analogy?

Thus, I find the 'weak equity axiom' of Sen (1973a, p.18) unacceptable. The axiom says: 'Let person i have a lower level of welfare than person j for each level of individual income. Then in distributing a given total of income among n individuals including i and j, the optimal solution must give i a higher level of income than j.' Thus, even if giving more income to i does not make her appreciably or even perceptively happier, while reducing j's income does make him enormously less happy (though still of higher welfare level than i), the axiom insists that i should receive more income than j. In my view, what is important is not the welfare levels of various individuals, but rather how much *increases* in welfare, to whomsoever they go (anonymity), we can have.

Another type of objection to WMP and the resulting use of just perceptible increments may now be discussed. First, it is argued that a just perceptible improvement may differ across different experiences even for the same individual. 'On many occasions, a just perceptible improvement in musical performance means much more to me than a just perceptible quantity of drink' (Mirrlees, 1982, p.69). This I think may be due to the difference in time period involved and/or to possible future effects. A just perceptible quantity of drink may last only a fraction of a second while the musical performance probably a couple of hours. Moreover, Mirrlees may also value the recollection of a high-quality musical performance. As it is, WMP is formulated in an atemporal basis and hence does not cover the complication introduced by differences in time period. With time as a dimension, one should then select a just perceptible improvement over a just perceptible length with neither future nor external effect as the standard unit, and use indirect measurement (Ng, 1975a, section 9) for experiences difficult to be so measured.

Now consider the following objection raised in a personal discussion by David Friedman (cf. Sen, 1970a, p.94; Pattanaik, 1971, p.150). If individual utility levels are continuous (which is the assumption used in Ng, 1975a), then even an indifference may involve a utility difference. It is thus not clear that a just perceivable increment of utility should be regarded as interpersonally equitable. For example, a person poor in perception or reporting may fail to notice or report a utility difference more significant in some subjective sense than one noticed or reported by another more perceptive person. On the other hand, if utility levels are discontinuous so that individual utility does not change until an increment of pleasure is perceived, then these discontinuous little jumps in utility may differ across individuals in some sense and hence should not be regarded as equivalent.

My reply to the above objection is several-fold. First, it may be noted that the above objection is not against the principle of the utilitarian SWF, but just against the way the various U^i should be best measured or interpersonally compared. In other words, if the marginal preference of a person half as perceptive (in terms of reporting a given amount of subjective utility) as another is counted twice as important, the above objection will presumably no longer apply. Thus, this objection is properly regarded as pointing to the difficulty of making interpersonal comparison of utility rather than as an objection against the utilitarian SWF as such.

Secondly, if we shy away from making any interpersonal comparison of cardinal individual utilities, then a SWF is impossible. Thus, for the question of which SWF to adopt, we must accept some form of comparison. Most methods of interpersonal utility comparison are rough estimates (if not guesstimates) perhaps partly influenced by personal value beliefs. It seems to me that the method of measuring the levels of just perceivable increments of pleasure offers to date the most promising objective way of making interpersonal comparison. (On some practical difficulties and ways to overcome them, see Ng, 1975a, Section 9.)

If we accept the above objection, it just means that even this best available method is not ideal. With finite sensibility (which is an indisputable fact) and without some form of interpersonal comparison, we cannot make a reasonable social choice except in the unlikely cases where every individual strictly prefers x to y. Even the indifference of one individual is sufficient to cloud the issue unless we are prepared to make the interpersonal comparison that any utility difference associated with his indifference is not strong enough to overshadow the preferences of others. Thirdly, even if it is true that a just perceivable increment of utility differs across individuals either due to different 'perceptive' powers or due to different 'jumps' in utility, how are we to know whose just perceivable increment is larger and whose smaller? In the absence of specific knowledge regarding this, it seems best to regard them as equal (cf. Lerner, 1944, pp.29ff; Sen, 1973b). If we adopt the convention of designing an average just perceivable increment of utility as one, then the just perceivable increment of any particular individual, in the absence of any specific knowledge, may be expected to have a probability distribution such as depicted in Figure 5.2, that is, the individual is just as likely (if at all) to have a lower as a higher than average value. We can thus minimise our mistake by taking this increment to be one, the average value (Ng, 1980).

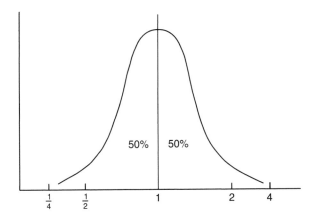

Figure 5.2

Our arguments for taking a just perceivable increment of utility as equitable across individuals (at least in the absence of an eudaimonometer) seem to be supported by the following argument of Harsanyi:

The *metaphysical* problem would be present even if we tried to compare the utilities enjoyed by different persons with identical preferences and with identical expressive reactions to any situation. Even in this case, it would not be inconceivable that such persons should have different susceptibilities to satisfaction and should attach different utilities to identical situations . . . , and identical expressive reactions may well indicate different mental states with different people. At the same time, under these conditions this logical possibility of different susceptibilities to satisfaction would hardly be more than a metaphysical curiosity. If two objects or human beings show similar behaviour in *all* their relevant aspects open to observation, the assumption of some unobservable hidden difference between them must be regarded as a completely gratuitous hypothesis and one contrary to sound scientific method. (This principle may be called the 'principle of unwarranted differentiation'.) In the last analysis, it is on the basis of this principle that we ascribe mental states to other human beings at all: the denial of this principle would at once lead us to solipsism. . . . Thus in the case of persons with similar preferences and expressive reactions we are fully entitled to assume that they derive the same utilities from similar situations.

Harsanyi, 1955, p.317

5.5 Utilitarianism and process fairness

There is an apparently very persuasive objection to utilitarianism raised by Diamond (1967; see also Kolm, 1998). I have not read any satisfactory answer to this objection. Consider a society of two identical individuals, 1 and 2, facing a choice between two alternatives x and y, with two equally probable states of nature, α and β; let the cardinal and interpersonally comparable individual utility indices be as shown in Table 5.1 (ignoring z for the moment):

Harsanyi's set of axioms implies that the society is indifferent between x and y. But many people may find y (strictly) preferable to x. If we ask why is y preferable to x, there may be two different answers. First, consider Diamond's explanation: 'I am willing to accept the sure-thing principle for individual choice but not for social choice, since it seems

Table 5.1

	x		y		z	
	α	β	α	β	α	β
1	1	1	1	0	0	0
2	0	0	0	1	1	1

reasonable for the individual to be concerned solely with final states while society is also interested in the process of choice' (Diamond, 1967, p.766). But the society *consists* of individuals. If all individuals are concerned with final states, why should the society be concerned with the process of choice? I can think of only two reasons why the society may be concerned with the process of choice that are consistent with individualism. First, some individuals in the society have views about the process of choice and will be hurt or feel happy by the adoption of certain processes. In this case, what needs to be done is just to amend the pay-off matrices or to construct a more complex one to take account of this feeling. This is then not a valid argument against the utilitarian SWF, provided the feeling about the process of choice has been taken into account in the utility calculus. (Cf. a similar but different resolution of the problem raised by Diamond's example by Broome, 1991, pp.111–15. Even *after* abstracting from feelings about the process of choice, Broome reconciles Diamond's preference with the sure thing principle by distinguishing the outcomes of 'death with fair treatment' and 'death with unfair treatment'. However, Broome's argument is not, nor is it meant to be, a defence of utilitarianism. Thus, my argument here and below differs from Broome's but Broome's defence of the sure-thing principle is very thorough.)

Secondly, even if no individual in the society now has any feeling about the process of choice as such, it may still be regarded as a legitimate concern since the process of choice may generate secondary effects and affect the utilities of individuals in the future who may not exist now. In this case again, what needs to be done is just to take account of the effects on individual utilities in the future as well. Thus, I cannot find any ground consistent with individualism that is a valid objection to utilitarianism on the grounds of the process of choice or the like. Let us turn to a different objection.

Even if the feeling for the process of choice, the welfare of future generations, etc. has been taken into account or has been abstracted away, some people may still regard *y* as preferable to *x* because *y* gives individual 2 a 'fair shake' while *x* does not. To be socially indifferent between *x* and *y* is thus regarded as being unfair against 2. But I fail to see why it is unfair if the society is also indifferent between *y* and *z* (see Table 5.1 above), as utilitarianism axioms dictate. Is it unfair against both individuals (!) to be socially indifferent between *x*, *y* and *z*, despite the fact that both individuals are indifferent between *y* and a 50–50 chance of *x* and *z*? It is probably difficult to convince those who still regard *y* as preferable to both *x* and *z*, but I hope that the following argument will persuade at least some of them to have a second thought.

Let us accept the reasonable assumption that social welfare is continuous in individual utilities (an infinitesimal change in individual utilities does not cause a big jump in social welfare). To prefer *y* over *x* and *z* then implies that if we change the utility indices of *y* sufficiently slightly, then this new alternative *y″* is still preferred to *x*. To see this more intuitively, note that we have to change the utility indices by a finite amount (due to continuity), say to *y′* (see Table 5.2; the precise figure is immaterial) to make it indifferent to *x*. We can then increase the utility indices back a little to *y″* which will then be preferable to *x* and *z*. I wish to show that the adoption of a SWF dictating this preference is detrimental to the utility of both individuals and hence irrational at least from the viewpoint of individualism, when individual preferences satisfy the Marschak (VNM) axioms.

We do not adopt a SWF to guide our social choice for one particular known instance only. Rather, once a SWF is adopted, it is used for all instances until, for some reason, it has been discarded in favour of another. Moreover, even if we consider a once-and-for-all choice only, we do not know which particular alternatives that choice will involve at the 'constitutional stage' or the 'original position'. Thus, on the

Table 5.2

	x		*y*		*z*		*y′*		*y″*	
	α	β	α	β	α	β	α	β	α	β
1	1	1	1	0	0	0	0.89	0	0.9	0
2	0	0	0	1	1	1	0	0.89	0	0.9

abstract problem of the ideal SWF, we must consider all possible instances of choice. For the particular instance of the choice between x and y'', the preference of y'' over x does not appear to be clearly unreasonable. The expected utility (EU^i) of both individuals being 0.45 with y'' (noting that $\alpha = \beta = {}^1\!/_2$) and $EU^1 = 1$, $EU^2 = 0$ with x. Since 2 gains 0.45 and 1 loses 0.55 in terms of expected utility by the choice of y'' over x, it does not necessarily appear to be a social loss to the non-utilitarians. Similarly, this is true for the preference of y'' over z. However, *ex ante*, we do not know whether we will be confronted with the choice between y'' and x or between y'' and z; both must be regarded as equally probable. It then becomes clear that if individual preferences satisfy the Marschak axioms, both individuals would be in favour of the adoption of a SWF preferring both x and z to y'' rather than the reverse, since the preference of y'' over x and z gives $EU^1 = EU^2 = 0.45$, while the reverse preference gives $EU^1 = EU^2 = 0.5$. Individualism thus clearly dictates the adoption of the utilitarian SWF.

It may be objected that the above argument is based on regarding (meta) social welfare as a function of expected individual utilities, i.e. $WE = W(EU^1, \ldots , EU^I) = W(\Sigma_j\theta_jU_j^1, \ldots , \Sigma_j\theta_jU_j^I)$ where θ_j is the probability of a state of nature times the probability of that choice instance. For example, confining only to the two equally probable choice instances x against y'' and z against y'', the probability of α prevailing in the choice instance x against y'' is ${}^1\!/_2 \times {}^1\!/_2 = {}^1\!/4$. In the presence of risk, perhaps it is better to maximise expected welfare as a function of *ex-post* individual utilities, i.e. $EW = \Sigma_j\theta_jW(U_j^1, \ldots , U_j^I)$. However, it can be seen that, even using this latter criterion, the choice of y'' over x and z is still clearly undesirable since $EW(y'') = {}^1\!/_2W(0.9, 0) + {}^1\!/_2W(0, 0.9)$ and $EW(x, z) = {}^1\!/_2W(1, 0) + {}^1\!/_2W(0, 1)$. Thus, $EW(x, z) > EW(y'')$ if W is increasing in individual utilities, i.e. if the Pareto principle is satisfied.

In the presence of risk, ignoring differences in (or incorrect) probability estimates (on which see Harris and Olewiler, 1979), there seem to be good grounds for either maximising social welfare as a function of individual expected utilities or maximising expected social welfare as a function of *ex-post* individual utilities. Within the framework of individualism, neither objective can be rejected as unreasonable. The reasonableness of both *WE* and *EW* can in fact be used as an argument for a linear SWF. If social welfare is a sum (unweighted or weighted with constant individual weights k^i) of individual utilities, then *WE* and *EW* are equivalent. Thus, $WE = \Sigma_ik^i\Sigma_j\theta_jU_j^i = \Sigma_j\theta_j\Sigma_ik^iU_j^i = EW$. If social welfare is not a sum of individual utilities, the maximisation of *EW* and *WE* will not, in general, yield the same result.[7] Thus, those who reject social welfare as a sum of individual utilities must explain why either *WE* or *EW* (but not both) is acceptable and the other is not. This is not an easy task within the individualistic ethics, ignoring incorrect probability estimates.

Now consider the argument of Holcombe (1997) that the absence of envy does not imply fairness as the fairness of the process of choice itself has to be taken into account. Consider the simple case of dividing two goods between two individuals involving no production and no difference in desert. The divide-and-choose (one person divides the total endowment into two bundles, the other chooses one bundle) may not be perfectly fair (though it may be a fair enough method to be practically useable most of the times) as it may involve a divider's advantage. If the preference of each person is known to the other, then the divider may divide the endowment in such a way that he will end up with a better bundle than if he is a chooser. Thus, if person J strongly prefers good X to Y and person K strongly prefers Y to X, then J, as the divider, may divide the bundle (of, say, $10X$ and $10Y$) into, say, ($2X + 6Y$ or $8X + 4Y$), knowing that K will prefer $2X + 6Y$, leaving her (J) with $8X + 4Y$. On the other hand, if K is the divider, he may divide the bundle into ($6X + 2Y$ or $4X + 8Y$), knowing that J will prefer $6X + 2Y$, leaving him with $4X + 8Y$. Thus, whoever is the divider ends up with 8 units of the preferred good and 4 units of the less preferred good, in contrast with the $6 + 2$ respectively for the chooser. This illustrates the divider's advantage. The divide-and-choose method is envy-free in the sense that no one prefers the bundle of any other person. However, it is not envy-free in the sense that the chooser prefers to be the divider. Given the assumption of known preferences and hence the divider's advantage, the chooser has the reason to envy the divider for being able to enjoy the divider's advantage. Nevertheless, if we stick to the traditional concept of envy-freeness referring only to the bundle of goods consumed, then Holcombe is correct that the absence of envy does not imply fairness. He attributed the 'problem with using freedom from envy as a criterion for fairness' to the fact 'that the criterion examines only the outcome of the process rather than the process itself' (Holcombe, 1977, p.801). In a sense, this is correct. However, in my view, the reason why the process of divide-and-choose is regarded as not a (perfectly) fair process and may not be envy-free in a wider sense is precisely due to the outcomes. (For cases where either the two individuals have the same preferences or no one knows the other's preferences, there is no divider's advantage, and the above objection to the divide-and-choose procedure does not apply. However, for the case of unknown preferences, a Pareto-inferior outcome may eventuate unless Pareto-improving exchanges are allowed after the divide-and-choose exercise. In particular, a risk-averse individual may divide the bundle equally which may not be Pareto optimal if preferences differ. The divide-and-choose with exchange may then be regarded as fair. The fairness or not of the rule depends on outcomes.) Hence, the point does not negate the acceptability of consequentialism in general and utilitarianism in particular, if these are not taken to narrowly refer only to the consequences on the consumption bundles, but to all relevant consequences.

6
A Dollar is a Dollar: Solution to the Paradox of Interpersonal Cardinal Utility

6.1 The paradox of interpersonal cardinal utility

As explained in Chapter 2, the impossibility theorems of Arrow (1951/1963), Kemp and Ng (1976), Parks (1976), and Sen (1969, 1970a) prove, and even just common-sense arguments demonstrate, that interpersonal comparisons of cardinal utility are necessary for making social choice which cannot reasonably be based on individual ordinal preferences only.

On the other hand, there is a long tradition in economics of regarding interpersonal cardinal utilities as impossible or meaningless and scientifically inadmissible (see, e.g. Kolm, 1993). As Wicksteed (1933) and Robbins (1938) put it, each mind is totally inscrutable to any other mind, making interpersonal comparisons of utility mere value judgments without any scientific status. I have argued elsewhere that interpersonal comparisons of utility are not value judgments but subjective judgments of fact and that economists are more capable in making those judgments of fact closely related to their field of study (Ng, 1972). I also argue (Ng, 1992b) that such views (apparently held by the majority of economists) on the conceptual impossibility of interpersonal comparisons of utility are based on the existence of souls (while a majority of economists, I believe, are philosophical materialists who don't believe in the existence of souls). I argue that individual utilities are not only cardinal and interpersonally comparable but there are also practicable (though imperfect) ways to measure and compare utilities (Ng, 1975a, 1979/1983, 1985, 1996a). However, I freely admit that the practical difficulties associated with cardinal utility measurement and comparison are orders of magnitude higher than those for ordinal preferences (which still exist and are significant, though ignored by most economists).

If we regard interpersonal cardinal utilities as impossible either in principle or in practice, a paradox is created as they are needed for making social choice. In the next section, a method is proposed that, to a very large extent, resolves the paradox of interpersonal cardinal utility.

6.2 The proposed solution

6.2.1 Using unweighted aggregate costs/benefits or a dollar is a dollar

The proposal to solve the paradox is to simply use the individual willingness to pay to obtain information on intensities of preferences, the unweighted aggregate willingness to pay in making social choice, plus the appropriate redistribution of total purchasing power to address the issue of equality. This frees us from having to obtain information on cardinal utilities and to compare them interpersonally, except in the decision on the appropriate redistribution of total purchasing power. Before justifying this solution, a number of clarifications are needed. (Some of these touch on some technical concepts; general readers may want to skip the rest of this section at least on first reading.)

1. There are some ambiguities and controversies associated with the measure of the willingness to pay and the issue whether willingness to pay (CV or compensating variation in income) or willingness to accept (EV or equivalent variation) (in lieu of something) should be the appropriate measure. This is related to the problems in the measurement of consumer surplus. I have discussed and resolved the issue elsewhere (Ng, 1979/1983, Chapter 4 and Appendix 4A). Basically, I argue that the differences between the various measures are usually minor and negligible in comparison to the inaccuracies of data collection and hence can be ignored in practice. Where the differences are large, I propose a better measure than either CV or EV called marginal dollar equivalent, defined as the number of times the relevant gain or loss is equivalent to that of a marginal dollar.[1]

2. Where external effects are important, the willingness to pay of the individuals directly involved may not be sufficient. The willingness to pay of the externally affected individuals has also to be included. Similarly, where factors such as second-best interconnections are relevant, they have to be appropriately taken into account. These ef-

ficiency issues do not change the principle of willingness to pay, they just require the principle to be applied more broadly.

3. Where ignorance of the individuals concerned are involved, the issue becomes more controversial. Personally, I believe that ignorance with minor effects should simply be ignored, partly to save administrative costs and partly because the violation of free individual choice has indirect costs (for being inimical to freedom). However, where ignorance results in big losses, individual willingness to pay may have to be overruled or revised. Thus, we have such cases like the prohibition of certain addictive drugs, the fluoridation of water, and subsidised milk for school children. (See Ng, 1979/83, Appendix 10 A.3, on the grounds for such merit and demerit goods.)

4. Even accepting the use of willingness to pay as the measure of intensity of preferences at the level of the individual, the acceptability of using *aggregate* (i.e. over a number of individuals) willingness to pay is still controversial, *even if* the issue of equality or distribution is ignored. This is so because, as shown by Boadway (1974) and Blackorby and Donaldson (1990), a positive aggregate willingness to pay (CV) need not ensure that the gainers can overcompensate the losers even given the feasibility of lump sum transfers. This difficulty is discussed in Ng (1979/1983, pp.96–8). Basically, it is argued that this difficulty is due to a change in relative prices as compensation takes place, possibly making aggregate willingness to pay not perfectly accurate as it is based on unchanged prices. Where changes in relative prices are not huge, as is true for most specific projects or measures, the inaccuracy involved is negligible. While aggregate willingness to pay does not correspond perfectly with a potential Pareto improvement, it corresponds closely for most cases.

6.2.2 The justification

The justification for using the unweighted (maximum) willingness to pay as a measure of the preference intensity of any individual (called 'a dollar is a dollar' principle for brevity) is based on the following two arguments. First, abstracting away certain difficulties mentioned in the previous section, the amount an individual is willing to pay to obtain a certain item reflects the intensity of their preference. The more intense is my preference for a certain performance, the higher is my maximum willingness to pay for it. This is less controversial.

Secondly, the reason we can use the *unweighted* willingness to pay is based on the argument that it is more efficient to do so and achieve whatever degree of redistribution desired through the general tax/ transfer system.[2] This point needs more elaboration.

The main reason people may be against the principle of a dollar is a dollar is that a dollar to the poor or the more needy meets more urgent needs than a dollar to the rich. In fact, I agree with this belief and am in favour of helping the poor (provided the costs of doing so are not excessive). However, unless factors such as ignorance, and external effects are involved (making it efficient to subsidise education and health care), it is more efficient to help the poor through the general tax/transfer system instead of overriding the principle of a dollar is a dollar in specific items, such as using distributional weights in cost–benefit analysis, using first-come-first-served in allocating car parking spaces. A counter-argument to this is that the tax/transfer system involves excess costs in the form of disincentive effects (the problem of administrative, compliance, and policing costs is discussed under 'trans- action costs' in Section 6.4 below). It is thus believed that it is better to achieve part of the redistribution through the progressive tax/transfer system, and partly through specific equality-oriented measures such as subsidising goods consumed disproportionately by the poor and using distributional weights in cost–benefit analysis. However, this counter- argument (held by most economists, including myself before I analysed the problem carefully) ignores the fact that the use of such specific, purely equality-oriented policies has the same disincentive effects as the tax/transfer system, but also has additional efficiency costs by dis- torting choice.

It is tempting for an economist to think that, since the substantial redistributive tax/transfer system has significant (larger than marginal) disincentive effects at the margin, it is better to shift some of the redis- tributive burden to specific items such as taxing/subsidising items con- sumed disproportionately by the rich/poor. Though some *marginal* efficiency costs of distorting choice are created, they are thought to be smaller than the reduction in disincentive effects due to relying less on the progressive tax/transfer system. This belief is incorrect. The reason is that, assuming rational individuals, the disincentive effects are in accordance to the total system of tax/transfer, taxes/subsidies, plus all other redistributive and preferential measures, instead of having a sep- arate and independent increasing marginal disincentive effects sched- ule for each of the separate measures. Rational persons, in their work/leisure choice, do not just ask how much post-tax income they can earn, but also have a rough idea the utility they can get from consuming goods and services purchased from the income. They are trading off the utility of leisure with the utility from work (which consists of the utility from consuming the higher income and the positive or negative utility of work itself). Moreover, the utility of consuming the higher income is affected by whatever specific redistributive or preferential measures are in place. Thus, the preferential treatment against the rich in government expenditure and other areas will *add on* to the progressive tax/transfer system to determine the total disincentive effects. Hence, even if only a marginal amount of specific equality-oriented measures are used, the disincentive effects involved are not just marginal. Thus, for the same degree of equality in real income (utility) achieved, the same degree of disincentive effects is incurred whether we use only the tax/transfer system or a combination of it and some specific purely equality-oriented system. But the latter alternative has the additional efficiency costs of distorting choice, and is thus inferior.

In Ng (1984b), the following proposition is proved.

Proposition A (A dollar is a dollar): For any alternative (designated A) using a system (designated *a*) of purely equality-oriented preferential treatment between the rich and the poor, there exists another alternative, B, which does not use preferential treatment, that makes no one worse off, achieves the same degree of equality (of real income, or utility) and raises more government revenue, which could be used to make everyone better off.

Under alternative B, a more (than alternative A) progressive tax/transfer system (designated *b*) may have to be used. By definition, progressivity in the tax/transfer system is not classified as 'preferential treatment' here. Section 6.3 below argues that complications such as administrative costs, political constraints, ignorance of benefits distribution, etc. either strengthen the proposition or do not affect the main thrust significantly.

In fact, proposition A can be generalised to any efficiency-inconsistent alternative A, not just an equality-oriented preferential treatment. The proof of the proposition is exactly unaltered if the preferential treatment is not equality-oriented but inequality-oriented. Instead of counting a dollar to the poor as worth *less* than a dollar to the rich in cost–benefit analysis, it is better to tax the rich less and tax the poor more (or subsidise them less). Similarly, an alternative based on random treatment, one based on tradition, etc. can all be shown to be inferior to some alternative B defined to compensate for the gains and losses in dismantling the efficiency-inconsistent methods used. Then, ignoring issues of practical difficulties, individual ignorance, irrationality, and procedural preferences (on the last item, see Ng, 1988), alternative B must be Pareto superior.

However, the *existence* of alternative B does not necessarily mean that it can be identified and implemented. If system *a* is *designed* to take account of second-best considerations, then system *b* can also be so designed. But system *a* may only be consistent with second-best considerations by *chance* rather than by design. In addition, the informational costs of designing a system consistent with the second-best considerations may be prohibitive.[3] Then we may not be able to identify system *b*. Thus, while alternative B may exist, it may not be *feasible* to implement. Thus, if we wish to strengthen Proposition A to be one about the existence of a feasible superior alternative B, it would apply only in a probabilistic sense. That it (the strengthened proposition) still applies in a probabilistic sense is due to the theory of third best. Just as it may be consistent with second-best considerations, system *a* may also be opposite to the requirement of second best. The theory of third best (see Ng, 1977) can then be used to show that the expected gain is negative. Hence, as far as the second-best consideration is concerned, the use of system *a* involves negative expected gains. Essentially, random divergence from first-best rules is as likely to be inconsistent as to be consistent with the requirement of second best. Due to the expected concavity in the relevant objective function, the gain when it is consistent is less than the loss when it is inconsistent. So the expected gain is negative. (See Ng, 1979/1983, Chapter 9 and Ng, 1984b for a more detailed demonstration of this.)

The half-a-century old argument of Little (1951) may be briefly discussed at this juncture. Basically, Little argues that one cannot say that a direct tax (on income) is better than an indirect tax (on some goods) on the ground that the former taxes all goods at the same rate. The reason is that there is another good, leisure, which is also untaxed under direct taxation. Taking the simple case of just two non-leisure goods (see the top half of Figure 6.1), an indirect tax on one of the goods creates a wedge (between relative costs and benefits) between that good (good 1) and the other good (good 2) as well as between that good and leisure. A direct tax causes a wedge between good 1 and leisure and between good 2 and leisure. Hence, no conclusion can be made on the desirability of direct versus indirect taxes without specific information on the interrelationships between the various goods and leisure. While this argument is formally correct in a certain sense, it is misleading in its conclusion. Thus, it is certainly true that an indirect tax on half of the (non-leisure) goods may be less distorting than a direct tax (equivalent to a uniform tax on all non-leisure goods) of equal revenue, *if* the former happens to concentrate on goods more complementary to leisure. However, if the former is just a random half, then it may be taken to be worse than the direct tax, at least in terms of average expectation. To see this, first consider a case where all goods are of equal degree of complementarity/substitutability to leisure. An indirect tax on half of the goods is then inferior to a direct tax of equivalent revenue. On the other hand, if (the first) half of the goods are more complementary to leisure than the other half, while an indirect tax on the first half is more efficient than the direct tax, this efficiency gain is less than the efficiency loss when the second half is taxed instead. (Both points are illustrated in specific mathematical examples available from the author.)

In terms of the 'wedge' argument of Little, we may say that, while a direct tax (of say 10 per cent) drives a moderate wedge between both goods and leisure, an indirect tax on half of the goods (typically in excess of 20 per cent to yield the same amount of revenue) drives a much bigger wedge between the taxed and untaxed goods, and between the taxed goods and leisure. (See Figure 6.1.) It is thus inferior to the direct tax at least in terms of expected value. If the goods taxed are randomly selected with respect to their complementarities to leisure, this bigger wedge between the taxed goods and leisure already induces, in terms of expected value, as big a disincentive effect (as the case of the direct tax). In addition, there is a distortion effect on individual choice between goods. Thus, in spite of Little's argument, a direct tax is better than an indirect tax not designed to take advantage of second-best considerations (complementarities with leisure). Our argument here is consistent with the general view in public finance that, other things being equal, a broader tax is a better tax.

Equality-oriented policies and other non-efficiency-oriented policies in the real world are, as far as I am aware, without exception, not based on the second-best consideration. Due to the non-taxability of leisure, goods highly complementary to leisure should be taxed more on the grounds of second best. Due to the higher income tax rates on the rich, the second-best consideration may suggest imposing taxes on the rich even higher than on others for the same leisure-complementary goods, and imposing higher taxes on leisure-complementary goods that are predominantly consumed by the rich. It may thus be thought that higher taxes on luxuries (defined as goods consumed disproportionately more by the rich) may be justified on efficiency grounds. However, it is equally true that goods highly substitutable to leisure should be sub-

Little's Argument

Direct Tax

Indirect Tax

(The ≠ sign signifies a wedge between MRS and MRT, i.e. relative benefits and costs)

Our Argument

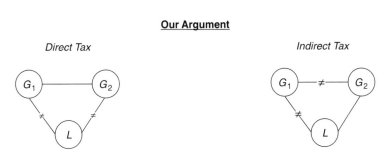

Direct Tax

Indirect Tax

Figure 6.1

sidised (or at least taxed less). Hence, due to the higher income tax rates on the rich, the second-best consideration also suggests giving *more* subsidies to the rich than others for the same leisure-substitutary goods, and giving higher subsidies on leisure-substitutary goods that are disproportionately consumed by the rich. Thus, luxuries as such do not justify higher taxes. (The proposal to impose high taxes on 'diamond goods' which are valued for their value is a separate matter of pure efficiency; see Ng, 1987a and Part II of this book which argues for more public spending partly based on this point.)

In practice, it is also informationally, politically, and administratively impossible to design and implement specific taxes/subsidies and other specific economic measures in accordance to the requirement of second best. This requires full information of the interrelationships of all relevant sectors in the economy. It may be informationally feasible to take account of the more important interrelationships, but political considerations may make it infeasible. For example, the political feasibility of giving higher subsidies on leisure-substitutary goods disproportionately consumed by the rich is certainly suspect. In addition, the adoption of the principle of a dollar is a dollar will save substantial administrative costs and achieve much simplicity. Its political feasibility, though certainly better than the second-best policies of subsidising the rich more than others for the same leisure-substitutary goods, has yet to be fostered through a long process of education, starting with the understanding of the argument of this chapter by economists.

Our proposed solution largely, but does not completely, resolve the paradox of interpersonal cardinal utility since interpersonal comparison of cardinal utility is still needed in determining the optimal tradeoff between efficiency (incentive) and equality in the general tax/transfer system. Moreover, for cases where individual willingness to pay cannot be used as a good reflection of welfare due to serious ignorance or irrationality (e.g. hard drugs), interpersonal comparison of cardinal utility may also be needed on specific decisions.

6.3 Economists should be in favour of reversed weighting!

At the risk of repetition, it should be emphasised that our argument for using the *unweighted* sum of willingness to pay or for treating 'a dollar as a dollar' is not based on valuing a dollar to the poor as worth no more than a dollar to the rich. In fact, personally, I value the former as worth much more than the latter. If manna were to fall from heaven (and regarded as once only, or at least as unrelated to income), I would certainly hope that they fall to the poor. However, if we adopt a policy of treating a dollar to the poor as worth more than a dollar to the rich, this will create disincentive effects and hence is inferior to using the tax/transfer system to reduce inequality. I am not against the attempt to reduce inequality, just against using inefficient methods to do so.

It is true that governments may not actively and optimally pursue distributive justice through income taxes and transfers. However, in the long run, some degrees of distributive balance are maintained. Even if this does not lead to an optimal tradeoff between equality and efficiency, it is incorrect to ignore that some degree of balance is being maintained. As far as I know, all those in favour of using distributional weights or inequality-averse criteria effectively ignore any degree of such a balance, or, at least they have not shown their awareness of the implication of such a balance on the appropriate distributional weights. Of course, they are aware of the existence of such a balance. However, this balance implies that the distributional weights should be less unequal (e.g. a dollar to the poor counted as only $1.20 instead of $2) than the case in the absence of any balance. In the presence of an optimal balance, no weights (or only equal weights) should be used. In the presence of an excessive balance (i.e. equality pursued at excessively high incentive costs), the distributional weights should be reversed (i.e. more weights to the rich than to the poor). Nevertheless, no advocate (as far as I know) of distributional weights or inequality-adverse criteria has explicitly shown some awareness in this respect. Many people probably believe that the distributional weights should be proportional to the social marginal utility of a dollar. However, this can only be justified if the use of distributional weights have no disincentive effects (which are efficiency costs over and above their direct distortive costs). I strongly suspect that many of those in favour of distributional weights simply ignore these disincentive effects.

It is possible that, despite some degree of balance between equality and efficiency, some economists may regard the balance as being far too inadequate. They may think that much more equality should be achieved despite the inefficiency costs involved. While this is certainly possible, the reverse case that an economist may believe that too high efficiency costs are being incurred to achieve equality should be even more likely, or at least as likely. As a group, economists are unlikely to be more equality-inclined than politicians, bureaucrats, or voters generally whose inclinations influence government policies. (In fact, there is evidence suggesting that economists are much more 'right-wing' in comparison to the general public; see, e.g. Ng, 1988.) Secondly, economists are more aware of the efficiency costs of pursuing equality, including administrative, compliance, policing, and disincentive costs. Thus, one should expect more economists to find the actual tradeoff between equality and efficiency being excessively in favour of equality than the other way round. So, one should expect more economists in favour of using reversed distributional weights than in favour of using the normal distributional weights. However, to my knowledge, not a single economist has come out in favour of the reversed weighting. In fact, the most radical in this respect is probably Posner (1981), a lawyer, who is in favour of wealth maximisation. (My argument of treating 'a dollar as a dollar' differs from Posner's as I allow for the achievement of equality through taxes/transfers beyond wealth maximisation.) These considerations support my suspicion that many economists in favour of distributional weights simply ignore the disincentive effects involved, not just because they are more egalitarian.

What about the minority of economists who are genuinely more egalitarian than the prevailing policy? In my view, they, as economists, should not be in favour of using distributional weights and purely equality-oriented policies. However, as citizens, they should campaign to move government policies towards more equality (preferably by using more efficient methods), while the majority of their fellow economists, as citizens, should campaign for less equality if, as argued above, they view the equality-efficiency trade-off as having been pursued to an excess.

6.4   Some qualifications

6.4.1   Political constraints on redistribution through taxation

It is argued above that, instead of using weighting, quotas, or other kinds of preferential treatment to achieve the objective of equality (not as second-best correctives); it is better to adopt a more progressive income tax schedule. What if the taxation system cannot be changed to the desired structure due to political constraints? If it is true that we can't change the taxation system but we can effect redistribution by other means, my conclusion may have to be qualified accordingly, though there is still the ethical question of the desirability of doing good by stealth. Yet, why should the political constraint act only to prevent redistribution through taxation and not redistribution by other means? Maybe because the voters are rather irrational. I suspect, however, that on this issue, voters are very rational and practical. The upper and middle classes will not only vote a government out of office for carrying out drastic changes in taxation but also for carrying out other drastic redistributive measures. Especially in the long run, the forces that operate to prevent redistribution through taxation will also operate to prevent redistribution by other means. If we are thinking in terms of a distributional equilibrium, the distribution should be considered not in terms of money income but in terms of real income. Naturally, if the rich are penalised in other ways they will have less tolerance with regards to the progressiveness of taxation. For example, had Australia been operating closer to the principle of 'a dollar is a dollar' in the past, the reductions in the progressiveness of its income tax schedule undertaken in 1978 and later would probably not have been required. Both the rich and the poor would probably have been better off.

It is true that actual political decisions are affected by a host of factors and not just by an impartial consideration of a balance between equality and efficiency. However, equality and efficiency are important considerations and the fact that preferential treatment is an inefficient tool to achieve equality and efficiency has to be pointed out.

6.4.2 Ineffectiveness in the tax/transfer system

If the tax/transfer system is not effective due to, say, tax avoidance/evasion while redistribution through certain specific measures is more effective, there may be a case for using such specific measures. This does not violate Proposition A (a dollar is a dollar) since the case for using such specific measures is not purely justified on purely equality-oriented considerations but also on that of effectiveness in getting the result. It may, however, be regarded as a practical qualification to the principle of a dollar is a dollar. (The argument of Kelsey, 1988, for putting eggs in many baskets due to uncertainty may be similarly viewed.) Nevertheless, the significance of the qualification may be questioned, at least for many cases. For example, if one may hide one's income to pay less taxes and get more transfers, one may also hide one's income to avoid penalty prices or to qualify for subsidies on specific items.

6.4.3 Transaction costs

Our analysis has been based on the assumption that the additional 'transaction' costs associated with redistribution through more progressive income taxation are not higher than the transaction costs of its alternatives. Apart from the disincentive effect (which has been taken into account and is not subsumed under transaction costs), the costs associated with income taxation seem to fall mainly under: (i) costs of administration on the parts of both the taxpayers and the collectors; (ii) costs involved in tax evasion and enforcement; and (iii) costs of tax lobbying activities and the like. It is recognised that all of these forms of costs are substantial. But the relevant amounts are not total costs, only marginal costs. For good or for bad, income taxation will be with us in the foreseeable future. The incremental costs of administration of a more progressive tax system seem trivial. The costs of a change from one system to another may not be trivial, but will probably not be substantial. However, at least in the long run, the relevant comparison is the cost of administering two alternative systems, the difference between which is probably quite negligible. A more progressive tax system may however involve higher costs in encouraging more evasion and more lobbying activities. But the increase in progressiveness is in lieu of some system of preferential treatment which itself is a subject of evasion and lobbying. While this is a subject where a precise conclusion can hardly be expected, it does not seem probable that costs involved in the latter (i.e. preferential treatment) will be much lower than costs involved in the former (i.e. a more progressive tax system). On the other hand, the costs of administering a pure taxation system are almost certainly significantly lower than those of administering a system of taxation combined with preferential treatment in government expenditure. Hence, consideration of transaction costs seems to strengthen, not weaken, our central conclusion.

There may be specific cases whereby the use of an apparently 'preferential' policy may be superior to making the income tax system more progressive because of the significantly lower transaction (evasion, lobbying, and administrative) costs of the former. But such a policy is justified on its efficiency consideration of lower transaction costs (relative to income taxation) and cannot be justified purely on the equality consideration advanced by egalitarian lobbyists.

6.4.4 Ignorance of benefit distribution

Our argument is based on the assumption that individuals know the distribution of costs and benefits in government expenditure across income groups, or the details of preferential treatment, so that the incentives are the same as an equivalent pure income taxation system. In practice, this knowledge is unlikely to be perfect. On the other hand, most individuals do know the scale of income taxation. Does this asymmetrical knowledge mean that the disincentive effects of income taxation are more severe than an equivalent preferential expenditure system, as, in effect, argued by Martin Feldstein (1974, p.152)? (However, de Bartolome, 1995 shows that at least half of the taxpayers underestimate their real marginal rates by confusing it with their average rates.)

In the absence of perfect knowledge, an individual has to base his choice on his estimates. From the fraction of knowledge he possesses, it seems that he is as likely to overestimate as to underestimate the degree of progressiveness implied in a given preferential expenditure system, depending on the psychology of the individual in question. Hence, on the whole, the degree of incentives is likely to be similar between the preferential expenditure system and the pure income taxation system.

6.4.5 Redistributive effects of the project itself

The argument for treating a dollar as a dollar does not imply that a billion dollars is always equal to a billion dollars. This point can be seen clearly by considering a simple example. Consider two alternative projects: project M will increase the incomes (after allowing for cost share) of one million individuals by $10 thousand each, and project N will increase the income of one single random individual by $10 billion. Ruling out costless lump sum transfers (that would make us indifferent between the two projects), it is clear that project M will be preferred to project N by all social welfare functions egalitarian in incomes. This preference is not based on valuing a marginal dollar to the rich as lower than a marginal dollar to the poor. Rather, it is based on treating the first dollar as more valuable than the 10 billionth dollar, to whomever they go. (Due to diminishing marginal utility, the same person typically regards the loss of $10,000 as more significant in utility terms than the gain of $10,000.) Hence, the equality-incentive argument used above does not apply here. However, the equality-incentive argument can be used to dispel the possible belief that, since a project that itself creates inequality is inferior to one with the same aggregate net benefits but which does not create inequality, a project that creates equality must be preferable to one with the same aggregate net benefits but distributionally neutral. Consider a third project O that will yield the same aggregate net benefits of $10 billion but be distributed across the economy in such a way that the poor will have much higher benefits and the rich have negative benefits. While this may seem to be a good thing in itself, the incentive argument will show that project O is in fact inferior to project M. If project O were to happen as a natural event, it would be preferable. But if it is chosen instead of project M, it will produce disincentive effects.

From the above, it may be said that, for projects whose redistributive effects are marginal, one can simply choose in terms of aggregate net benefits; for projects whose redistributive effects are significant, we should prefer the one with less redistributive effects, given the same aggregate net benefits. This seems to lend support to the concept of a conservative social welfare function discussed by Corden (1974, p.107).

6.4.6 Preference for working

If an individual prefers to have his income by earning it instead of receiving it as a transfer welfare payment, then a cost–benefit analysis that does not take this preference into account may be misleading. (This has been emphasised by Skolnik, 1970. For an analysis of the social norm of living on one's work, see Linbeck *et al.*, 1999.) This kind of complication can be taken care of by appropriate shadow pricing. For example, in the particular case considered here, the main difference is the possible preference of an individual for earning his income instead of receiving some kind of dole money. This can largely be taken care of by putting an appropriate shadow price on employment. For a single person without dependents, his income from a low-paid job is likely to be sufficient to preclude him from receiving a subsidy. All that is needed is a low or zero income tax, so he will not have to suffer the feeling of being on the dole. For families with dependents, the subsidy can be effected in the form of, say, substantial child-endowment payments differentiated according to income levels. A fixed child-endowment is used in Australia with no one feeling ashamed of receiving it and the introduction of differentiation is unlikely to change this substantially.

6.4.7 Unexpected emergencies

In times of unexpected emergencies such as earthquakes, wars, etc. certain necessities may be in very short supply. In principle, we could impose appropriately higher taxes on the rich and those who happen to own the goods in short supply and pay subsidies to the poor and the victims of the disaster. Then the policy of 'a dollar is a dollar' could still be best. However, due to time lags, imperfect information, and the like, it may be practically infeasible to effect the required changes in taxes/subsidies in time. Rationing of basic necessities such as medical supplies (which also involves external economies) may then be the best practical solution. However, the possible desirability of violating the principle of 'a dollar is a dollar' in such emergencies does not mean that the same is true for normal times.

6.4.8 Non-income indices for preferential treatment

Our analysis concentrates on the use of income as the index for preferential treatment and redistributive taxation. But surely income is an imperfect measure of 'deservingness', and non-income variables such as health and age status are likely to enter distributional objectives. In particular, the use of age as an index for preferential treatment will create few, if any, disincentive effects, since one cannot change one's age. However, we can similarly use age as an index for the purpose of tax-subsidy. The purpose of giving assistance to the aged, for example, can be achieved without the additional efficiency costs of, say, giving free milk as some may not wish to drink milk. (Subsidised milk to schoolchildren may, however, be justified on the efficiency ground of merit wants; on merit wants as a possible efficiency ground, see Ng, 1979/1983, Section 10A.3). The consideration of non-income factors does suggest that a single tax based on incomes only may not be sufficient; the tax-subsidy system may have to take non-income factors into account.[4]

A related problem of using income as the basis for taxation is that measured income may be a poor indicator of actual earning potential due to savings, risk bearing, etc. Thus, persons of the same earning potential may be taxed more if they are more willing to bear risk, to save, etc. However, this imperfection applies also to the use of measured income for the purpose of preferential treatment and hence does not affect our argument. In general, to the extent that a better index is available for use as a basis of preferential treatment, it can also be used for the tax-subsidy purpose. Unless there are asymmetrical transaction costs (see 6.4.3 above), no qualification to our central argument is necessary.

From the discussion above, it may be concluded that none of the complications seems to change our central argument significantly.

6.5 Concluding remarks

The argument of this chapter has far-reaching implications. It justifies the separation of equality and efficiency considerations in public policy. On all specific areas, public policy needs only be concerned with efficiency, leaving the objective of equality to be achieved through the general tax/transfer system. This creates a tremendous simplification in the formulation of all public policies and in cost–benefit analysis in particular. (On the case and actual uses of distributional weights in cost–benefit analysis, see Little and Mirrlees, 1974, Adler and Posner, 1999, and references therein.)

However, the argument of this chapter does not deny the possibility that some measures may improve efficiency and equality simultaneously and some measures may harm both simultaneously due, for example, to such considerations as the physiological effect of income on work effort (Strauss and Thomas, 1995), the principal–agent problems and imperfection in the credit market due to informational asymmetry which may be lessened by the use of collaterals that the very poor lack (Binswinger *et al.*, 1995; Hoff and Lyon, 1995 and Hoff, 1996), moderation of tax progressivity on wage demands of unions (Hersoug, 1984; Creedy and McDonald, 1990 and Lockwood and Manning, 1993), the discouragement of investment of high inequality which increases the difference between median and average incomes and hence the median voter demand for higher tax rate (Persson and Tabellini, 1994; but see Perotti, 1996 on the negative empirical evidence for the mechanism, though the negative relationship between inequality and growth appears valid; see Birdsall *et al.*, 1995), and the crime-reduction effect of equality (Eaton and White, 1991 and Grossman, 1994). (For a summary of empirical evidence on the relationship between inequality and growth, see Bénabou 1996. On other related issues, see Haveman, 1988; Murphy *et al.*, 1989; Schmid, 1993; Bowles and Ginitis, 1996; Baland and Platteau, 1997; Breen, 1997; Le Grand, 1997; Devins and Douglas, 1998; Nagel, 1998; Putterman *et al.*, 1998; Aghion and Williamson, 1999; and Lee and Roemer, 1999. Also, Ackerman *et al.*, 1997 contains a large selection of readings in related normative, social and other 'extra-economic' issues in summary form; it provides enlightening reading, though an economist will typically find most of the points made not inconsistent with economic analysis and some are even misleading or just a difference in terminology.) Our argument is also consistent with the idea of regulating or taxing more heavily the incomes of superstars in sports and entertainment, as they earn more than their marginal contribution since their role may be assumed by the runners up without significant losses (Borghans and Groot, 1998).[5] We also ignore the possible role of increasing returns in affecting the efficiency–equality relationship. (See, e.g. Brown and Heal, 1979 which shows that the efficiency of marginal-cost pricing may depend on distribution in the presence of increasing returns.) Our argument also does not deny the need to take account of indirect effects, including external effects and those arising from a change in preferences. (On preference changes, see Bowles, 1998.) It may also be noted that Congleton (1997) has an interesting argument for the equal protection of the law due to its *efficiency* in avoiding the differential enforcement of the law for the interest of the governing coalition. This argument may be misleadingly regarded as a counter-example to the principle of a dollar is a dollar. However, the equal protection of the law is really a second-best solution to the violation of the principle of 'a dollar is a dollar' (from the viewpoint of the whole population) by a subset of the population, the governing coalition, at a greater cost to the non-governing sections of the population. Thus, there is really no violation of the principle.

7
Economics versus Politics

In Chapter 6, it is argued that a dollar should be treated as a dollar to whomsoever it goes to achieve efficiency, leaving the objective of equality to the general tax/transfer system. This proposition of 'a dollar is a dollar' can be generalised to show the Pareto inferiority of any efficiency-inconsistent alternative A, not just an equality-oriented one. Interpreting this generalisation widely, the principle of 'a dollar is a dollar' can be applied to areas outside the traditional confines of economics. Then, what prevents the application of the simple efficiency principle from being used in political issues like the election of a president or members of a parliament, where the principle of one person one vote seems to be universally accepted?

It is tempting for one to believe that the answer lies in the need to limit the power of the rich. Using the simple efficiency principle of 'a dollar is a dollar' would allow the rich too much power in political decisions. This answer is incomplete, to say the least. The main point can be explained simply. If we limit the range in which the market or efficiency principle apply, we need to have more inequality in income distribution to maintain the same degree of incentives since the range of things income can be spent on has been reduced. Thus, if the same degree of incentives is to be maintained, the poor cannot be made better off. In fact, every income group will be made a little worse off due to the inefficiency of restricting the working of the market. On the other hand, if we are prepared to reduce the degree of incentives in order to make the poor better off, we could do this more efficiently by just making the tax/transfer system more progressive, without restricting the working of the market. This point is shown more precisely in a simple mathematical example available from the author, showing that the random restriction of the range of market operation makes both the rich and the poor worse off.

In fact, the point can be seen without the mathematical example. To see it more clearly, abstract from the effects of changes in relative prices (which could go either way) by considering a case of fixed earning abilities and fixed prices (as could be facilitated by constant returns, small country, etc.). Starting from a situation where some of the goods (private, no external effects) are not subject to market allocation but are supplied in fixed amounts by the government to everyone (possibly equally), dismantle the government provision and allow these goods to be allocated in the market. The savings of the government from not having to provide these goods are then used to pay each individual, with each individual getting the worth of the previously allocated amounts of these goods in money and free to buy whatever quantities desired. Then obviously no individual will be worse off as she can buy the previously allocated quantities if so desired. (It is assumed that the transaction costs of market allocation are not higher than that of government allocation.) Those choosing to buy different combinations (including buying more or less of some or all goods) of these goods are made better off.

The market economy can be shown to function perfectly efficiently in the sense of Pareto optimality mainly under the assumptions of perfect competition, adequate information by the market participants, and the absence of external effects. Thus, possible reasons for government intervention or even replacing the market include objectives beyond Pareto efficiency on the one hand and certain serious violations of the above assumptions (called 'market failures' below) on the other. In my view, a valid objective beyond Pareto efficiency is distributional equality. (See Ng, 1988, 1990a for arguments on the unacceptability of many other proposed objectives.) However, as argued above, the objective of equality may justify a progressive tax/transfer system but does not justify specific efficiency-inconsistent measures. It is true that this argument assumes the feasibility of the appropriate tax/transfer system. Where such a system is politically or administratively infeasible or subject to very important uncertainty in its effects (Kelsey, 1988), it may be efficient to supplement the tax/transfer system with other specific equality-oriented measures, including commodity taxes (Cremer and Gahvari, 1995). While such a possibility cannot be completely ruled out, problems of administrative costs and political difficulties are likely to be more serious for the specific equality-oriented measures, as argued in

Section 6.4 above. Thus, we have to look to market failures for valid reasons for replacing the market.

Different degrees of market failures prevail all over the place, most requiring no or only limited intervention instead of supplanting the market altogether. Thus, the existence of some market failures is not enough; we have to look for very substantial, even overwhelming, extent of market failures. I do not think we can find this with respect to market power and ignorance. The wealthiest person may be able to wield many times more influence than an average person if willingness to pay is taken into account, but in most countries, no single person earns a substantial fraction of the GNP. While substantial ignorance is involved in political voting, it is not substantially alleviated by going for the one-person-one-vote solution. This leaves external effects as the possible source of substantial market failure.

Three distinct types of external effects may be associated with political decisions. First, political decisions taken may externally affect people beyond the jurisdiction and people in the future. This external effect has little to do with the issue here, since the choice of either one-person-one-vote or willingness-to-pay has negligible effects on these external effects. Secondly, political decisions, being concerned with public issues, involve the public-good external effect. Both the choice (usually in elections) of public officials and the decisions of the public officials on public issues (including law and order, other regulations, provision of public goods) are related to the public-good problems, including that of free riding. Thus, if voters are allowed to actually pay money to express their willingness to pay, most of them may pay nothing, preferring to free-ride. However, this problem only makes the willingness-to-pay principle difficult to put into effect, it does not make the principle undesirable. If we have more sophisticated method of inducing self-interested voters to express their true willingness to pay, such as the use of the Vickrey–Clarke–Groves incentive-compatible mechanism on a carefully selected sample of voters (Ng, 1979/1983, Section 8.3), the free-riding problem could be overcome. Thus, I see the next external effect as the most important stumbling block to the use of the efficiency principle in political decisions.

The third type of external effects associated with political decisions is less similar to the normal external effects familiar in economics; it may even be controversial to describe it as an external effect. The functioning of a modern society, including its economy, requires political stability, the maintenance of law and order, and preferably also a high degree of social cohesion. These elements may also be desirable for the psychological well-being of individuals in the society. These desirable elements are fostered by a political system using the one-person-one-vote principle in its political process instead of the willingness-to-pay principle, except for a society where the majority of its citizens are as good economists as you (i.e. the likely readers of this book), and this is well nigh impossible, at least in the foreseeable future. The use of the efficiency principle in political process is likely (if not certainly) to generate feelings of apathy, antagonism, and the like against the government, the wealthy, and law and order among the poorer classes and those in the political fringe. This will increase the difficulties or costs of maintaining law and order and will likely reduce stability and cohesion. Thus, the exercising of the preference intensities through the willingness to pay in traditionally political sphere, especially by the rich, may be said to entail important external costs. In most cases, this consideration makes the use of one-person-one-vote principle optimal in the political process despite the existence of the normal inefficiency associated with supplanting the market. This is the most important factor, as far as I can see, in explaining the separation of political and economic spheres. However, since this factor depends on the attitude of the people, as this attitude changes with time and with the understanding of economics, the optimal sphere of economics will gradually expand. Nevertheless, knowing the difficulty of teaching basic economic principles even to university students, I am not at all optimistic about the speed of this expansion and about the ultimate conquest.

PART II

How Much Should the Government Spend?

> The central public finance question facing any country is the appropriate size of its government.
>
> Feldstein, 1997, p.197

It is not the intention here to discuss all issues relevant to this central question of public finance. Important questions like the relative efficiency of government versus private supply, the feasibility of the private production of public goods, informational asymmetry, etc. are not addressed except in passing. Instead, some neglected and perhaps more important issues are focused. After reviewing the basic theory on the appropriate size of government spending on public goods and some empirical considerations, Chapter 8 argues for higher public spending based on the importance of diamond goods, relative-income effects, and environmental disruption effects, the unimportance of absolute income for welfare at the social level at least for developed economies, and the high welfare potential of public spending especially in research (the example of a possible quantum leap in welfare through brain stimulation is discussed in Appendix A). With reasonable assumptions, it is shown that the optimal relative (to the GDP) size of public spending increases with per capita income (Appendix C). Chapter 9 addresses the question: Should the benefit–cost ratios for public projects exceed one by a sufficient margin to account for the distortionary costs of raising government revenue?

8
A Case for Higher Public Spending

Co-author: Siang Ng

I like to pay taxes. With them I buy civilization.
Justice Holmes in Eisenstein, 1961, p.5

Saunders (1993) shows that the share of public expenditure reached a peak in most countries in early to mid-1980s, stabilised and then declined. (See also Bohl, 1996 and Payne and Ewing, 1996 on international evidence on the Wagner's law on the increase in the share of the public sector.) The decline is sharper in terms of the real size of the public sector due to a higher relative price; see the end of Section 8.2 below. This decline is associated with the worldwide movement towards privatisation and the use of the market mechanism. While accepting that there are some valid reasons (such as the inefficiency of the public sector) underlying this movement, this chapter discusses some neglected factors that provide some offsetting considerations. Before doing so, the basic theory on the appropriate size of public spending on public goods and some related considerations are reviewed.

8.1 Some simple theories of government spending

8.1.1 Government spending as providing public goods

It is clear that a major part of the spending of most governments is on items (e.g. the maintenance of law and order, defence, etc.) that are uncontroversially public goods in the Samuelsonian sense (non-rivalness in consumption). Others are more controversial. A major part of government spending is paying the public employees. However, if these employees are largely necessary for the government to perform the functions of providing public goods, this part of government spend-

105

ing may also be regarded as the cost of providing public goods. In many countries, governments spend a lot on transfer payments such as old-age pensions and unemployment benefits. These are regarded as redistributive spending rather than spending on public goods. While these items certainly have redistributive effects, they also have some public-goods aspect. Thus, keeping the unemployed paid reduces crimes and a more equal distribution of income increases social cohesion and enters positively into many people's utility function. Hence, while the aspect of public goods provision does not exhaust the function of government spending, it is the major one for most countries. For simplicity, only this major aspect is focused here.

A public good is non-rivalrous in consumption. My tuning to a radio or TV broadcast in no way affects your reception of it. Thus, in contrast to the equation of the marginal benefit of each and every consumer to the marginal cost for a private good, the optimal supply of a public good is based on equating the *aggregate* marginal benefit (vertical sum of individual marginal benefit curves) to the marginal cost of provision, as is (should I just say 'should be') now well known to all undergraduates in economics. A simple theory on the appropriate size of public spending may then be stated thus. Sum the aggregate marginal benefit curves of all relevant public goods *horizontally* to give the aggregate marginal benefit curve of public spending in general. The intersection of this curve with the marginal cost curve of public spending then determines the optimal size of public spending.

Due to the heterogeneity of different public goods, a convenient way of measuring public spending is by the dollar amount spent. Then, a change in the efficiency in supplying public goods will be reflected in different physical quantities for the same spending. This will be reflected in a shift in the aggregate marginal benefit curve rather than in the cost curve. However, despite the dollar definition of public spending, the marginal cost of a unit of public spending need not be one dollar. Taking account of the excess burden (also called deadweight loss or distortionary cost) of taxation and other excess costs of raising government revenue (administrative, compliance, and policing cost), the marginal cost of a dollar of public spending is typically regarded as exceeding one dollar by a considerable margin. Feldstein (1997) gave an estimate as high as $2.65. (On the marginal cost of public funds, see also Fortin and Lacroix, 1994 and references therein.) With a higher marginal cost of public spending, the optimal size of public spending is smaller, given the marginal benefit curve. However, contrary to this traditional view,

Kaplow (1996) argues that the benefit–cost ratio for public project only needs to exceed one. Chapter 9 addresses this issue. (If we ask the wider question whether a higher public sector increases unemployment and/or reduces the rate of economic growth, it seems that the evidence is inconclusive; see, e.g. Dowrick, 1993; Karras, 1996; Phelps and Zoega, 1998, pp.788–9.)

8.1.2 Growth in public spending and the median-voter model

Assuming that government spending is determined by the preferences of the median voter, the standard model is:

$$\log G = a + b\log Y_m + c\log P_m$$

where G is government spending, a, b, c are constants (with b positive and c negative), Y_m is the income of the median voter, and P_m the marginal 'price' of public goods to her (related to the marginal tax rate on her). (See, e.g. Jackson, 1993, p.29 on some problems of this model; de Bartolome, 1995 on the point that there are as many individuals who mistakenly use the average rates as the relevant marginal rates; Turnbull and Chang, 1998 on an empirical test supportive of the median voter model.)

In terms of the above model, the long-term growth in the share of government spending may be explained by (as summarised by Atkinson and Stiglitz, 1980, pp.326–7):

A. Increasing per capita real income, with public expenditure being a superior good (income elasticity being larger than one).
B. A redistribution of income that raises the median relative to the average income.
C. A decrease in the perceived tax burden of the median voter. This may be caused by a change in the tax structure or due to a higher fiscal illusion.
D. A decrease in the relative price of public sector output.

Extending beyond the median-voter model, we have additional factors:

E. An increase in voting participation of lower income groups.
F. An increase in the activities of interest groups lobbying for more public spending.
G. Changing ideology of political parties and shifts in sources of financial support for political parties.

This list does not include some important considerations (discussed below) that may explain the increase in public expenditure. (On the growth of government spending, see also Baumol, 1967; Levitt and Joyce, 1987; and West, 1991 on the increase in costs relative to the private sector; Peltzman, 1980 emphasising the role of equality, Meltzer and Richard, 1981 emphasising inequality and the democratic process in increasing transfer payments; Kau and Rubin, 1981 on the increase in efficiency in collecting taxes, Ferris and West, 1996 on the empirical test of the various theories, Rodrik, 1998 on the risk-reduction role of public spending for open economies, Marmola, 1999 on a utility-interdependence explanation of the constitutional choice of the set of public goods, Mueller, 1989, Chapter 17, for a discussion of several public-choice theories including interest groups and bureaucracy, and Lybeck and Henrekson, 1988 on some conceptual and empirical issues.)

8.2 Inefficiency in public spending may increase its optimal level

As pointed out at the beginning of the last section, public spending is measured by the monetary amount, and a change in the degree of efficiency in providing public goods is reflected in a shift in the marginal benefit curve of public spending. Does this mean that the inefficiency in public provision necessary shifts the marginal benefit curve downward and hence decreases the optimal level of public spending? The answer is no (at least 'not necessarily') even ignoring the possible more subtle interaction between benefits and costs and holding the cost side unchanged. (For simplicity, it is also assumed that the degree of provision inefficiency is independent of the level of public spending; the relaxation of this complicates the analysis without changing the possibility that optimal public spending may increase with provision inefficiency.) The reason is that the inefficiency in public provision may *increase* the marginal benefit at the relevant margin, even though it decreases the marginal benefit at the initial range.

This simple point is shown in Figure 8.1 where the *MB* curve measures the marginal benefit of public spending assuming a given degree of efficiency (including that of perfect efficiency as a special case) in public provision of public goods. With the given *MC* curve, the optimal level of public spending is at g^*. Now consider a decrease (say halving) in the degree of efficiency in the provision in the sense that the same amount of spending results only in half of the previously amount of public goods provided. Then, the marginal benefit of the first marginal unit is halved. The marginal benefit curve must thus shift downward in its initial range to become *MB'*. The value of (the new) *MB* (i.e. the height of the *MB'* curve) at any given level of public spending *g* is only half of the original value of *MB* at half that level of public spending $g/2$; e.g. the height of *A'* is only half that of *A*. This is so because, by halving provision efficiency as assumed, the *g* amount of public spending provides only $g/2$ amount of public goods previously provided, and a marginal increase in *g* also results in half of the previous increment. This results in a downward shift in the marginal benefit curve for the range where the curve is elastic in the sense of a demand curve (i.e. if a more than 1% increase in *g* is associated with a 1 per cent reduction in the marginal benefit, which must be true starting at $g = 0$; note that the *MB* curve being elastic in the sense of a demand curve really means that the fall in *MB* is proportionately small with respect to an increase in *g*). However, for the range where the marginal benefit curve is inelastic, a decrease in provision efficiency shifts the *MB* curve upward. Thus, if the *MC* curve intersects the *MB* curve at the inelastic range as shown in Figure 8.1, inefficiency in public provision may in fact increase the optimal level of public spending. (This is subject to the condition that the decrease in provision efficiency is not so large as to make non-provision optimal or to make a shift to private provision optimal.) We thus have (see Appendix F for a formal demonstration):

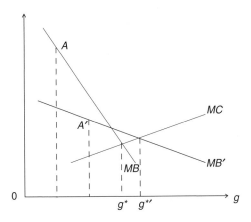

Figure 8.1

Other things being equal, an increase in inefficiency in provision increases/decreases the optimal level of public spending if the marginal benefit of public spending (or good) decreases proportionately more/less than the increase in public spending (or the physical amount of public good provided).

The part in parenthesis also holds because the (proportionate) responsiveness of the marginal benefit to the level of public spending (in dollar terms) is the same as the responsiveness of the marginal benefit to the physical amount of public good, under the simplification that the degree of inefficiency does not depend on the level of public spending, as shown formally in Appendix F.

The result may be seen in an alternative way. If we measure the *physical* amount of public spending along the horizontal axis (Figure not shown here), a (uniform) decrease in provision efficiency may be taken as an proportionate upward shift in the *MC* curve. This necessarily reduces the optimal physical amount of public spending (ignoring some possible interaction in the *MB* and the *MC* curves). However, if the *MB* curve is inelastic, the reduction is proportionately less than the increase in cost, leading to an increase in the monetary amount of public spending.

The reason that inefficiency in provision may increase the optimal level of public spending may be put in the following intuitive terms. Inefficiency decreases the (total) benefit but increases (by underprovision physically) the need for public spending. Needless to say, an increase in efficiency is desirable for all cases (i.e. whether the *MB* curve is elastic or inelastic).

Distinct from but similar to the inefficiency in provision is the increase in cost of providing public goods relative to private goods. As pointed out by Baumol (1967), this increase in relative cost increases the size of the public sector even if it remains unchanged in real terms. As calculated by Gemmell (1993, p.7), the share (as a percentage of GDP) of general government consumption expenditure in the UK at current prices increased from 16.5 per cent in 1950 to 21.7 per cent in 1980 (and declining back to 19.9 per cent in 1990) but *decreased* at constant 1985 prices from 25.7 per cent in 1950 to 21.9 per cent in 1980 (and further decreased to 19.1 per cent in 1990). The difference is caused by an increase in the relative price of government from 64.2 (using that of 1985 = 100) in 1950 to 99.1 in 1980 and 104.2 in 1990. In the presence of the increase in cost, if the demand for public spending is inelastic, the optimal size of public spending increases.

8.3 General taxation may be more corrective than distortive

A reason why the marginal cost of public spending is regarded as rather high is explained by Feldstein (1997, p.209): 'the deadweight loss caused by a change in tax rates is not a small triangle but a much larger trapezoid because we start with an existing tax distortion'. This is a valid argument within the orthodox framework where taxes are raised just to pay for the public spending and serves no other useful purposes. Within this framework, it is also quantitatively a very important consideration as the existing level of tax revenue accounts for more than 30 per cent of GDP for many countries. However, there is one consideration that may offset this important factor. In the production and/or consumption of most if not all goods and services, significant environmental disruption effects (including pollution, deforestation, littering, and congestion) are created either directly or indirectly (through intermediate goods). Few, if any, corrective taxes have been imposed on these activities. Thus, the usual income and consumption taxes, while designed for revenue-raising purposes, may serve as a rough correction to the environmental disruption effects of production and consumption. While the rate structures are far less than ideal in an abstract sense, this is a much smaller problem when the issue of feasibility and/or administrative costs are taken into account, though higher tax-rates on more disruptive activities should still be imposed. (See Ballard and Medema, 1993, on the different figures for the marginal cost of public fund raised by output, consumption, income, and Pigovian taxes.) Given the severity of the environmental problems (recalling the recent report of the big ice crack in the Antarctica due to global warming) and the very long-term nature of the effects, an average corrective tax-rate of around 30 per cent may not be excessive, though more reliable estimates should be done. At least, this consideration significantly offsets the trapezoid effect of higher tax rates, if not making the distortionary costs of taxation negative!

8.4 Diamond effects and burden-free taxes

It is widely known that corrective taxes on external costs such as pollution may yield negative excess burden, as argued in the last section, though the point is seldom brought up with respect to the optimal size of public spending. It is almost completely unknown, even among economists, that there exists a class of goods, taxes on which impose not only no excess burden but no burden at all. Ignoring administrative costs, the extent of negative excess burden is 100 per cent.

Given the quality, the utility (i.e. the extent of usefulness) of a good to a consumer depends on the quantity consumed. This is true for most goods that yield intrinsic consumption effects, e.g. nutrition, warmth. However, for many goods, it is the value (price times quantity) of the good rather than the quantity that is important. A notable example is diamond. Though beautiful, the utility of diamond to the (household) consumer is mainly due to its value. Cubic zirconia looks exactly like top-quality diamond but costs only a tiny fraction. Someone mixed a few stones of cubic zirconia with top-quality diamonds and gave them to diamond experts for verification. The expert declared all stones imitations. The willingness of people to pay high prices for diamonds cannot be explained by their intrinsic consumption utility, but by their values. For convenience, I call goods valued purely for their values 'pure diamond goods'.

People value goods for their values for a number of reasons. First, they can be used as items of conspicuous consumption, demonstrating one's wealth. Secondly, they are given as gifts of value. Thirdly, they are kept as a convenient store of value. Refugees cannot carry their shops and factories but could carry diamonds and gold when leaving in an emergency. One might add the speculative motive but these days speculation is largely done in paper (or rather electronic) transactions.

When someone gives a diamond ring or some other gift of value, it is the value of the ring rather than the size of the stone that is really important. The same is true for items of conspicuous consumption and for store of value. If gold is doubled in value, one may just half the physical quantity to achieve the same purpose. In fact, it makes carrying a large value of gold less cumbersome. Inconvenience in dealing with tiny quantities for smaller transactions can be avoided by using less valuable stones and metals like silver. Thus, ignoring transitional and distributional issues, if pure diamond goods are heavily taxed causing much higher prices, consumers suffer no loss in utility. Thus, efficiency requires arbitrarily high taxes on pure diamond goods, as demonstrated in Ng (1987a). (See also Ng, 1993 on mixed diamond goods with upward compensated demand curves and welfare-improving taxes.)

However, not many goods are pure diamond goods. Even diamond itself has some intrinsic uses. Nevertheless, many goods have significant components of the diamond effect. Thus, efficiency requires the imposition of higher taxes on these goods. This seems to be ignored in the present climate with emphasis on broad-based uniform taxation.

It should be emphasised that our case for higher taxes on goods with significant diamond effects is purely efficiency based, not equality based. In fact, as argued in Chapter 6, the objective of equality is more efficiently achieved through the general tax/transfer system rather than through specific measures.

8.5 Relative-income effects bias against public expenditure

Over a certain biologically minimum standard of living, the welfare of people depends more on non-material factors such as personal relationships and outlook in life. As far as personal or household incomes are concerned, it is more the relative level than the absolute level that is important. Since the early 1960s, per capita real income in OECD countries has more than doubled. However, the average person now is not really much happier than those in the 1960s. If they are, it is unlikely due to the much higher per capita income. In fact, the average Australian probably feels economically worse off now, mainly because of a drop in their relative position internationally, despite their bigger house, technically more sophisticated car, etc. than in the 1960s. For its own interest and as an extreme manifestation, it may be noted that even mortality may be more a function of relative than absolute income (Wilkinson, 1997).

The importance of relative-income effects and the relative unimportance of absolute incomes (beyond a certain level) are of course well known and have been discussed by economists and psychologists, including Rae (1834), Veblen (1929), Duesenberry (1949), Easterlin (1974), Hirsch (1976), Kapteyn and Wansbeek (1985), Frank (1985, 1999), and Cole *et al.* (1992). However, the implications of this on relevant economic policy issues, especially on the optimal size of public spending, have been largely ignored by economists. (There are some specific policy implications made, e.g. Ireland, 1994 notes the possibility of taxing status-seeking signals.)

For a single person, an increase in income increases both their absolute income and relative income. It is thus perceived to be of substantial importance. However, for the whole society, an increase in the relative income of some implies the reduction in others. If income levels of all increase proportionately, relative-income levels remain unchanged. Hence, from a social viewpoint, only the absolute component is relevant. This component is not of very high welfare significance for countries of high per capita incomes. Thus, in the presence of relative-income effects, the usual method of estimating the optimal level of public expenditure (equating the sum of individual marginal valuations to the marginal cost) is likely to lead to a sub-optimal level (Ng, 1987b). In most estimates, the marginal benefit of private expenditure is likely to be taken to include the intrinsic consumption effects and the internal or direct relative-income effect (as these two taken together constitute the worth of a private good as it appears to each individual), but not to include the external or indirect (through reduction in the relative incomes of others) relative-income effects. This creates an over-emphasis in favour of private expenditure, leading to a sub-optimal level of public expenditure. This is shown more formally in Appendix C where it is also shown that, under reasonable assumptions, the optimal size of public spending relative to GDP increases with per capital income.

8.5.1 Policy implications ignored by economists

While economists recognise the importance of relative-income effects, the relevant policy implications are ignored even when undertaking cost–benefit analyses relevant to actual policy decisions in the real world. As a specific example, we may consider the otherwise competent cost–benefit analysis of Portney (1990) who concludes that 'Congress and the President are about to shake hands on a landmark piece of environmental law [The Clean Air Act] for which costs may exceed benefits by a considerable margin.' However, the analysis of costs and benefits is based on ignoring the existence of relative-income effects, the full consideration of which may change the cost–benefit ratio substantially.

8.5.2 Rat-race for material growth may reduce welfare

In fact, it may be reasonably argued that, unless environmental protection and other welfare-improving measures are increased, economic growth may reduce welfare. Taking absolute income, relative income, and environmental quality as important for individual welfare, an individual places a higher value on the contribution of an increase in their income to their welfare than the value by which a general increase in incomes for the whole society could really increase social welfare. This is so because for an individual, an increase in income contributes to their welfare both through the absolute and the relative-income components. For the whole society, only the absolute-income component is relevant. Moreover, if this absolute component is relatively unimportant, and if economic growth is not accompanied by appropriate environmental protection measures such that environmental quality deteriorates significantly, the growth may be welfare reducing from the world perspective, though each individual and even each nation may find growth important, as argued in more details in Ng and Wang (1993). Appendix C goes further to show that welfare-reducing growth may prevail even if the government chooses the optimal level of public spending and the optimal amount of spending on environment-disruption abatement.

8.6 The unimportance of absolute income

While absolute income is not as important as indicated by the rat race for making money, it seems to be still of considerable importance in terms of utility or preference. In terms of happiness or welfare, the importance of absolute income is even more doubtful.

It is true that happiness is more difficult to measure and compare objectively than some more objectively measurable magnitudes like GDP. However, conceptually, it is cardinally measurable (Chapter 2 above). A practical method has also been developed and used to measure happiness cardinally and interpersonally comparably (Ng, 1996a). Though most existing measures of happiness have more problems with their comparability, they are not completely useless. Different researchers arrive at largely consistent results which also correspond with alternative measures like the opinions of friends. (See Veenhoven, 1984, 1993.) If one wants to be pedantic in insisting on perfect accuracy, even the measurement GDP is open to query on its accuracy and comparability.

Studies by psychologists and sociologists show that, both within a country and across nations, the happiness level of people increases with the income level, though not very significantly. For example, using regional and cultural classifications, the Northern European countries with high income also score top on happiness, followed by the group of English-speaking US, UK, Australia, and Ireland. Central and South-American countries including Brazil come next, followed by the Middle East, the Central European, Southern and Eastern European (Greece, Russia, Turkey, and Yugoslavia), the Indian Sub-continent, and Africa which does not, however, come last. Southern and Western European (France, Italy, and Spain) score significantly lower than Africa. And the last group is East Asia, including the country that leads in income, Japan. Singapore has an income (per capita) level 82.4 times that of India. Even in terms of purchasing power parity instead of using exchange rate, Singapore still has 16.4 times higher income than India. However, the happiness scores of both countries are exactly the same, both significantly higher than that of Japan. (See Cummins, 1998.)

While there are notable cases like Japan and France that are far off the regression line, statistically significant positive relationship between happiness and income exists cross-nationally *globally*. However, this is due mainly to the *inter-group* difference between the high-income and high-happiness advanced and free countries *and* the others. The analysis by Schyns (1998) shows that there is no positive relationship between income and happiness within either of these two groups. Kenny (1999, p.12) reports a similar lack of relationship within each group by splitting all countries into two groups of below and above $8,000 in per-capita income.

The relationship between happiness and income level intertemporally within the same country (at least for the advanced countries which have such data) is even less encouraging in terms of giving a positive relationship. For example, from the 1940s to 1994, the real income per capita of the US nearly trebled. However, the percentage of people who regard themselves as very happy fluctuated around 30 per cent, without showing an upward trend; another measure of average happiness fluctuated around 72 per cent. Over the period 1958–88, the per capita real income level in Japan increased by more than five times (Summers and Heston, 1991). However, its average happiness measure fluctuated around 59 per cent, also without an upward trend. (See Veenhoven, 1993; Myers, 1996, p.445; Diener and Suh, 1997; Oswald, 1997; Frank, 1999.) In fact, 'if there is any causal relationship in rich countries, it appears to run from happiness to growth, not vice-versa' (Kenny, 1999, p.19). Also, recent research suggests that individuals who strongly value extrinsic goals (e.g. fame, wealth, image) relative to intrinsic goals (e.g. personal development, relatedness, community) have less happiness (Ryan *et al.*, forthcoming).

Kenny (1999, pp.4–5) also puts the point of fast diminishing marginal utility of income in more objective terms thus:

Compare Mozambique, China and the USA. In turn, the countries' GNPs per capita in 1992 were $80, $470 and $24,740. Infant mortalities were 145.6, 30.5 and 8.6 per 1,000 live births, respectively. Life expectancies were 47, 69 and 76 years. Thus, going 1.6 percent of the distance between Mozambique and the United States in terms of wealth, so reaching China's income, we move 84 percent of the distance in terms of infant mortality and 76 percent of the distance in terms of life expectancy.

On the other hand, there are factors that affect or at least correlate with happiness much more significantly than income, including being married or single (Myers, 1996, p.510), being employed or not (Winkelmann and Winkelmann, 1998), and having a religious belief and church attendance.

For those who do not trust the more subjective measure of happiness and opt to use more objective indicators of the quality of life, the picture is not much different. Analysing a panel dataset of 95 quality-of-life indicators (covering education, health, transport, inequality, pollution, democracy, political stability) covering 1960–90, Easterly (1997) reaches some remarkable results:

1. While virtually all of these indicators show quality of life across nations to be positively associated with per capita income, when country effects are removed using either fixed effects or an estimator in first differences, the effects of economic growth on the quality of life are uneven and often nonexistent. '*For the fixed effects estimator applied to 95 indicators, the coefficient of income was significant at the 5% level for 40 indicators. This is not so bad, except that only 23 of these 40 show improvement in the quality of life associated with rising income. It is distressing that almost as many indicators show significant deterioration in quality of life*' (Easterly, 1997, p.18).

2. Most of the exogenous time shifts (69 out of 95 indicators) improve the quality of life and time shifts are more important than growth effects in the majority (62% of the 79 available indicators) of indicators. Even for the only 22 out of the 95 indicators with a significantly positive relationship with income under fixed effects, time improved 10 out of these 22 more than income did.

The surprising results are not due to the worsening income distribution (there is some evidence that the share of the poor gets better with growth). Rather, the quality of life of any country depends less on its own economic growth or income level but more on the scientific, technological, and other breakthroughs at the world level. These depend more on public spending than private consumption.

If higher income does not really increase happiness, why do people put so much emphasis in making money? Apart from the importance of relative-income effects and the public bad aspect of environmental disruption, individual ignorance and/or irrationality may also have a role to play. Apart from the discussion in Chapter 4 (Section 4.2 in particular), some further remarks may be added here.

First, there is the animal spirit for accumulation mentioned by Keynes. This is similar to the accumulation instinct of some animals, like the storage of food by rats, the burial of nuts by squirrels. Such instincts are selected as they generally help the species to survive. We are a much more 'rational' species. (A species is defined to be more 'rational' than another if its behaviour is more affected, than the other species, by the calculation of reward and punishment and less by hard-wired instincts. See Ng, 1996b where it is argued that the evolution of more 'rational' species makes the environment more complex which in turn makes more 'rational' species more selectable, leading to a virtuous circle culminating in our species of *homo sapiens*, partly explaining the fast rate of evolution, the speed of which is doubted by creationists.) However, we are still partly affected by our animal spirit of accumulation instinct. In times of scarcity, this helps us to survive better. However, in our present era of material plenty (but environmental-quality scarcity), our animal spirit may make us irrational. Is it rational to sacrifice friendship, love, and family, or to take the high risk of losing freedom, fame, and jobs by engaging in corruption, robberies, murders, etc. just to make some more money which is not that important to one's happiness, especially in the long run? Those who can see through this may call themselves 'not deluded'. (Confucius said, 'I became independent at thirty, not deluded at forty.')

Secondly, there are studies by psychologists and sociologists suggesting that people are typically ignorant and/or irrational. For example, most people believe that winning a big sum of money will make them very happy. Thus, many people spend a lot of money and time buying lottery tickets. However, there is evidence that lottery winners are no happier than non-winner controls (Brickman, *et al.*, 1978). For another example, most or at least many people also believe that losing one's legs or eyesight in an accident is worse than being killed. However, studies show that quadriplegics are only slightly less happy than healthy people (Brickman, *et. al.*, 1978). After an initial period of adjustment, maimed victims can still enjoy life and are glad that they were not killed. Also, people typically underestimate the negative/positive effects of current enjoyment/suffering on future ability for enjoyment. (See Headley and Wearing, 1991.) Eating sufficiently salty, sweet, or tasty food now may yield more utility now than the slight health hazard involved. Shifting to healthier food may incur too big a loss in present pleasure. However, our taste will adjust to the blander and coarser but healthier food. I changed from white bread to wholemeal bread a long time ago on health reasons. Initially, I was not really sure that the gain in being healthier justified the loss in taste. However, after months of eating wholemeal bread, I began to enjoy that more than white bread even just on taste. Those still on white bread are strongly urged to shift. Also, making children accustomed to white bread may be very unwise.

An ancient Chinese poet had a line: 'Having seen the big blue sea, it becomes difficult to appreciate waters [i.e. lakes become less impressive]'. Thus, the long-term utility of seeing the blue sea may not be that high as it lowers the utility of seeing other less impressive waters in the future. However, most people fail to take adequate account of such effects, including myself. When I was on my first leave, my family and I visited the top attractions in the world like the Great Wall, Niagara Falls, and the Grand Canyon. After that, sightseeing is no longer exciting. 'Except for that in the Wu Mountains, no cloud is attractive', so says the second line of the poem. Thus, another Chinese sage advised that one should eat sugar-cane from the less tasty end, proceeding to the more tasty parts gradually.

8.7 Welfare-improving public expenditures

While noting that the rat race for material growth may be welfare reducing, I am not anti-growth. Instead of hoping for a slower growth or even a depression, as some environmentalists do, a healthy growth with an appropriate increase in environmental protection measures seems a much superior option. Moreover, if economic growth is conducive to a higher degree of civilisation by providing more resources to support scientific and technological advances conducive to welfare, it may be welfare-improving despite some negative environmental effects. For example, the advance in science and its applications to medicine, engineering, etc. have contributed much to a comfortable and enriched life, the relief of pain, and the cure of many illnesses. The development of the Westminster and other forms of democratic government and the rule of law, the prevalence of modern communications and social interaction have also helped create a freer and more peaceful world. The understanding of the working of the market mechanism has contributed to the collapse of the communist totalitarian system and to the end of the Cold War. Higher education is becoming more widespread. Looking into the future, one can be reasonably confident that further advances in these and related areas will be forthcoming. Moreover, there are likely to be significant or even dramatic improvements in welfare from sources most people do not dream of now. For example, the techniques of electrical brain stimulation (discussed in Appendix A) and genetic engineering could be used, after more intensive experimentation and with careful management, to increase welfare by quantum leaps.

Despite the above-mentioned promises, it remains true that a pure increase in GNP (even without any deterioration in income distribution) may be welfare-reducing unless environmental protection and other welfare-improving measures are facilitated. In rich countries, what is important is not simply growth in GNP and the resulting higher consumption per head but how welfare-improving measures (environmental protection, scientific advances, etc.) can be increased. Thus, despite the excess costs (excess burden, administrative, compliance, and policing costs) of raising public revenue, more public expenditures in the right areas (including research) may yet be most welfare improving. This is especially so in view of the importance of environmental disruption effects, relative-income effects and diamond effects (with the associated burden-free or at least less burdensome taxes) which may be expected to be increasing in importance, absolutely and relatively.

8.8 Concluding remarks

It is shown more formally in Appendix C that, with reasonable assumptions, the optimal relative (to the GDP) size of the public sector increases with higher per capita income. Thus, one may say that the historical increase in the relative size of the public sector is consistent with and is partly explained by this. In fact, we may go further than this and argue that, despite the higher relative size of the public sector, it is still lower than the optimal level. This may be so for a number of reasons.

Environmental quality is to a large extent a global public good. The big mountain fire in Indonesia recently (1997) affected the air quality, climate, and even visibility of neighbouring countries within days/ weeks and is fairly certain to affect the air quality (though to a lesser extent) of the whole world for a very long time to come. Decisions by separate national governments based on national interests are unlikely to take full account of the global effects unless there is adequate international coordination. The latter is only starting to emerge and is far from being adequate.

Environmental quality is a very long-term problem. Many pollutants remain in the environment for a long time. The warm-house effect could threaten the coastlines of low-lying cities perhaps decades or centuries from now through the melting of polar ice. In contrast, politicians in both democratic and authoritarian countries are likely to have much shorter time horizons.

In assessing the relative benefits of public versus private expenditures, people are likely to overestimate the true importance of the latter. (See Section 8.5 above.) Affected by the working of relative-income effects including the desire to keep up with the Joneses, people find private spending very important. If most of your child's classmates are given expensive birthday gifts you will then feel pressurised into giving your child a substantial gift. However, most people ignore the fact that, if the whole society devotes more resources to supply public goods, on average everyone will have less to spend on private items. Then, despite a lower post-tax income, one can still keep up with others.

Research, especially fundamental research, is also largely a global public good and hence is under-funded by national governments. However, once a basic level of consumption has been attained, happiness cannot increase significantly with higher private consumption (especially at the social level due to relative-income effects as already discussed) given the level of knowledge. Many of us can easily double our private consumption. (For those who cannot, many can halve their consumption without much real loss in happiness.) But what is the point? If you are already well-fed, well-clothed, well-accommodated, increasing private spending does not increase your happiness significantly but imposes significant negative externalities in the form of environmental disruption and relative-income effects. Is it really very important to spend many weeks holidaying in far-away places living in 5-star hotels, when you can walk or jog in nearby parks and read fascinating books or watch interesting programmes on TV? Is having a beer in a local pub or a cup of tea with a few friends at home significantly less enjoyable than dining in expensive restaurants or drinking wine at US$500 a bottle? Rather than spending extravagantly, our welfare can certainly increase much more if the cities become safer, the environment becomes cleaner, a cure is found for some illness, or the method of stimulation of the brain can be improved for common use. (On the quantum leap in welfare with the last method, see Appendix A.) Most of such items need public spending.

Due to the inefficiency of public organisations, privatisation in certain areas and de-regulation of counter-productive regulations may make a lot of sense. It is also easy to find particular areas of waste and ineffectiveness in public expenditures. (This is so since public expenditure is unlikely to be optimally distributed among different items and also unlikely to be provided in the most efficient way.) However, due to the above considerations, the recent global trend towards the checking of public expenditures, especially in the funding of research, may be very negative in terms of social welfare, especially globally and in the long term.

This negative effect may consist to a large extent in the failure to attract talented people to work in the welfare-improving areas of research and the public sector. Top students used to stay to do PhDs and remain in the academic world. Now, many good students leave to work for business firms where real talents are largely wasted in competitive rivalry at both the production and consumption levels. True, talents are also needed to have efficiency in production and innovation. However, the very best talents are needed to do research and to serve in the public sector, especially after the satisfaction of basic needs when increases in private consumption without an increase in knowledge are not very welfare-conducive. Many people are sceptical of the productivity of increased funding for research, being aware of many ill-conceived projects and many publications of doubtful usefulness. However, one piece of useful research out of a hundred may make it all worthwhile. Moreover, long-term social welfare may be improved by raising the rewards and working conditions of researchers and other public-sector employees so as to attract real talents back from the business sector. The market fails here partly because of the public goods externality and partly because of factors like relative-income effects (also a form of externality) discussed above.

Combining the analysis of this chapter (and that of Appendix C) with the evidence reported in section 8.6 above (especially the remarkable results of Easterly, 1997), a strong case may be made for international cooperation to dramatically increase public spending on global public goods including environmental protection and research. A few examples may be given to indicate that much more research is needed to increase welfare.

- The very topic of the appropriate size of the public sector, regarded by Feldstein (1997) as the central public finance question, is very under-researched. For example, few, if any, researchers relate the important issue of relative income to this central question. While I have discussed this and other related issues above, a lot more quantitative studies are needed.
- While studies on the effects of specific drugs and ingredients have been done, it seems that a general study tracing the different types

of food, drugs, and activities taken by a big enough sample of people (at least thousands) of different ages and health conditions (not just those hospitalised) over a long period (at least decades) to discover the desirable and undesirable effects may be most rewarding. Though the study would be very costly, we may gain very useful knowledge on millions of factors simultaneously.

- The stimulation of certain pleasure centres in the brain can induce intense pleasure without the effect of diminishing marginal utility. This has been known since the mid-1950s. Why has the method not been perfected for common use? (See Appendix A for details.)

Much useful research and development are undertaken in the private sector. However, by and large, it is effective only at the level with immediate or close to immediate application. Nowadays, most fundamental research is undertaken in the public sector:

It was a government research program that produced the mathematical algorithms that led to the computer. The Internet was created by researchers in US universities under contract to the Defence Department. The laser, the electric telegraph – research has always been a public responsibility. And, as we move to a knowledge economy, its role has become central to the economy

Joe Stiglitz, reported in the *The Age*, (Melbourne), 27 Mar. 1999

Despite the negative evidence discussed in Section 8.6, I believe that happiness has increased. (It is likely that people's standards for describing themselves as 'happy' or 'very happy' have increased, hiding an increase in real happiness. This increases the importance of using the proposed more interpersonally comparable measure of happiness (Ng, 1996a).) However, I remain convinced that happiness could be increased by shifting resources from the largely competitive private consumption to items of public spending that benefit the whole world for a long time.

9
The Appropriate Benefit–Cost Ratio for Public Spending

The optimal level of public spending is related to what public spending/projects are regarded as appropriate. This is in turn related to the benefit–cost ratio used to assess public projects. The use of a benefit–cost ratio more stringent (i.e. larger) than one would generally lead to a smaller level of public spending. Recently, some prominent economists have expressed apparently rather contrasting views on this issue. This chapter reconciles and qualifies their arguments.

9.1 The conventional view

The conventional view of economists is that the optimal level of public spending should be less than that indicated by the use of the simple benefit–cost ratio of one, since the financing of public revenue involves distortionary costs. This view dates from at least the time of Pigou (1928), who stated that the benefits of public goods must exceed their direct costs by an amount sufficient to outweigh the distortionary cost (also called deadweight loss or excess burden) of taxation. An authoritative modern textbook (Stiglitz, 1988, p.140) puts the Pigovian principle this way: 'Since it becomes more costly to obtain public goods when taxation imposes distortions, normally this will imply that the efficient level of public goods is smaller than it would have been with nondistortionary taxation.'[1]

It is known that the Pigovian principle is subject to qualifications due to the presence of considerations like second best, including complementarity/substitutability between public and private goods. (See, e.g. Atkinson and Stiglitz, 1980; King, 1986; Batina, 1990 and Chang, 1997.) Wilson (1991) goes as far as establishing a case where the second-best public-goods level exceeds the first-best level. However, he assumes the feasibility of financing public spending through a general lump-sum tax (or a reduction in the lump-sum subsidy) without which, Wilson (1991, p.153) himself recognises, the abnormal case 'normally will not happen'.

Christiansen (1981) identifies a set of sufficient conditions for the applicability of the simple benefit–cost ratio of one, namely similar individual preferences except for the influence of different earning a bilities (a standard assumption in the Mirrlees, 1971 framework), weak separability of the public good and the *numeraire* private good from leisure/work, the absence of commodity taxation (in whose presence, an additional condition on the independence of the marginal valuation of the public good is needed), and the operation of an optimal (in general) non-linear income tax. Using the self-selection approach (a high-ability person may choose to work less and pay less tax), Boadway and Keen (1993) derive a modified (Samuelsonian) benefit–cost rule for public goods, explaining and confirming Christiansen's important result for the specific case. Using his approach to analyse commodity tax reform, Konishi (1995) generalises Christiansen's result to any smooth non-linear income tax, optimal or not. However, Christiansen's case for the simple benefit–cost rule is meant as applicable to a special case.

Feldstein (1997) presents the orthodox position on the distortionary costs of taxation most comprehensively and clearly, reviewing some very important contributions by himself and other researchers (including Stuart, 1984; Ballard *et al.*, 1985; Browning, 1987; Auten and Carroll, 1994; Feldstein, 1995a, 1995b; Feldstein and Feenberg, 1996 and Slemrod and Yitzhaki, 1996). At the risk of over-simplification, Feldstein's position may be summarised by the following quotation:

> 'First, higher tax rates may reduce the supply of labor and, in the longer run, the supply of capital. . . . Second, higher tax rates change the forms in which individuals take their compensation. A higher marginal tax rate on labor income induces a substitution of untaxed fringe benefits and more pleasant working conditions for taxable cash income . . . [Third,] higher marginal tax rates reduce taxable income by inducing more spending on things that are tax deductible (including . . . charitable gifts, and health care) . . . many economists believe that an increase in tax rates would cause only a small dead-weight loss . . . as a "small" triangle. . . . That line of reasoning is wrong for four reasons. First, the deadweight loss caused by a change in tax rates is not a small triangle but a much larger trapezoid because

we start with an existing tax distortion. . . . Second, the relevant labor supply elasticity is much larger than the traditional estimates imply. . . . Third, . . . other ways of reducing taxable income . . . [Fourth, the] same kind of wasteful distortion is also true for spending on things that are tax deductible. . . . The total cost per incremental dollar of government spending, including the revenue and the deadweight loss, is thus a very high $2.65. Equivalently, it implies that the marginal distortionary costs per dollar of revenue are $1.65.'

Feldstein, 1997, pp.201, 209–11

(Other estimates, e.g. Ballard *et al.*, 1985, usually give a much lower figure of around 30 per cent, but Browning, 1987 gives a bigger range. See also Snow and Warren, 1996 for a more general analytical analysis.)

9.2 Kaplow's argument and the principle of 'a dollar is a dollar'

While some recent literature has qualified the Pigou principle, a full-scale onslaught is presented by Kaplow. He argues that public goods can be financed without additional distortion by using an adjustment to the income tax that offsets the benefits of the public good. The:

preexisting income tax schedule is adjusted so that, at each income level, the tax change just offsets the benefits from the public good. By construction, an individual's *net* reward from any level of work effort will be unaltered; any reduction in disposable income due to the tax adjustment is balanced by the benefits from the public good. Because an individual's after-tax utility as a function of his work effort will thus be unchanged, his choice of work effort – and utility level – will also be unaffected.

Kaplow, 1996, p.514

For example, if the benefit of a public good is proportional to the income level of the taxpayers, it may be financed by a (or an increase in) proportional income tax. The proportional income tax itself may involve a disincentive effect. However, the tax plus the public good together involve no disincentive effect. For example, suppose the benefit of police protection of properties is proportional to the income level of the taxpayers. With a higher degree of police protection financed by a higher proportional income tax, a person benefits more (in comparison to a lower degree of protection and lower tax) and pays more by the same amount if she earns more, leaving the incentive structure unaffected.

If the benefit of a public good is a constant amount across all income levels but it is financed by a proportional income tax, then a disincentive effect may be involved. But then 'it will be accompanied by a countervailing change in redistributive benefits that has been ignored' (Kaplow, 1996, p.525). To this observation, it may be added that, in the reversed case, e.g. where a public good with benefit proportional to income is financed by a lump-sum tax, a *negative* redistributive benefit will be involved, but it will be accompanied by a *negative* disincentive effect, reasonably assuming that a tax increasing in income is already in existence for redistributive purposes. If the income-tax schedule has been designed to approximately achieve an optimal balance between the redistributive benefits and the distortive costs of taxation, the redistributive benefits (positive or negative) of non-benefit-proportional financing of a (non-huge) public good will be approximately offset by its distortionary costs (positive or negative). For a huge public good or the cumulative effects of a large number of public goods, either benefit-proportional financing may be used or a change to the income-tax schedule may be made to redress any significant divergence between redistributive benefits and the distortionary costs of taxation.

For the case where the benefits of the public goods increase with the income level, it may be interpreted as a case where there is significant complementarity between the public good and the taxed goods. In this case, some recent analysis allows for certain offsetting effect on the extent of distortionary costs. (Intuitively, an increase in public goods then increases the demand for the taxed goods, generating more tax revenue and offsetting the under-consumption of these taxed goods.) However, while this complementarity is unambiguous in reducing the distortionary costs, it is ambiguous in affecting the optimal size of public good provision due to the following counteracting effect. An increase in public good provision necessitates higher taxes on the taxed goods, leading to higher prices of these goods which reduces the marginal valuation on and hence the optimal size of the public good through complementarity. Substitutability has the reversed effects. (See Batina, 1990 and Chang, 1997.) Since the Kaplow principle is concerned with the size of the required benefit–cost ratio for public goods rather than on the level of public spending directly, it is not affected by the counteracting effect through complementarity on the marginal valuation on public goods. Moreover, most of the recent contributions in optimal taxation/expenditure, using a single representative consumer model, ignore the countervailing change in redistributive benefits for cases where the distortionary costs are not offset by complementarity to become zero.[2]

The argument of Kaplow may be compared with my argument (Chapter 6) for treating a dollar as a dollar whomsoever it goes to or comes from (in particular, irrespective of income groups) in the assessment of any change, policy, project, etc. (except in the general income tax/transfer system). If a project benefits the rich by $10 m and costs the poor $8 m, the pure efficiency principle of a dollar as a dollar dictates its adoption but most people will not regard it as desirable. However, it is Pareto-superior to adopt the project and adjust the tax schedule such that the rich have to pay $9 m more and the poor has to pay/receive $9 m less/more. Most economists do not believe that this is Pareto superior because making the tax schedule more progressive increases the disincentive effects of taxation. This belief ignores the fact that the policy of rejecting such a project also has higher disincentive effects.

Despite the similarity of my 'a dollar is a dollar' argument with Kaplow's argument (both involving offsetting income tax/transfer adjustment), I must admit that I failed to see the Kaplow principle (that the benefit–cost ratio for public goods only need to exceed one) for two decades after formulating my 'a dollar is a dollar' principle (seminar presentations at Monash in 1976, at VPI, New York, and Yale in 1978; the principle appeared to be so right-wing that the paper could not be published until 1984) until I read Kaplow. In a sense, one may say that the Kaplow principle is a specific application of the 'a dollar is a dollar' principle to the case of public goods/projects. Since a dollar should be treated as a dollar whomsoever it goes to or comes from, the costs and benefits of any project (private or public) should be counted equally and hence the benefit–cost ratio needs only exceed one for any project (private or public). However, before reading Kaplow, I thought that requiring the benefit–cost ratio for a public good to exceed one by a sufficient margin is based on the efficiency principle as a dollar of public revenue costs the economy more than one dollar. In other words, I accepted the conventional position here completely. Thus, I find Kaplow's paper extremely important and hope that it will be given the attention it deserves.

One obvious qualification to the Kaplow principle and the principle of 'a dollar is a dollar' is: What if the higher public spending cannot be financed by offsetting benefit taxation and if the existing progressivity in income tax/transfer system is not optimal or cannot be adjusted to offset the shift to the efficiency principle, due to political constraints or other factors? While we may try to do good by stealth in the short run and proceed to use, say, distributional weights, in the long run this will be known and cause disincentive effects. Moreover, the same political forces that prevent the increase in progressivity may then work to *decrease* the degree of progressivity as actually happened in many countries in the past few decades, when incentives have been reduced by the use of distributional weights and other non-efficiency, purely equality-oriented policies. We then end up with less efficiency and no more equality. (See Section 6.4.)

Kaplow also mentions two qualifications to his simple analysis which also applies to my 'a dollar is a dollar' principle. However, neither qualification affects the central thrust of either the Kaplow principle or the principle of 'a dollar is a dollar'. First, when second-best considerations such as different degrees of complementarity with leisure are taken into account, the simple cost–benefit rule or the 'a dollar is a dollar' principle should be adjusted or be defined to include such indirect costs/benefits through second best or external effects. It might then, for example, be argued:

> that there should be smaller public libraries than otherwise would be efficient, because libraries make leisure more attractive, reinforcing the adverse incentive effect of the income tax. Conversely, there perhaps should be greater police protection of private property than otherwise would be efficient, because this increases the value of goods that are purchased from the fruits of labor. . . . This qualification . . . does not justify the type of adjustment to cost–benefit analysis.
>
> Kaplow, 1996, p.518

This would require a higher benefit–cost ratio for all public goods or a distributional weighting system favouring the poor and against the rich for all specific cases. (For the case of libraries, I believe that there are counteracting benefits, including indirect external economies and merit goods, justifying higher levels of provision. But this is a separate issue. On indirect externalities, see Ng, 1975b.)

The second qualification refers to heterogeneity of preferences for people on the same income. It is not feasible to design income tax schedules and public spending programmes that differ between people on the same income but of different preferences. Thus, the construction of compensating tax/transfer changes in either Kaplow's or my argument can only make people on each income *as a group* no worse off. People who differ in preference significantly from the average (at that income level) one way or the other may either gain or lose. However, the gainers within each income level could compensate the losers fully (with some overall gains left over). This is called a quasi-Pareto social improvement in Ng (1984b). Objections to the compensation tests are mainly based on the distributional consideration that a gain valued at $2 million by the rich need not be more important than a loss valued at $1 million by the poor if the compensation is not actually paid. For a quasi-Pareto social improvement, full compensation is possible within each group of the same income level. The rich-poor issue does not apply. (The minor problem of possible inconsistency in the application of compensation tests is also discussed in Ng, 1984b.) Thus, the problem of heterogeneity of preferences does not cause a big problem. A more important qualification to the Kaplow principle (but not to the 'a dollar is a dollar' principle) is discussed below.

9.3 Reconciling Kaplow and Feldstein

The positions of Kaplow and Feldstein (and that of most other economists, including myself before I read Kaplow) appear to be diametrically opposite, with Kaplow arguing for the adequacy of the simple benefit–cost principle and Feldstein emphasising the need to account for the big deadweight loss of raising revenue for public spending. However, I wish to argue in this section that we may adopt an interpretation that makes both sides basically correct, subject to some important qualifications.

Subject to an important comment mentioned below, Feldstein is basically correct that, given the various ways individuals adjust to the higher tax rates, raising an additional dollar of public revenue (by, say, a marginal proportionate increase in tax rates across the board) *on its own* does impose, in general, a significant (say, 100 per cent) distortionary cost over and above the revenue collected. However, this does not mean that the benefit–cost ratio for a public project has to exceed 2. There are offsetting benefits at the spending side (on top of the direct benefits of the public goods).[3] If the valuation of the higher public spending is the same as the extent of the higher taxes at each and every income level, then the higher disincentive effects of the higher taxes will be exactly (subject to the qualifications mentioned at the end of Section 9.2 above and another qualification to be mentioned presently) offset to give no net increase in disincentive effects, as shown by Kaplow. This is so because when people reckon in terms of the total package of the higher taxes and spending, the gains offset the losses at each income group. Putting it differently, the fact that people at higher income levels place higher values on the public goods makes the spending side possess *negative* disincentive effects or positive *incentive* effects, offsetting the disincentive effects of the higher taxes, when the higher taxes do cause disincentive effects.[4] On the other hand, if the degree at which the valuation of the higher public spending increases with income is less than the degree at which higher taxes increases with income, such that there are higher disincentive effects for the total package (of higher taxes and higher spending), there exist offsetting distributional gains (since the poor gain and the rich lose in net terms). In the opposite case where the poor lose and the rich gain in net terms, there are distributional losses. But then the combined disincentive effects of the total package are negative. In any of these three cases, the Kaplow principle applies.

However, apart from the qualifications mentioned at the end of Section 9.2, the Kaplow principle is subject to another important qualification. (See Appendix C of Ng, forthcoming b, on another more complicated consideration.) Kaplow's analysis ignores the behavioural responses to higher taxes except through the income (consumption)/ leisure choice. As Feldstein (1997) emphasises, there are other responses including substitution into less tax-assessable spending like luxurious offices. This encouragement of inefficient choices does increase the distortionary costs of higher taxes despite Kaplow's argument. Higher taxes encourage people at each and almost all income levels (especially those facing high marginal tax rates) to use less-beneficial though more tax (avoidance)-effective ways of spending money. This *extra* distortion is not offset by any extra benefit of the higher public spending. This qualification to the Kaplow principle applies also to illegal means of tax evasion: higher tax rates encourage more evasion. Here, the loss in tax revenue itself is not a distortionary cost as it is offset by the gain of the taxpayers. The distortionary cost consists in the fact that the taxpayers would prefer to have the higher incomes legally, without having to go into the dubious, time-consuming, and likely less beneficial means that are more tax-effective. In practice, this may be the most important qualification to the Kaplow principle.

A query may arise: Why do the higher benefits of the higher public spending, financed by the higher compensatory taxes, offset the higher tax-rates to produce neutrality (no extra disincentive effect) in income/leisure choice, but do not offset the higher tax-rates to also produce neutrality in tax evasion and other similar choices? This is so because if an income earner decides to have more leisure and earn less income, she forgoes not only the after-tax income but also the benefits (e.g. protection of more property) associated with higher incomes. (For the case where the benefits from public spending is related to the publicly unobservable earning abilities rather than incomes, a qualification may be needed as discussed in Ng, forthcoming b.) On the other hand, when a person under-reports the income she actually does earn, she does not forgo, by and large, the benefits (from higher public spending) associated with higher (actual) incomes. Those parts of the benefits of higher public spending that only apply to *reported* incomes will in fact offset the higher tax-rates and reduce the incentives for tax evasion. If all the benefits depend on reported than on actual incomes, then the qualification to the Kaplow principle being discussed is not needed.

It may be noted that the above qualification to the Kaplow principle due to non-leisure behavioural responses need not apply to the principle of 'a dollar is a dollar', for the following consideration. While higher taxes/transfers on the rich/poor in lieu of specific equality-oriented policies tend to encourage more tax evasion and avoidance, the specific equality-oriented policies themselves also encourage evasion and avoidance. Just as one may pretend to be on low income to pay less tax, one may also pretend to be on low income to have access to specific benefits for low income-earners. Unless there is asymmetry in the extent of losses in the 'wrong' direction, no qualification to the principle of 'a dollar is a dollar' is needed here. I discussed this and similar issues under 'transaction costs' in Section 6.4 and concluded that the asymmetry is actually in the 'right' direction, with an *a fortiori* case against specific equality-oriented policies.

Another query may arise: Why is the Kaplow principle subject to the qualification of non-leisure behavioural responses while the principle of 'a dollar is a dollar' is not? This may be explained thus. The more progressive tax/transfer system used in the argument for the principle of 'a dollar is a dollar' is *in lieu of* a system of specific purely equality-oriented policies that is itself subject to similar behavioural responses. For the Kaplow principle, the higher taxes are used to finance for *extra* public spending that does not exist yet. The losses due to the behavioural responses to the higher tax rates have thus to be taken into accounted in assessing whether the extra public spending is worth undertaking.

The argument of Feldstein regarding the extra distortionary costs due to the various non-leisure responses of individuals has itself to be subject to an important qualification. Two different types (for simplicity, we take the two polar types, though various degrees of mixture of the two types may be involved in practice) of (legal or illegal) tax-free (or lower tax-rates) spending should be distinguished. First, there are various items that the government wants to (or should) encourage for some social purposes, including the efficiency consideration of external benefits (e.g. health care, the prevention of communicable diseases in particular) and the distributional one of poverty reduction (e.g. charitable gifts). If the higher taxes encourage people in genuinely spending more on these items that the society wants to encourage, there is no extra deadweight loss. (If the increase in taxes is so huge that the extra spending becomes too excessive, the degree of tax deductibility may need to be reduced to revert to optimality.) This is so because the reduced benefits to the taxpayers are offset by the increased gains of external benefits or distributional benefits.

Secondly, the higher tax rates may also encourage people to spend more on those items that the government does not really want to encourage but nevertheless has to treat them as tax-deductible due to the difficulties of distinguishing them from items that genuinely should qualify for tax-deductibility. These include (but may not be confined to): 1. pretended, non-genuine spending on deductible items, e.g. claiming private dining as business expenses; 2. excess spending on deductible items, e.g. big offices. These types of spending create extra distortionary costs as explained by Feldstein. They do not produce compensating benefits like external or distributional benefits like the first type of tax-free spending.

Even without accepting Kaplow's argument, the estimation of the distortionary costs of taxation should reflect those due to behavioural changes of the second (encouragement-not-intended) type but not the first (encouragement-intended) type. Feldstein includes items like charitable gifts and health care in his discussion of behavioural responses. These items clearly largely belong to the encouragement-intended type. Also, his method of estimating taxable income elasticities (used in turn to estimate the distortionary costs) by the blanket comparison of actual tax revenues before and after tax-rate changes necessarily lump the two types of responses together. Thus, if the method is used, a separate estimate of the part due to the first type of response should be made and deducted from the total to give an appropriate estimate of the true distortionary costs, before considering Kaplow's point. The need for the separate treatment of the two types of responses is established in a more formal analysis in Ng (forthcoming b).

9.4 Concluding remarks

Putting the above arguments and those of Chapter 8 together, it means that, in estimating the distortionary costs of taxation for determining the appropriate excess (of unity) benefit–cost ratio for public spending, the relevant positive (i.e. in favour of a positive excess) effects are the non-income responses of type two (those not purposefully encouraged by the society) and the relevant negative effects include the bias due to the importance of relative-income effects and the corrective nature of most existing taxes due to environmental disruption of most production and consumption. Before a reasonable estimation of these opposing effects, it is difficult to say whether the appropriate benefit–cost ratio for public spending should exceed or fall short of unity. I agree with Feldstein (1997, p.197) that the 'central public finance question facing any country is the appropriate size of its government' and that economists should put more effort in trying to help answer this question. Our discussion indicates that both a comprehensive consideration taking all relevant issues into account and much more quantitative estimation of the relevant factors are needed.

10
Concluding Remarks

Discerning readers may have noticed that Part I of this book is somewhat 'rightwing' while Part II is 'leftwing'. Thus, Part I argues strongly for utilitarianism (Chapter 5) and against pure egalitarianism (Appendix B), and for the principle of 'a dollar is a dollar' (Chapter 6). On the other hand, Part II argues for higher public spending, especially on research and environmental protection. However, though the two parts may be opposite in their political philosophy, they are not inconsistent with each other. For example, the fact that the principle of 'a dollar is a dollar' is consistent with the argument for higher public spending may be seen easily as the latter is based purely on the efficiency considerations of relative-income effects, environmental disruption effects, the negative disincentive effects of public spending (the Kaplow principle), the global public-good nature of research, etc. I may be schizophrenic in the sense that my heart is leftwing and my head is rightwing. However, there is no inconsistency in my arguments. In fact, the opposite political inclinations of the two parts demonstrate that I follow the dictates of my logical analysis wherever they take me, without sticking to a political preconception.

While there is no inconsistency, there may be some tension between different arguments. For example, my allowance for the difference between preference and welfare due to non-affective altruism (or malice), ignorance, and irrationality (Chapter 4) and the use of the willingness to pay (Chapter 6) need some explanation. As should be clear from Chapter 3 and Chapter 4, I view happiness or welfare as the appropriate ultimate objective. However, partly because it is more difficult to obtain information on happiness than on willingness to pay, especially on economic issues, and partly because of the possible negative effects of overriding people's preferences even for their own welfare, I have gone along with the economist's convention of using preference or utility instead of welfare in much of the discussion. However, if there is a big conflict between the two, I would opt for welfare at the ultimate level. For example, if it is true that economic growth does not increase happiness or even certain objective indicators of the quality of life much (Chapter 8), the calculation based on willingness to pay may have to be adjusted a lot to arrive at something appropriate for the pursuit of the objective of welfare. Such adjustments may include not only such factors as relative-income effects, environmental disruption effects, etc. discussed in Chapter 8, but also ignorance and irrationality if these prove to be substantial. That there is not much agreement on these issues reflects mainly our lack of knowledge than our ideological differences. (In fact, the so-called ideological differences arise from the lack of precise knowledge, making each person having then to resort to some estimates based on one's experience, education, upbringing, and psychology.) This just shows how much more research is needed.

Appendix A
Electrical Brain Stimulation: a Case Showing the Importance of Public Spending in Research

Cutting government funding on research is starving the goose that lays the golden eggs. In a developed economy like ours, it is research that contributes most to social welfare and further economic growth. Without sufficient safe-guard on protecting the environment and without increasing welfare-improving measures like research, pure increases in income and consumption may well be welfare-decreasing.

A1 Misconceptions on the costs of public spending

With the perceived needs inflated by comparison to neighbours, friends, class-mates of children, colleagues, etc. most people still strive hard to get more money even in our affluent society where most essential needs have been more than sat-isfied for most people. Politicians respond to this rat race to material abundance by emphasising private disposable income and consumption. However, after a certain minimum level of consumption, competition between individuals for higher income and consumption are largely self-defeating from the social view-point. More importantly, the belief that taxation causes excess burdens or inef-ficiency is also questionable. Thus, as argued in Part II in the text, our welfare can be increased much more by public spending to safeguard the environment, to acquire and spread knowledge through research and education which also have positive feedbacks on economic growth.

Imagine a trebling in your income but without access to computers, tele-vision, phones, modern medical facilities, etc. wouldn't your welfare be reduced significantly? We are on the brink of massive scientific–technological break-throughs that will increase our welfare by quantum leaps. Such leaps in welfare can be brought forward to be enjoyed by people of this generation if research activities are significantly increased. Tantalising possibilities abound in the field of genetic engineering, though caution is needed in such areas. However, this appendix focuses on the wonderful potential of electrical brain stimulation.

A2 Direct access to intense pleasure

It has been known for more than four decades that electrical brain stimulation (EBS) can relieve acute pain, induce intense pleasure, and promote a sense of well-being without the undesirable health effects of drug addiction. However, apart from isolated research experiments and limited therapies (see, e.g. Devinsky *et al.*, 1993), the enormous potential benefits of EBS have neither been adequately explored nor widely discussed. Much increased research effort and eventual widespread use of EBS are called for.

Positive reward associated with EBS leading to voluntary self-stimulation was discovered by Olds and Milner (1954) when they observed that a rat returned to the place where it received direct electrical stimulation of certain parts of its brain. Further research established sites that induce pleasure (medial forebrain bundle, septal, limbic and hypothalamic areas), pain, and ambiguous or mixed feelings. Stimulation of the pleasurable sites clearly produces positive reward as suggested by experiments in which rats were willing to cross a painful shock grid in order to obtain the stimulation, and as confirmed by human subjects. Moreover, the pleasure induced is so intense that rats prefer EBS to food and sex, and if not stopped by experimenters, will continuously seek stimulation until exhaustion. In humans, 'patients who were having emotional or physical pain experienced such intense pleasure with stimulation that the pain was obliterated' (Heath *et al.*, 1968, p.188).

A3 Enormous benefits

Apart from relieving pain and inducing pleasure, EBS may also be used as a 'primer' in improving well-being. For example, Heath (1964, p.236) reported, 'strong pleasure [from brain stimulation] was associated with sexual feelings, and in most instances the patient experienced spontaneous orgasm. . . . This patient, now married to her third husband, had never experienced orgasm before she received . . . stimulation to the brain, but since then has consistently achieved climax during sexual relations'. Once the right neurons have been excited, they become excitable more easily. The right neural pathways have been established.

Among the important social problems of our time are drug addiction, crimes and (mental) depression. These social problems, and possibly others, seem to be largely solvable with the widespread use of EBS. In comparison to EBS, the use of addictive drugs like heroin is a very inefficient and dangerous method of achieving a 'high'. If one has easy access to pleasurable sensations by just turning on the electricity, there seems little reason left to try dangerous alternatives like heroin. Just as intractable pain may be relieved by EBS, mental depression should also be largely removable by positive EBS. Since most depressions are caused by failure to achieve happiness one way or other, the availability of happy sensations by EBS should provide a definite relief. Among others, the amelioration of stress (Patterson *et al.*, 1994), reduction of stress ulcers (Yadin and Thomas, 1996), improved performance in a maze (Jiang *et al.*, 1997), and the treatment of alcoholics (Krupitskii *et al.*, 1993) have been reported.

A4 Safe and long-lasting pleasure

Though EBS is not physically addictive, it might be psychologically addictive. However, in contrast to heroin addiction, EBS addiction is not dangerous to health. From the quite large amount of evidence we have, the proper use

(Patterson and Kesner, 1981) of EBS over a sustained period for a long time (e.g. a few hours daily over a number of years) has proved to be quite safe. Thus EBS addiction is only a problem if it leads to the serious disregard of other duties such as to threaten the welfare of (mainly) other people (especially the future generations). While the pleasures induced by EBS can be intense, I doubt that psychological addiction of such a magnitude would occur. Rats choose to use EBS until exhaustion but humans only for 'up to half an hour daily' (Sem-Jacobsen, reported in Delgado, 1976, p.484). Relative to other pleasures and objectives, the pleasure of EBS does not seem to be compelling for humans (Bishop *et al.*, 1964; Valenstein, 1973, p.28). If one believes in creation, perhaps God made us this way so that we could eventually provide happiness not only for ourselves but also for animals. In the unlikely event of serious addiction, the problem could be solved by using legal and/or technical devices restricting the unlimited use of EBS.

While EBS addiction is unlikely to be so serious as to threaten the survival of a civilised society, it may be feared that it would significantly reduce mutual human relationships. If one could obtain pleasure by simply turning on the electricity, there might be little motivation left for the cultivation of personal relationships. This is unlikely to happen. Even if one could obtain a variety of pleasurable sensations by EBS, there would still be the innate need for companionship left. Secondly, the pleasure from EBS to humans does not seem to be as fulfilling as, say, a full sexual relationship with its simultaneous stimulation of a number of areas and close personal contact, nor as rewarding as spiritual fulfilment of the highest order. Thirdly, the provision of pleasure which might otherwise be unavailable in sufficient amount may in fact create many happy and easy-to-go-with individuals. This may remove many personal conflicts and promote better mutual relationships. Fourthly, even if personal relationships were reduced, the benefits of EBS would still likely to more than compensate for the loss. For example, the introduction of television probably has significantly reduced conversation. But that does not necessarily make it a bad thing. Its benefits have to be taken into account as well.

In this connection, the long-lasting nature of pleasure from EBS definitely gives it a big advantage. Inventions like television usually appear to have enormous potential benefits around the time of their initial introduction. After prolonged usage, some of their disadvantages are discovered though some other beneficial usages may also be found. More importantly, the novelty value has disappeared. For example, while watching television is very enjoyable for those just getting access to it, it may become a second best option after its novelty value has disappeared. The benefits of television probably still outweigh its costs by a very wide margin, but not by as much as it would be if the novelty value could be maintained. With EBS, the situation would be different. Since EBS is the *direct* stimulation of the brain, the pleasure during stimulation does not depend on any novelty value. Moreover, the intensity of pleasure from EBS does not diminish with prolonged stimulation (either continuously or daily over a number of years). Thus the enormous increase in happiness brought about by EBS could be expected to be maintained largely unabated, and in fact could be greatly increased through better techniques of stimulation.

EBS may be regarded as unnatural in the sense that it does not occur in the course of our natural biological survival. But most civilized products, institutions, medical treatments, etc. are unnatural in this sense. This does not make them bad. To improve our welfare, we have invented many 'unnatural' things. EBS is a recent invention that if properly made use of widely, possesses welfare significance surpassing all previous inventions put together.

Many people from the West may find, upon first contact, the culture, tradition, and ways of enjoying life in the East and in some primitive tribes degrading. The same is true for people from the East on some Western ways of life. But we have learned from liberalism to be more tolerant towards different cultures and ways of life as long as they are not harmful. Many liberals would go further in tolerating individual freedom of action even for those actions which are harmful to the actors themselves. EBS is about the least harmful way of inducing intense pleasure and should never be regarded as degrading by anyone who has the slightest adherence to liberalism.

Will God approve EBS? If one does not believe in God, the question does not arise. If one believes in God, then the answer seems to be affirmative. For example, the ten commandments do not include: Thou shall not engage in EBS. Nor do they include: Thou shall not enjoy yourself. Moreover, if God does not want us to use EBS, why did He create us in a way that EBS can induce intense positive reward?

If higher funding for research could result in such spectacularly welfare-improving discoveries and inventions as EBS, the present writer would be prepared to halve his post-tax income to help pay for them.

Appendix B
Pure Egalitarianism: a Critique

Egalitarianism has made much headway. When utilitarianism was first proposed by classical utilitarians in the 19th century, it was regarded as a radical philosophy used to justify egalitarian policies through such arguments as diminishing marginal utility. (For a modern statement of this, see Hare, 1997.) Now, most people writing on related issues (e.g. Rawls, 1971; Dworkin, 1981; Nielsen, 1985; Sen, 1992 and Roemer, 1996) seem to view utilitarianism as a conservative philosophy; they prefer much more radical egalitarianism. In this appendix, it is argued that this is based on questionable reasoning. On the other hand, there are writers arguing for something much to the right of utilitarianism. For example, Nozick (1974) argues for liberty and against equality; Posner (1981) argues for wealth maximisation. Such extreme divergence of views is, at least partly, based on the confusion of non-ultimate considerations with basic values, rather than just on the difference in basic value judgements.

For example, as argued in Chapter 6, for whatever degree of equality-efficiency tradeoff aimed at, it is more efficient to pursue efficiency or wealth maximisation (treating a dollar as a dollar whomsoever it goes to) on specific issues of public policy, leaving the equality objective to be pursued through the general tax/transfer system. However, as the ultimate social objective, wealth maximisation is clearly unacceptable. (Another example of confusing non-ultimate considerations with basic values is the concern, e.g. Kappel, 1997, for simultaneous inequality with life-time equality.)

At the non-ultimate (e.g. political, day-to-day) levels, liberty, efficiency, equality of incomes (or resources, primary goods, capabilities), etc. are all important considerations. However, they typically may be in conflict and need be traded-off with each others. At the ultimate level, the optimal tradeoff should be decided by the maximisation of aggregate individual welfares, as argued in Section B1. This is also a form of egalitarianism, equality in the weights attached to the welfare of all individuals. This is the only appropriate equality to insist on at the ultimate level (Section B2). At this ultimate level, the arguments of the libertarians (Section B3), Rawls (Section B4), various forms of egalitarianism including resource and welfare egalitarianism (Section B5) and capability egalitarianism (Section B6) are shown to be unacceptable.

B1 Why is happiness the only ultimate consideration?

As argued in Section 4.4 in the text, things we want in life like money, position, relationships, health, etc. are not wanted for their own sake. Only extreme misers want money for money's sake. In fact, it may be argued that even misers do not want money for money's sake. They just feel happy by looking and knowing that they possess a lot of money. We all want money, health, etc. in order to be happy. But we do not want happiness for the purpose of obtaining anything else. Happiness is good in itself.

We do not have to ask why is happiness valuable or good because we all enjoy our happy feelings and suffer from unhappy feelings. We are like this because of biological reasons. We are intelligent beings capable of making choices. (This is also true for at least some animal species higher up in the phylogenetic scale.) Due to this capability, God (or evolution) found it necessary to ensure that we make the 'right' choices (from the viewpoint of survival and reproduction, i.e. biological fitness). Thus we are genetically programmed to want to do the fitness-enhancing things by being awarded with pleasures when eating fresh and nutritious foods when hungry, when mating with fertile members of the opposite sex, and penalised with pain when we injure ourselves.

It may also be true that we have an instinct for justice or morality. At least we have a sense of morality which may be partly inborn and partly learned. As long as the sense of morality is formed by nature and/or by nurture, we also feel happy/unhappy in doing/seeing/suffering something morally good/bad. Such happiness/unhappiness should of course be included in the utilitarian calculus. However, moral principles are ultimately valuable only because of their contribution to welfare, as argued in Section 4.1.

Like other non-ultimate objectives like freedom, democracy, etc. equality is a valuable objective if and only if it contributes, directly or indirectly, to the ultimate objective of happiness or welfare. (Individual welfare is defined to be the net happiness of the individual.) Generally, equality is a highly valuable objective as it contributes to welfare in several important ways, including through the undisputed fact of diminishing marginal utility, through fostering better social cohesion, and through our sense of justice. Thus, I regard myself as a utilitarian egalitarian. To the extent that the pursuit of equality does not harm too much other valuable objectives like liberty and efficiency, it contributes to welfare.

Consider the hypothetical situation where most people do not like equality in the distribution of income (or primary goods, etc.). They find equality dull. Each of them would rather be one of the poor in a society of income inequality than be one in a society of equal income, even at a higher average income. Then, even abstracting from disincentive effects, equality itself may make everyone worse off. Clearly, in this case, equality is not good for the society even if efficiency, liberty, and other valuable objectives are not diminished. Thus, it is clear that, ultimately speaking, equality is only of instrumental value; it is not valuable in itself.

While the above example is hypothetical, it is true in the real world that people ultimately want happiness, not equality in itself. They do want equality but only to foster their welfare and perhaps also the welfare of others. Some evidence may be adduced to support this claim. First, surveys indicate that people view happiness as their ultimate objectives (Veenhoven, 1984 and Ng, 1996a). Secondly, people from very poor countries of less unequal distribution still eagerly seek to migrate to countries of higher incomes even if more unequally distributed, and even if they would become one of the poorest class if they are successful in migrating. Thirdly, most readers can convince themselves by asking what they themselves value ultimately. Be persistent and try to go to the truly ultimate. If you think you value equality, ask, 'Why?' Answer: 'equality is good'. Then ask: 'why is equality good?' or 'is equality good if it makes everyone suffer enormously?', etc.

B2 Equality in the welfare weights

In a sense, virtually everyone is in favour of some form of equality. The important question is: 'equality *in what*?' This was realised as early as Aristotle (see Pojman and Westmoreland, 1997, p.3) and emphasised by Sen (1992). Thus, Nozick (1974) wants equality of libertarian rights, the utilitarians want equality in the weights attached to each person's welfare, Rawls (1971) wants equal liberty and equality in the distribution of primary goods (unless inequality makes everyone better off), Dworkin (1981) wants equality of resources, Sen (1992) wants equality in capability, Arneson (1989), Cohen (1989) and Roemer (1996, 1998) want equality of opportunities, Nielsen (1985) and Kolm (1996) want equality in welfare. So, why is equality in welfare weights the right equality at the ultimate level?

The answer is (partly) that resources, income, primary goods, capability, etc. are not our ultimate objectives, it is welfare that is our ultimate objective. (A problem faced by most if not all non-welfare objectives is the index number problem of how to aggregate different bundles of say primary goods into a commensurable measure.) If equality in resources, income, etc. decreases the welfare level of everyone, then it is clearly undesirable. But then why not the equality of welfare? The answer is that equality of welfare may also result (in fact it is almost certainly true in most real-world situations due to individual differences in endowment and capability and due to the disincentive effects of attempts to equalise welfare) in very low welfare levels for most people. We want high welfare levels, not equal welfare levels with others. I hate receiving lower incomes than others. If the incomes of all others are doubled and mine only increases by 10 per cent, I will probably be made worse off. However, if the welfare levels of all others are doubled and mine only increases by 10 per cent, I am still 10 per cent better off! I would love that if it were possible.

We all want higher welfare levels. Thus, for the society, treating everyone's welfare on an equal footing and maximising the equally weighted (equivalent to unweighted) sum of individual welfares is the morally right objective. Moreover, as outlined and argued in Chapter 5, there are morally compelling reasons in favour of maximising the unweighted sum of individual welfares.

B3 The libertarians

No doubt, liberty is extremely important. At the political level, it makes sense most of the times to insists on liberty as if it is sacrosanct. The sacrifice of liberty on some grounds of expediency may increase welfare at the moment but is likely to produce undesirable side effects and hence undesirable in the long run even from the viewpoint of welfare maximisation. Thus, again, I regard myself as a utilitarian libertarian. However, liberty is not our ultimate objective. If we have included all the side effects, most people, like me, would rather be happy but not free than be free but unhappy.

Nozick (1974) emphasises the appropriate methods by which properties are acquired rather than the equality in their distribution. Obviously, this is extremely important for the orderly functioning of society and the adequate incentives for productive activities. However, Nozick believes that this liberty to acquire wealth by appropriate methods should be given unlimited scope. If someone is endowed by the lottery of birth with a sexy voice that attracts millions of teenagers and hence can earn millions of dollars by singing a few songs, he is just enjoying his liberty. Others who are endowed with no income-earning abilities only have their bad luck to blame. Provided that there is no unjust method in the acquisition of wealth, the resulting distribution, no matter how unequal, is just and the government should not try to make the distribution more equal. Doing so is an infringement on liberty. This is so even if, by a marginal infringement (e.g. by a mildly progressive income tax/transfer), the poor could be helped by an enormous amount.

A person may be poor as a result of squandering away his inherited wealth or spending his time watching TV rather than learning and working. Most people are not sympathetic towards such a person. On the other hand, a person may be poor due to sheer bad luck in his endowments and opportunities, despite his hard work. Similarly, a person may be rich by contributing a lot or by sheer luck in endowment and opportunity. Inequalities in the distribution of income, wealth, other primary goods, capabilities, etc. due to unjust methods are abhorrent, but those due to sheer luck also need addressing. (For the argument that, if the fruit of labour is understood to include only 'that subset of the . . . product of one's labour which is due to his choices rather than luck', redistributive taxes from the lucky rich to the unlucky poor does not violate self-ownership as claimed by Nozick, see Michael, 1997.)

B4   Rawls

In contrast to the libertarians, Rawls (1971) does not accept the justice of unequal endowments. But he goes to the other extreme in believing that primary goods (i.e. income, wealth, opportunities, the social bases of self-respect, etc.) should be distributed equally unless inequality makes everyone better off.

Rawls' (1971, 1982) theory of justice may be summarised into two principles:

1. Each person has an equal right to a fully adequate scheme of equal basic liberties which is compatible with a similar scheme of liberties for all.
2. Social and economic inequalities are to satisfy two conditions. First, they must be attached to offices and positions open to all under conditions of fair equality of opportunity; and secondly, they must be to the greatest benefit of the least advantaged members of society.

I am prepared to accept the first principle on the following understanding:

- that it is adopted *because* it promotes the general welfare;
- in circumstances where it is disastrous to the general welfare, it may have to be suspended;
- in deciding what is the 'most extensive total system' and what is 'compatible . . . for all', the ultimate criterion is the general welfare.

A sex maniac may be in favour of freedom to rape and claim that this is compatible with everyone's freedom to rape.[1] It may also happen that the sex maniac is the person of the lowest welfare level such that freedom to rape for all will maximise the welfare of the worst off, hence consistent with the spirit of Rawls' second principle to be discussed below. However, if freedom to rape results in the reduction of the welfare of those raped and scared of being raped by more than (in aggregate) the welfare gain of the rapists (even though the former still have higher welfare levels than the latter group even with freedom to rape), then freedom to rape should be regarded as not compatible with the freedom of not being raped. The 'most extensive total system of basic liberties' should then not include the freedom to rape. However, thus interpreted, the first principle is really a device to promote the general welfare. It is not ultimate. The first part of Rawls' second principle may be similarly accepted as the first principle.

Now, consider the second part of maximising the benefit of the least advantaged, with advantage being judged by the possession of primary goods. This maximin principle is in direct contrast to the utilitarian principle of maximising the unweighted sum of welfares. The latter gives equal weights to all while the former gives an infinite weight to the welfare of the least advantaged. Being the least advantaged, they probably have very high marginal welfare of income. Giving equal weights to their welfares already implies valuing a dollar to them as worth more than to the more advantaged groups. Giving an infinite weight implies the willingness to sacrifice the welfare levels of all others enormously (provided that none of them becomes more disadvantaged than the least advantaged) for a marginal increase in the welfare of the least advantaged. This is morally unacceptable. In fact, if I were the least advantaged person, I do not want any person/group in the society to sacrifice a big welfare loss just to increase my own welfare a little. (For an interesting argument on the unacceptability of the Rawlsian version of egalitarianism as it implies: 'that redistribution ought to aim to equalize the life expectancy of men and women by making men have longer and women shorter lives . . . to employ fewer men and more women in . . . undesirable jobs. Men . . . ought to have shorter working days and longer vacations than women', see Kekes, 1997, p.661.)

B5 Pure and welfare egalitarianism

Pure egalitarians insist on the equality in certain things (typically resources) irrespective of the consequences. For example, Watson (1977, p.123) argues that equality of resources is such a transcendent value that, if equal distribution of food were to result in no one getting enough to eat, we should nevertheless choose the annihilation of the human race rather than an unequal distribution. This is clearly an unreasonable position to take. As remarked by Pojman and Westmoreland (1997, p.5), 'if equality is a transcendent value . . . [the thoroughgoing egalitarian] would have to dumb down the brilliant, infuse the healthy with disease, and blind the sighted'.

Welfare egalitarians want not just equal weights on the welfare levels of all individuals but equality in the welfare levels. For example, Ake (1975) regards that justice in society as a whole ought to be understood as a complete equality of the overall level of benefits and burdens of each member of that society.

Nielsen (1985) is also in favour of radical welfare egalitarianism. Sen (1992) is not explicitly a welfare egalitarian. However, one may argue that, pursuing his logic in moving (from some form of resource egalitarianism) to capability egalitarianism to its logical conclusion, one will end up in welfare egalitarianism (next section).

Welfare egalitarianism is patently unacceptable as it may end up making everyone substantially worse off. Suppose that the relevant utility feasibility frontier is as illustrated in Figure B1 and the initial point determined by the given endowment (of individual talents, etc.) after Nozick-just acquisitions and exchanges is at point N. Libertarians insist on the point N even if the welfare of the poor (represented as U^p on the vertical axis) could be increased a lot with the welfare of the rich (represented as U^r on the horizontal axis) reduced only marginally, taking everything into account. In contrast, Rawlsians would go all the way to R where no further increase in U^p is possible. Worse, pure and welfare egalitarians would insist on E even if both the rich and the poor would be significantly worse off than the initial point N. The equally absurd maximax point M has also received some support (e.g. Temkin 1987).

Roemer (1986, 1996, Chapter 7) argues that resource egalitarianism implies welfare egalitarianism. This argument is based on an axiom unacceptable from the viewpoint of social welfare maximisation with welfare contours allowing some trade off between the individual welfare levels of different persons. However, since this axiom is compelling from the viewpoint of resource egalitarianism, Roemer's argument remains valid. Nevertheless, the following explanation not only shows how Roemer can reach his rather strong conclusion but also why both resource and welfare egalitarianism are unacceptable, at least from the viewpoint of social welfare maximisation with tradeoff. The relevant axiom of Roemer is Resource Monotonicity which requires that no individual welfare level should decrease with an increase in resources for the whole society. The

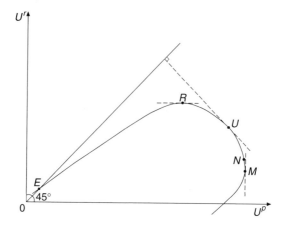

Figure B1

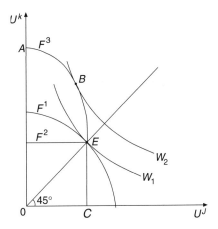

Figure B2

point that this apparently innocent axiom is objectionable and the point that it (together with other reasonable axioms) leads to welfare egalitarianism may be illustrated together in Figure B2.

First, suppose that, in situation 1 with a given amount of resources and the utility functions of the two persons, we have the *symmetrical* utility feasibility frontier (UFF) F^1. (Points on and within the frontier are feasible to attain; points above or beyond the frontier are not feasible.) The reasonable axiom of symmetry assumed by Roemer then dictates the choice of the equal welfare/utility point E. The assumed concavity in the individual utility functions without interdependence and the abstraction from production considerations may mean that the UFF is concave (the feasibility set is convex). However, since no upper limit is placed on the degree of concavity, we have as the limiting case, F^2 as a possibility. The point E still has to be chosen given F^2 (from either symmetry or from the Pareto principle). Now suppose that the amount of resources increases unambiguously but in a way that increases the utility possibility of person K only, such that the new UFF F^3 is the curve ABEC. Resource Monotonicity requires that, in this new situation with F^3, no individual utility can be lower in comparison to the situation at F^1 or F^2. This means that E still has to be chosen from F^3. There is no upper limit as to how steep the section BE of F^3 may be, except that it is downward sloping. If BE is steep enough, any SWF allowing for some tradeoff between utility levels of different persons, including those satisfying symmetry, such as one represented by the welfare contours W_1 and W_2, will choose a point B from F^3 that is northwest of E. This shows that Resource Monotonity, by insisting on E, is unreasonable.

Consider a concrete example. Suppose that the two persons concerned are my brother and myself and that no other sentient will be affected. Suppose first that we are endowed only with food which we enjoy equally with diminishing marginal utility. It makes sense to share the food equally. (The issues of desert and incentives do not arise by assumption.) Now, suppose that we also have a ball (assumed not exchangeable into food). I hate ball games while my brother loves them. It makes sense to let him have the ball. However, he enjoys playing with the ball only if he has enough to eat; the more he plays with the ball, the hungrier he becomes. Thus, his utility can only increase substantially if he has more than half of the food. Ball games increase his marginal utility of food dramatically. It makes sense for me to agree to let him eat more than I do. The increase in endowment of a ball should in this case result in an optimal outcome involving my having less welfare. Is this unfair on me? I genuinely think not. If the increase in endowment is in the form of a sword with which I like to play very much and which my brother hates, then I should similarly have more to eat to be able to enjoy the sword. Provided this will also be done, there is no unfairness. My welfare and that of my brother has the same weight in the social welfare function of our two-person society. By maximising the unweighted sum of utilities, the society maximises the expected utility of each individual under the veil of ignorance. This is fair and moral.

B6 Sen and capability egalitarianism

Sen (1985, 1992) argues for the equality in capability rather than in objective resources or subjective welfare. He regards Rawls as making an advancement in going from just equality in income and wealth to wanting equality in the distribution of primary goods (unless inequality makes the least advantaged better off) which also include opportunities and the social basis of self-respect. However, Sen regards this as insufficient. People who are disadvantaged physically, mentally, or socially need more resources and opportunities to be able to perform the various valuable functions. These functionings: 'can vary from most elementary ones such as being well-nourished, avoiding escapable morbidity and premature mortality, etc., to quite complex and sophisticated achievements, such as having self-respect, being able to take part in the life of the community' (Sen, 1992, p.5). The disadvantaged should be given more resources and opportunities to allow them to have equal capability to achieve these functionings than others.

I regard Sen's emphasis on capability and functioning and the need to pay special attention to the disadvantaged as very important at the political level, as it may be a good practical way to increase overall social welfare. However, if viewed at the ultimate level, capability egalitarianism is not an acceptable objective as it violates the Pareto principle. (It should be noted that Sen also emphasises other desirable aspect of human conditions including opulence or wealth, happiness, and agency goals as discussed below.) To see this, consider Figure B1 again, but now using the axes to measure the capability levels of the two groups. The capability feasibility frontier may look like the UFF curve. To achieve equality in capability, we may have to tax the advantaged rich so much that the disincentive effects will be so big as to make all groups having a lower capability level at *E*. To avoid this Pareto inferior outcome, perhaps the capability egalitarians may make a concession like Rawls in going for maximin than for complete equality in capability. This is still unacceptable. If I were the least capable person, I would not think it is morally right for the society to incur huge costs to improve my capability marginally.

Sen (1992, p.84) argues that: 'Capability represents freedom, whereas primary goods tell us only about the means to freedom.' I will similarly argue that 'welfare is the ultimate objective, whereas capability tells us only about the means to welfare'.

Sen does not go for equality in welfare for two reasons. One is the issue of responsibility also emphasised by others (e.g. Dworkin, 1981). The society should compensate the disadvantaged for circumstances for which they are not responsible, not for something for which they are responsible, including inequalities from the exercise of personal preferences. The other one is Sen's view that people are not only concerned with welfare. Let us come to this second point later and assume now that people are only concerned ultimately with welfare. Then, the following argument is reasonable. A person is no less disadvantaged and no more accountable if he is unlucky enough to be born with some handicaps in performing valuable functions than if he is unlucky enough to have lower inborn earning abilities and/or is less lucky in business. This may justify the movement from equality in (objective) resources to equality in primary goods and in capability. However, following this logic to its logical conclusion compels us to welfare egalitarianism. If people want to maximise their own welfare and, with equal capability,[2] end up with different welfare levels, this must be due either to different abilities in making appropriate choices (if this ability is included in the definition of capability and is equalised, only the next reason applies) or to differences in luck. Differences in ability to make appropriate choices are not different morally from differences in ability to earn income and in capability to perform functionings. Luck in obtaining higher welfare levels is no different morally from luck in earning higher incomes. Thus, if we should move from resource egalitarianism to capability egalitarianism, we should also move from capability egalitarianism to welfare egalitarianism. (Cf. the arguments of Arneson, 1989/1995.)

Sen will object to the argument of the above paragraph on the ground that people do not just want to maximise welfare/happiness but have other objectives as well, including opulence (wealth) and agency goals. Even for misers, wealth or money is not wanted for its own sake. While most people want money to buy goods now or in the future (for the purposes of consumption, security, power, rivalry and indication of success), misers derive so much pleasure from looking at the money that spending money is seriously curtailed. But no one wants money for its own sake. Some people may enjoy the process or the fact of making money. Still, it is the enjoyment, the prestige, etc. that counts. These all increase the happiness for them to be valuable. Thus, opulence is not an ultimate objective.

People also want to do certain things, to accomplish certain achievements, and prefer to do so themselves. For example, I want the moral compellingness of utilitarianism at the fundamental level to be generally accepted. If I myself contribute to this acceptance, all the better. This is what Sen means by agency goals. This is important enough, but again not at the fundamental level. I like to contribute to this enlightenment myself because it makes me feel good and also increases the respect of others for me which again makes me feel good and more likely to be successful in other activities which are in turn pursued for the purpose of increasing welfare (including my own and that of other sentients). Thus, I see no conflict of rational agency goals (or any other rational objectives) with welfare, ultimately speaking. (For further arguments in favour of welfare as the ultimate objective, see Chapters 3 and 4. In particular, welfare-inconsistent preferences such as myopia, dangerous sexual practices, and achievement for achievement's sake are argued to be irrational preferences that may have some biological and educational explanation, i.e. nature plus nurture. Natural selection, through our unfeeling genes, programmes us to incline to maximise our survival fitness which may be inconsistent with our welfare which we, in contrast to our genes, should maximise.)

Even with only welfare as the ultimate objective, some people may choose partly with the welfare of others in mind. Then, with differences in the degree of genuine altruism (see Section 4.1 for a compelling argument on its existence), people with the same capability may end up with different welfare levels, even with no differences in the ability to choose and in luck. Abstracting from unexpected outcomes contrary to intention, the more altruistic typically end up with less welfare levels. On this point, capability egalitarianism seems to be morally inferior to welfare egalitarianism. However, it has been argued above that both forms of egalitarianism are unacceptable as the ultimate social objective.

B7   Concluding remark

This appendix has examined several views regarding egalitarianism, including the libertarian, the Rawlsian, welfare egalitarianism, and capability egalitarianism and has found them to be unacceptable as an ultimate social objective. That such extremely different views are held by intelligent and reasonable authors may be explained by the confusion of non-ultimate considerations with basic values. For example, the reason why Nielsen (1985, p.45, p.53) is in favour of having 'the income and wealth . . . be so divided that each person will have a right to an equal share' is to avoid giving 'one person power or control over another'. Presumably, being subject to the power and control by others is bad for welfare. Thus, when we reckon at the ultimate level, we may take into account such negative effects of inequality of wealth and analyse using the ultimate objective of welfare. Then, the society should not go for equal welfare but for maximum aggregate welfare as individuals want more welfare for themselves, not equal welfare with others.

Liberty, equality of resources, of capability, etc. may be desirable aspects usually conducive to the general welfare when other things are held unchanged. However, they are not the appropriate ultimate objective for the society. As argued here and elsewhere in this book, the appropriate ultimate social objective should be individual happiness or welfare. The maximisation of the unweighted (equivalent to equal weights for all individuals) sum of these individual welfares (i.e. utilitarianism) is the appropriate form of egalitarianism. In fact, Section 5.2 shows that Rational Individualistic Egalitarianism implies utilitarianism.

Appendix C
Economic Growth Increases the Optimal Share of the Public Sector

Joint Author: Siang Ng

There are two very important observations, one well known to all economists and uncontroversial and one not well known and may be controversial. The first is that government spending as a share of GDP (or GNP) increases historically and increases with per capita GDP both intertemporarily and cross-nationally. (See Section 8.1.) The second is that, for rich countries, the level of happiness does not increase with per capita income. (See Section 8.5.) The main purpose of this appendix is to provide a simple but reasonable analytical model that simultaneously explains these two apparently unrelated observations. The main results are summarised into two propositions below.

Without intending to be exhaustive, some important factors affecting the welfare of a person are included in the analysis proposed below. First, we accept the traditional variables focused most closely by economists, personal consumption c (in real terms, as also true for all variables discussed in this appendix) and leisure x. Secondly, the amount of public goods provision g is included. Obviously, apart from personal consumption, one benefits from the provision of law and order and other public goods and facilities. This has also been well recognised and analysed by economists. Thirdly, as discussed in Section 8.5 in the text, we include relative consumption or relative income r. (For our purpose here, it does not really matter which one is used.) Fourthly, environmental quality E is included. Again, in the current era of heavy pollution, congestion, deforestation, and other forms of environmental disruption, the importance of this factor needs hardly any justification.

Of course, there are other factors affecting happiness; they are not analysed here. Also, we ignore the possible existence of ignorance, imperfect foresight, and other possible divergences (non-affective altruism and irrationality) between preference (represented by a utility function) and happiness (represented by a personal welfare function). Arguments on the existence and implications of these divergences have been discussed in Chapter 4.

We thus take the utility or welfare function of an individual as

$$U = U(c, x, r, g, E); \quad U_c, U_x, U_r, U_g, U_E > 0 \tag{C1}$$

Where $r \equiv y/Y$, y is the income of the individual concerned and Y is the average income of the relevant society, a subscript denotes partial differentiation, e.g. $U_c = \delta U/\delta c$. An individual maximises (C1) subject to:

$$c = (1-t)y \tag{C2}$$

$$y = (1-x)w \tag{C3}$$

taking g, E, t, w as given; where t is the proportional (assumed for simplicity) income tax, and w is the exogenously given earning ability, and the time constraint is normalised to be unity. Assuming an interior solution (compelling as starvation and exhaustion are both unacceptable), the first-order solution is:

$$U_x = (1-t)wU_c + (w/Y)U_r \tag{C4}$$

Now consider the effect of personal enrichment. In our model, this is an increase in one's own earning rate w. Differentiating (C1) with respect to w, taking t, g and E as given (as viewed by the individual), we have:

$$\frac{dU}{dw} = U_c \left(\frac{dc}{dw} \right) + U_x \left(\frac{dx}{dw} \right) + U_r \left(\frac{dr}{dw} \right) \tag{C5}$$

Substituting in dc/dw and dr/dw from the differentiation of (C2), (C3) and $r \equiv y/Y$, taking Y as given, and substituting in (C4) (which makes the term associated with dx/dw equals zero; intuitively, as the individual starts with an optimal position with respect to the choice of leisure x, a marginal change in x has no first-order effect on utility), we have after multiplying through by w/U to express in proportionate or elasticity terms:

$$\sigma^{Uw} = \eta^{Uc} + \eta^{Ur} \tag{C6}$$

where $\sigma^{Uw} \equiv (dU/dw)w/U$ is the proportionate total response of U with respect to a change in w ('total' in the sense of allowing other relevant variables to change endogenously; but g, E, Y are not relevant variables here), $\eta^{ab} \equiv (\delta a/\delta b)b/a$ for any a and b is the proportionate partial response of a with respect to a change in b ('partial' in the sense of holding other variables unchanged). Equation C6 indicates that the degree of importance of enrichment for an individual equals the sum of the intrinsic consumption effect and the relative-income effect. For the poor, the intrinsic consumption effect is big though the relative-income effect may be at least relatively small; for the rich, the relative-income effect is big though the intrinsic consumption effect may be small. Thus, for almost all people, making more money seems very important, explaining why most people, in rich and poor countries alike are engaging in the rat race.

For the whole society, economic growth increases the earning ability not only of one person but also of most persons. Ignoring distributional changes, we consider the situation of the representative individual whose earning ability w increases at the same rate as that of the average earning ability W, i.e. we have $w = W$, $dw = dW$, $x = X$, $Y = (1 - X)W$, etc. where capital letter indicates the average value of the relevant variable. A more complicated formulation in terms of a continuous distribution of individuals of different earning abilities does not change the central conclusions. Differentiating (C1) with respect to W, at $w = W$, $dw = dW$, and allowing the aggregate variables Y, g, E to change correspondingly, we have:

$$\frac{dU}{dW} = U_c \left(\frac{dc}{dw} \right) + U_x \left(\frac{dx}{dw} \right) + U_g \left(\frac{dg}{dW} \right) + U_E \left(\frac{dE}{dW} \right) \tag{C7}$$

Note that U_r does not appear in (C7) as y and Y change by the same proportion, leaving r unchanged. We should now introduce the determination of government spending on public goods g and environmental quality E. In our simple model, these are:

$$g = N(1 - \alpha)tY \qquad (C8)$$

$$E = E(A, Y); \quad E_A > 0, \quad E_Y < 0 \qquad (C9)$$

where N is the given number of individuals, α is the proportion of tax revenue used for the abatement (A) of environmental disruption, leaving the proportion $(1 - \alpha)$ for spending on public goods. That $E_Y < 0$ captures the environmental disruption effect of most production and consumption. We also have:

$$A = \alpha tYN \qquad (C10)$$

Substitute dc/dw, dg/dW, dE/dW from the differentiation of (C2), (C3), (C8), (C9), taking N, t and α as given, we have, after simplification using (C4) (but we cannot get rid of all the terms associated with dx/dw this time, as Equation C4 is not in general optimal from the social viewpoint) and multiplication with W/U to express in proportionate terms:

$$\sigma^{UW}\big|_{t,\alpha} = \eta^{Uc} + \eta^{Ug} + \eta^{UE}(\eta^{EA} + \eta^{EY}) + \left(\frac{x}{1-x}\right)\sigma^{XW}[\eta^{Ur} - \eta^{Ug} - \eta^{UE}(\eta^{EA} + \eta^{EY})]$$

$$(C11)$$

where $\sigma^{ab} \equiv (da/db)b/a$ and $\eta^{ab} \equiv (\delta a/\delta b)b/a$ for any a, b as before, and $|t, \alpha|$ indicates that t and α are being held constant. The first three terms in the RHS of (C11) are the direct effects of an economy-wide increase in earning or productivity, including an intrinsic consumption effect η^{Uc} as the higher productivity allows higher per capita consumption, a public-good effect η^{Ug} as higher national income allows more spending on public goods, and an environmental disruption effect $\eta^{UE}(\eta^{EA} + \eta^{EY})$. For this last effect, the environmental quality effect η^{UE} has to be multiplied by both the abatement effect η^{EA} and the disruption effect η^{EY} because an increase in production both increases the disruption and the abatement (through the higher tax revenue a constant share of which is used for abatement). The last complex term in (C11) is the indirect effect through σ^{XW}, the (proportionate) effect of earning ability W on leisure X. As everything in (C11) is put in proportionate terms, this has to be multiplied by $x/(1 - x)$, the ratio of leisure to working hours. The rest of this complex term, i.e. $[\eta^{Ur} - \eta^{Ug} - \eta^{UE}(\eta^{EA} + \eta^{EY})]$, captures the external effects of individual income/leisure choice. An increased consumption of leisure reduces one's own income and hence benefits others through the relative-income effect η^{Ur}, but harms others through a reduction in public goods provision (hence *minus* η^{Ug}), and may benefit or harm others through the environmental effect η^{UE} depending on whether $(\eta^{EA} + \eta^{EY})$ is negative or positive. It is perhaps not unreasonable to assume that $(\eta^{EA} + \eta^{EY})$ is negative. Even if a given proportion (provided not excessively large to begin with) of tax revenue is used for abatement, an increase in production still causes more disruption to the environment.

The RHS (right-hand side) of (C11), in contrast to that of (C6), is of ambiguous sign. An individual may rationally engage in the rat race for making money. For the society, an increase in productivity may not be an unmixed blessing even if the higher production finances more public goods provision and more abatement.

So far, we have assumed that the tax rate t and the proportion of tax revenue used for abatement α are being held constant. However, as productivity W increases, the government may wish to change these ratios. Allowing t and α to change with W, we have, instead of (C11):

$$\sigma^{UW} = \sigma^{UW}{}_{|t,\alpha|} - \left(\frac{t}{1-t}\right)\sigma^{tw}\eta^{Uc} + \left[\sigma^{tw} - \left(\frac{\alpha}{1-\alpha}\right)\sigma^{\alpha w}\right]\eta^{Ug} + \left(\sigma^{tw} + \sigma^{\alpha w}\right)\eta^{UE}\eta^{EA}$$

(C12)

where $\sigma^{UW}{}_{|t,\alpha|}$ is as given in (C11).

Now, suppose that t and α have been both chosen optimally to maximise U, with W given. Differentiating U in (C1) with respect to t, allowing endogenous variables c, x, y, g, E to change but taking α as given (one thing at a time; this does not really matter since, if we allow α to vary, we will just get some additional terms which sum to zero when we take account of the first-order condition for the optimal choice of α), and allowing the average values to change with the individual values ($dy = dY$, etc.), we have, after substituting in (C4) and multiplying through by t/U to express in proportionate terms:

$$\sigma^{Ut} = \eta^{Ug} + \eta^{UE}\eta^{EA} - \left(\frac{t}{1-t}\right)\eta^{Uc} + \left(\frac{x}{1-x}\right)\sigma^{Xt}[\eta^{Ur} - \eta^{Ug} - \eta^{UE}(\eta^{EA} + \eta^{EY})]$$

(C13)

where σ and η to the double superscripts are as defined under (C11). Similar to (C11), the first three terms in the RHS of (C13) are the direct effects and the last term is the indirect effect. While the indirect effect is completely analogous to that in (C11) and has the same interpretation, the direct effects (of an increase in tax rate t) consist in a public goods provision effect η^{Ug}, an (environmental disruption) abatement effect $\eta^{UE}\eta^{EA}$ (as a higher tax revenue finances for both public goods provision and abatement), and a (reduced) consumption effect $\left(\frac{t}{1-t}\right)\eta^{Uc}$. The last effect has the term $[t/(1 - t)]$ because of the proportionate nature of all terms in (C13). For this particular effect, it is easier to see its rationale in non-proportionate terms. If we multiply both sides by U/t to undo the proportionality, we have, showing in the RHS the reduced consumption effect only:

$$\frac{dU}{dt} = \ldots \frac{y\delta U}{\delta c} \ldots$$

(C13′)

In this form, it is clear that an increase in t reduces utility at the rate y through the consumption effect as an increase in t reduces c at the rate y.

Similarly, differentiating U in (C1) with respect to α, we have:

$$\sigma^{U\alpha} = \eta^{UE}\eta^{EA} - \left(\frac{\alpha}{1-\alpha}\right)\eta^{Ug}$$

(C14)

Obviously, the RHS of (C14) indicates that an increase in α entails a benefit of increasing abatement and a cost of reducing the provision of other public goods. Reasonably assuming continuity and interior solutions for t and α, optimal choice of t and α entails setting (C13) and (C14) to zero. Substitute the resulting equations into (C12), yielding:

$$\sigma^{UW}{}_{|t^*,\alpha^*|} = \left\{1 + \left(\frac{t}{1-t}\right)(1-\sigma^{tW})\right\}\eta^{Uc} + \eta^{UE}\eta^{EY} + \left(\frac{1}{1-\alpha}\right)\sigma^{tW}\eta^{Ug}$$

$$+ \left(\frac{x}{1-x}\right)(\sigma^{XW} - \sigma^{xt})\left[\eta^{Ur} - \eta^{UE}\eta^{EY} - \frac{\eta^{Ug}}{1-\alpha}\right] \tag{C15}$$

where $|t^*,\alpha^*|$ indicates that the tax rate and the proportion of revenue used for abatement are being optimised. Thus, (C15) gives, in proportionate terms, the effect of an exogenous increase in productivity on utility, while both the tax rate and the abatement ratio are being optimised before and after the increase. Despite this optimisation, the RHS of (C15) is of ambiguous sign. The first term (consumption effect) is positive (but likely to be small for rich economies), the second term (environmental disruption effect) is negative (and likely to be absolutely sizeable for rich economies), the third term is positive/negative if the optimal tax rate t increases/decreases with W, and the last term is of ambiguous sign. With likely opposing income and substitution effects, both σ^{XW} and σ^{xt} are of ambiguous sign. The term $\left[\eta^{Ur} - \eta^{UE}\eta^{EY} - \frac{\eta^{Ug}}{1-\alpha}\right]$ is itself of ambiguous sign, consisting of the first two positive parts and a negative (and enlarged absolutely, as $1/(1-\alpha)$ is larger than one) third part.

If the negative environmental disruption effect is large absolutely and both the consumption and public goods effects (first and third terms in the RHS of Equation C15) are relatively small, the first three terms may sum to be negative. If, in addition, leisure does not respond substantially (as has been the case empirically; see Pencavel, 1986), the last term fails to make a big difference, leaving the RHS of (C15) possibly negative. From the contrast between the unambiguously positive (and likely large for both poor and rich economies alike) RHS of (C6) and the possibly negative RHS of (C15), we may conclude

Proposition 1: Reasonably assuming the existence of important environmental disruption effect and relative-income effect, economic growth may decrease happiness even if the provision of public goods and disruption abatement are being optimised, and even though all individuals are rationally engaging in the rat race for making more money.

Proposition 1 came to us as a surprise, at least with respect to the optimal choice of the tax rate t. At one stage, we thought that proposition is true only if t is held constant. If t can be increased at will to shrink the private sector and expand the provision of disruption abatement and public goods, we thought that this should ensure the sufficiency of the utility-enhancement effect of productivity growth. After ensuring the correctness of our mathematics, we discovered the intuitive reason for the insufficiency. This is related to the fact that we allow production Y, rather than just private consumption C to enter (negatively) into the environmental quality function E. This means that the production of the public sector itself is environmentally disruptive. This is a reasonable assumption. However, this means that, if a higher tax rate does not discourage work significantly (σ^{xt} not large), the instrument of income tax is powerless in reducing the higher environmental disruption of higher production (through higher productivity W) except through the financing of more abatement. However, if abatement is not very effective in reducing disruption or in improving environmental quality (η^{EA} not large), even optimal abatement may fail to fully offset the higher disruption effect of more production.[1] To avoid this undesirable outcome, the direct taxation of environmental disruption may be needed.

If the provision of public goods is not environmentally disruptive, we may revise our model by letting consumption C rather than production Y enter the function E. Then, similar to the derivation of (C15), we may derive:

$$\sigma^{UW}{}_{|t;\alpha\eta} = \left\{1 + \left(\frac{t}{1-t}\right)(1 - \sigma^{tW})\right\}(\eta^{Uc} + \eta^{UE}\eta^{EC})$$

$$+ \left(\frac{x}{1-x}\right)(\sigma^{tW} - \sigma^{xt})[\eta^{Ur} - \eta^{Ug} - \eta^{UE}(\eta^{EA} + \eta^{EC})] \qquad (C15')$$

Now, even if $\eta^{Uc} + \eta^{UE}\eta^{EC}$ is negative (i.e. the environmental disruption effect dominates the consumption effect) and the responses of leisure negligible, (C15') may still be positive by having a large enough σ^{tW}. If the provision of public goods is not environmentally disruptive, a sufficient increase in tax rate must be sufficient to check the higher disruption effect of higher productivity and to provide more abatement and other public goods to ensure higher utility with growth. Of course, different public goods may have different degrees of environmental disruption effects. Then, it means that growth may be utility-enhancing if it finances extra provision of public goods that provide more benefits than disruption.

The growth in governments

Using the simple model above, it may be shown that under plausible assumptions, the growth in the public sector (relative to the private sector) with the increase in productivity is required for optimality. The needed assumptions are:

A. With higher productivity, the importance of intrinsic private consumption effect decreases, i.e. η^{Uc} decreases with W (through a decrease in the former with c which increases with W).
B. The environmental quality effect η^{UE} increases with higher productivity.
C. The importance of the public-goods effect η^{Ug} and the abatement effect η^{EA} do not significantly decrease with higher productivity.
D. A change in the proportional tax rate t has negligible effects on the working hours.

Actually, we only need either A *or* B, with the other remaining unchanged. Assumption D is justified partly on the conceptual point that the substitution and the income effects tend to offset each other and partly on the empirical observation of roughly unchanged working hours for many decades despite big increases in net wage rates.[2] It should be noted that the intrinsic private good consumption is mainly important at low consumption levels, and that environmental quality and most public goods are likely to be non-inferior goods, Assumptions A to C are also reasonable.

To analyse how the optimal relative (to total production) size of the public sector (indicated in our model by the proportional tax rate t), set the RHS of

(C13) equal to zero (for optimal t) after substituting in $\sigma^{xt} = 0$ from Assumption D. Totally differentiate the resulting equation, yielding:

$$\frac{\eta^{Uc}}{(1-t)^2} \cdot \frac{dt^*}{dW} + \frac{t}{1-t} \cdot \frac{d\eta^{Uc}}{dW} = \frac{d\eta^{Ug}}{dW} + \eta^{UE}\left(\frac{d\eta^{EA}}{dW}\right) + \eta^{EA}\left(\frac{d\eta^{UE}}{dW}\right) \qquad (C16)$$

From Assumption A, the second term in the LHS of (C16) is negative. From Assumption B, the last term in the RHS of (C16) is positive and from Assumption C, the rest are either negligible or positive. Since $\dfrac{\eta^{Uc}}{(1-t)^2}$ is positive, $\dfrac{dt^*}{dW}$ must be positive. We thus have

Proposition 2: With economic growth, the optimal size of the public sector increases relative to the private sector.

Intuitively, with higher productivity/income, environmental quality becomes relatively more important and the intrinsic private consumption effect less important. Optimality then requires the use of more resources for environmental protection and the provision of other public goods.

Appendix D
Non-Affective Altruism: When the Pareto Principle Is Unacceptable

This appendix argues that, there is a particular set of circumstances where the Pareto principle in terms of preferences, even in its weak form (dictating a social preference only when there is a unanimous strong preference by *all* individuals), is clearly unacceptable, even in the absence of ignorance and undesirable effects on the future or the like. The unacceptability of the Pareto principle in the presence of altruism or the need to exclude 'external' preferences in social choice have been remarked by a number of authors (e.g. Hammond, 1987/1995; Harsanyi, 1995, p.325), but no distinction has been made between affective versus non-affective altruism. While non-affective altruism should be excluded in social choice, affective altruism should not.

D1 The Pareto principle

There has been some ambiguities in the interpretation of the Pareto principle. For example, some people (e.g. Nath, 1969, p.228) interpret it to mean that a sufficient condition for a social improvement is for the rich to get richer and the poor remaining at the same income levels. With such a debatable interpretation, it is obvious that the principle is not acceptable as the negative relative-income effects on the poor may make them sufficiently worse off to more than offset the gain of the rich. However, Pareto (1935, p.1466n) himself spoke of 'benefit' and 'detriment', not 'richer'. Moreover, most economists interpret the principle to refer to preference rather than to income. Thus, I shall follow this orthodoxy. With this accepted interpretation, it seems that the principle is compelling, as argued, for example, by Ng (1979/1983, pp.30–2). However, there is a specific set of circumstances where the principle is unacceptable.

A natural reason for rejecting the Pareto principle is where there is important ignorance involved in individual preferences. However, I shall ignore ignorance, imperfect foresight, misinformation, inconsistent preferences, and the like. Another natural reason for rejecting the Pareto principle is due to unfavourable effects on the future and on others (including people in other countries, animals, etc.) For example, if everyone now prefers depletion to conservation (of, say, some essential resources), one may still not go along with the Pareto principle for the benefits of future generations. One may argue that in this case the Pareto principle is not really satisfied, as people in the future would be against depletion now. To avoid these sort of complications, let us assume that there are no effects on the future or on any other possibly controversial subjects like animals. Also to avoid getting into the issue of optimal population, let us assume that the set of people concerned is fixed. With these assumptions, it seems that the Pareto principle is compelling. The discovery of a set of circumstances where the Pareto principle is clearly unacceptable even under these assumptions is thus remarkable.

It is possible for an individual to prefer x to y even if she will be happier at x than at y, even without ignorance and irrationality, since the individual may have a concern for the welfare of others, as argued in Section 4.1. In other words, an individual may be altruistic in reason, on top of being altruistic in emotion or affection. In emotional or affective altruism, one's welfare (i.e. happiness) is increased by an increase in the welfare levels of others. In 'rational' or non-affective altruism, one's utility is increased by an increase in the welfare levels of others *over and above* the affective altruistic effect through one's own welfare level. In the presence of such non-affective altruism, it is possible that the society should prefer y to x even if every individual prefers x to y, since social preference should then take account of individual welfare rather than individual utility levels to avoid multiple counting, as argued in the next section.

D2 When the weak Pareto principle is unacceptable

The existence of non-affective altruism makes the weak Pareto principle unacceptable under a certain set of circumstances even in the absence of ignorance. Since the existence of affective altruism does not cause a problem here, it is abstracted away for simplicity. Consider a simple case of three individuals where person 1 is an egoist with $u^1 = w^1$ and persons 2 and 3 both strong non-affective altruists with respect to the welfare of person 1, with $u^i = w^i + \frac{2}{3}w^1$; $i = 2, 3$, where u = utility (representing preference) and w = welfare (representing happiness) and a superscript indicates the person concerned. It should be noted that the existence of a reasonable social welfare function or the general possibility of a reasonable social choice presupposes interpersonal comparable cardinal utilities, as argued in Chapter 2. It is difficult to obtain individual cardinal utilities/welfares and to compare them interpersonally. However, to concentrate on the main point, let us abstract from these difficulties and assume the existence of interpersonal comparable cardinal individual welfares and utilities. The non-acceptability of the Pareto principle may be shown even under this simplification. Consider the choice between social alternatives x and y for a situation depicted in Table D1, where the welfare and utility figures may be taken as being in interpersonally comparable cardinal units.

It is clear that every person prefers y to x, i.e. $u^i(y) > u^i(x)$ for all i. According to even the weak Pareto principle, the society should prefer y to x. However, I

Table D1

	w^1	w^2	w^3	$u^1 = w^1$	$u^2 = w^2 + \frac{2}{3}w$	$u^3 = w^3 + \frac{2}{3}w$	Σw^i	Σu^i
x	6	12	18	6	16	22	36	44
y	18	5	12	18	17	24	35	59

wish to argue that the weak (and *a fortiori* the strong) Pareto principle is not acceptable in such circumstances and that the society should prefer *x* to *y*.

We should also abstract away the complications of indirect or long-term effects by assuming that the individual welfares and utilities figures for *x* and *y* in the above figures capture all relevant outcomes and that there are no other effects. If we focus attention on individual welfares only, it is clear that *x* is preferable to *y*. Not only is the sum of individual welfares higher in *x* than in *y*, all social welfare functions of individual welfares that is anonymous and increasing in individual welfares must obviously rank *x* higher than *y*. However, should the social welfare function be a function of individual welfares or of individual utilities?

If the individual welfare figures in Table D1 already capture all relevant effects as mentioned above and if the welfare levels of all other sentients are abstracted away or assumed unchanged, Section 4.1 argues that social choice should be based on individual welfares than on individual utilities. Here, a more compelling and simple case can be made due to the fact that individual welfares and utilities differ here because of only a specific reason by construction.

In the example of Table D1, misinformation, ignorance, and all other reasons that may cause the utility (representing preference) of a person to differ from her welfare have been abstracted away, except non-affective altruism. Person 1 is assumed to be not altruistic non-affectively so that his utility does not differ from his welfare. Persons 2 and 3 are both assumed to be strongly non-affectively altruistic towards person 1. (We do not need such a high degree of non-affective altruism to establish the point if we have more individuals.) Each of them has a higher welfare level at *x* than at *y* but prefers *y* to *x* because of a non-affective concern for the welfare of person 1. However, for social choice, since the welfare of person 1 is already fully taken into account as w^1 in any reasonable (including the property of anonymity) social welfare function, it should not be taken into account again as components of u^2 and u^3. Otherwise, multiple counting is involved. To see this point more clearly, consider a simpler case of just two persons depicted in Table D2.

For this case, it is obvious that, taking account of the welfare levels of the individuals, any anonymous social welfare function increasing in individual welfares ranks *x* above *y*. However, if the utility figures are taken as relevant for social choice instead, any anonymous and non-anti-egalitarian social welfare function (such as $W = \Sigma u^i$) prefers *y* to *x*, as *y* has a more equal utility profile with a bigger sum than *x*. Nevertheless, the social preference of *y* to *x* is patently unfair to person 2. The welfare of person 1 is only counted once while that of person 2 is

Table D2

	w^1	w^2	$u^1 = w^1$	$u^2 = w^2 + w^1$	Σw^i	Σu^i
x	2	7	2	9	9	11
y	7	1	7	8	8	15

counted twice, once as the component w^1 in u^1, and once as the component w^1 in u^2, because person 2 has a perfect concern for the welfare of person 1. If she were to make the choice herself, she would choose in accordance to $w^2 + w^1$. If person 1 had a similar perfect concern for the welfare of person 2, the use of Σu^i would rank x above y. Due to the asymmetrical degrees of non-affective altruism, the use of utility figures instead of welfare figures biases social choice in favour of persons of lower degrees of non-affective altruism, effectively penalising persons with higher degrees of non-affective altruism. The example of Table D2 shows clearly that, where the difference between utility and welfare levels is due only to non-affective altruism, social choice should be based on individual welfare rather than utility figures.

Coming back to Table D1, the agreement to the use of individual welfare figures for social choice means that any anonymous and increasing SWF will rank x above y, despite the fact that every individual prefers y to x. As the society should prefer x to y even when every individual prefers y to x, the Pareto principle, even in its weak and hence more compelling version, is not acceptable in this set of circumstances.

D3 The case of affective altruism

It should be noted that, while non-affective altruism may cause the Pareto principle to be unacceptable, affective altruism does not. In this case, the altruists also *feel* better off by, say, seeing the higher incomes of those they are altruistically minding for. Thus, the welfares of the altruists are also higher. There is thus no ground to reject the Pareto principle due to this. To see the point clearer, consider the case illustrated in Table D3 where m^i is the (real) money or income of person i. Non-affective altruism and ignorance are both assumed absent.

Here, person 2 is an affective altruist who is happier with her income reduced from 6 at x to 4 at y as she, say, thinks that person 2 has more need to get more income and feel good knowing that he gets a higher income of 8 at y. Both persons prefer y to x and are happier at y than at x. Assuming that Table D3 already includes all relevant effects as should be, there is no ground for the society not to prefer y to x. The Pareto principle should be respected in this case. The fact that x has a more equal distribution of income is not a valid reason for preferring x to y socially. This is so because income is not an ultimate end. Hence, equal distribution of income is only desirable if it increases our ultimate end – happiness. In the case of Table D3, the equal distribution at x (in comparison to

Table D3

	m^1	m^2	w^1	w^2	u^1	u^2
x	6	6	6	6	6	6
y	8	4	7	7	7	7

y) decreases the welfare of all individuals. It may be argued that unequal distribution may have undesirable long-term consequences. If so, that should be included into the welfare figures in Table D3. Then, we can judge according to the figures inclusive of all effects.

D4 Should voters be asked to suppress their non-affective altruism?

It has been shown that even the weak Pareto principle may not be acceptable in the presence of non-affective altruism which is strongly argued to exist. This raises some perplexing questions. For one thing, it is generally believed that altruism increases social welfare and improves the social decisions undertaken. This may certainly be true for decision-making by key persons with altruism. However, for the processes of revealing individual preferences which are then used as the information ingredients for making social decisions, non-affective altruism may be counter-productive. For example, in the case of Table D1, if non-affective altruism is excluded from individual preferences, the correct social ranking of x over y is likely to be made. On the other hand, if individual preferences inclusive of non-affective altruism are used, the incorrect social ranking of y over x is likely. Thus, despite the general beneficial effects of altruism, it may be desirable to request voters to vote in accordance to their welfare, or their preferences exclusive of non-affective altruism. However, such a practice may decrease the degrees of altruism in the long run and that may be detrimental to social welfare. Hence, a kind of a dilemma is present.

Appendix E
The Bergson–Samuelson Tradition Implies Individualism, Independence, and Ordinalism

By the 'Bergson–Samuelson tradition' we do not mean the general formulation of a SWF in Bergson (1938) which, in the words of Osborne (1976, p.1003) 'in some mysterious fashion maps S (social states) directly into social welfare'. Rather, we refer to the widely used version introduced by Bergson under the label 'fundamental value propositions of individual preference'. According to that version, social welfare derived from any social state is a function only of individual preferences in that social state:

$$W(x) = W[u_1(x), u_2(x), \ldots u_n(x)] \tag{E1}$$

where u_i is the utility function representing the ordinal preferences of individual i, and x is a social state.

While this formulation is in terms of social welfare, it may also be regarded as a social choice formulation if it is agreed that the social ranking of social states is to be in accordance with the value of social welfare, i.e. if $xRy < = > W(x) \geq W(y)$, where R indicates weak social preference.

That the Bergson–Samuelson tradition as represented in (E1) implies individualism is obvious, since social welfare depends only on individual utilities. That it implies independence is also not difficult to see, since $W(x)$ depends only on individual utilities at the social state x, and this is so for any x.

It cannot be inferred from (E1) alone that the Bergson–Samuelson tradition relies on ordinalism for the u_i could represent cardinal utilities. Rather, ordinalism is imputed from statements made by Bergson and Samuelson. Bergson (1938) himself writes: 'In my opinion the [cardinal] utility calculus introduced by the Cambridge economists [referring to Marshall, Pigou, etc.] is not a useful tool for welfare economics' (as reprinted in Arrow and Scitovsky, 1969, p.20). And interpreting Bergson, Arrow writes: 'Bergson considers it possible to establish an ordering of social states which is based on indifference maps of individuals, and Samuelson has agreed' (Arrow, 1951/1963, p.5, emphasis added). Samuelson is even more forthright than Bergson. He repeatedly asserts that a Bergson–Samuelson SWF 'does exist. . . . No cardinal intensities are ever involved' (Samuelson, 1977, p.86). If we interpret the u_i in (E1) as purely ordinal, the Bergson–Samuelson tradition thus implies ordinalism as well.

Appendix F
Inefficiency in Provision May Increase Optimal Public Spending

Ignoring the possible interaction between benefit and cost, we may choose g to maximise net benefit N:

$$N = B[a(g)] - C(g) \tag{8.1}$$

where B = (total) benefit, a = actual or physical amount of public good provided, g = monetary amount of public spending, C = (total) cost. The use of this general cost function allows for possible excess burden in financing for g:

$$a(g) = Ag \tag{8.2}$$

where A is an index on the efficiency in the public provision of public goods. Assuming the satisfaction of the usual conditions (differentiability of the functions, B' and $C' > 0$, $B'' < 0$ and $C'' > 0$), the maximisation of (8.1) with respect to g, using (8.2) gives:

$$B'A = C' \tag{8.3}$$

Totally differentiating (8.3) with respect to A, we have, after using the total differentiation of (8.2):

$$dg*/dA = (B' + aB'')/(C'' - A^2B'') \tag{8.4}$$

Since the denominator of the RHS is positive, the sign of $dg*/dA$ is the same as that of the numerator. As $(B' + aB'')$ is positive/negative if and only if $B' >/< -aB''$ or $1>/< - (\delta B'/\delta a)a/B'$, we have Proposition 8.1 in the text. To show that the (proportionate) responsiveness of marginal benefit is the same whether we use the monetary level of public spending g or the physical level of public good a (given that the provision efficiency A is independent of g), note that, from the B function in (8.1) and from (8.2) we have $B_g \equiv \delta B/\delta g = B'A$ from which we have, $\delta B_g/\delta g = B''A^2$, and hence $(\delta B_g/\delta g)g/B_g = (\delta B'/\delta a)a/B'$. Thus, the marginal benefit is equally responsive proportionately either with respect to the monetary amount of public spending g or to the physical amount of public good a.

Notes

Chapter 3

1. A different welfarist reason for including such apparently 'non-welfarist' indicators into the short-run SWF is their effects on welfare in the long run. For example, a less unequal distribution of income may promote social harmony.
2. See also Sen, 1967. I define basicness somewhat differently: 'a value judgement [is] basic to a person if it is not derived from some other value judgement and he believes in it for its own ethical appeal' (Ng, 1979/1983, p.19). Whether this definition differs from Sen's depends on the interpretation of 'all conceivable circumstances' in Sen's definition.
3. As an example of the importance of this practical consideration, see Creedy (1996) who argues that the maximisation of the utilitarian objective of the unweighted sum of individual welfares in the long run may be close to, in the short run, the pursuit of Rawlsian maximin or the use of target efficiency in poverty reduction.
4. However, perception and affective feelings probably evolved simultaneously. As I hope to argue elsewhere, perception without affective feelings also serves no evolutionary purposes. Here, perception is defined as involving subjective consciousness, not just in the wider sense 'reception and interpretation of signals from the environment', regarded as evidenced in the bacterium *E. coli*, see M. Delbrück, 1986.
5. This leaves a little vague as to whether non-affective malice is rational or irrational. I prefer to regard non-affective malice as irrational. Since both irrationality and non-affective altruism/malice are excluded by Axiom 1, this vagueness does not affect the argument below.

Chapter 4

1. This chapter is largely based on Ng (1999).
2. In this simple formulation of the utility function, it may appear that some subtle differences such as whether the higher welfare levels of others are caused by one's own actions or not (Sen's 'agency' problem) are not distinguished'; however, certain relevant activities such as one's own contribution to charity may be allowed to enter one's welfare function in the text below.

Chapter 5

1. Fleming only lists postulates ensuring the existence of a social ordering. With continuity, this ensures the existence of a SWF as well. Continuity and the existence of a SWF is implicitly assumed in Fleming's derivation. The existence of a social ordering alone is not sufficient for Fleming's purpose as a lexicographic social ordering cannot be represented by a SWF at all.

2. Or, rather, if they had an equal chance of being 'put in the place of' any individual member of the society, with regard not only to his objective social (and economic) conditions, but also to their subjective attitudes and tastes. In other words, they ought to judge the utility of another individual's position not in terms of his own attitudes and tastes but rather in terms of the attitudes and tastes of the individual actually holding this position (Harsanyi's note).
3. This proviso is redundant if we accept Rational Individualism (Axiom 1) which implies welfarism.
4. This has to be so as non-welfare variables are being held constant; also, non-affective altruism/malice is to be excluded in social choice from Axiom 1d2.
5. From the continuity of preference, one should really use one to measure the welfare difference of a just imperceptible indifference, and anything larger than one will be perceptible preference (Ng, 1975a). However, since a just imperceptible indifference is continuous with a just perceptible preference, we will ignore this pedantic point.
6. The difference between individual preferences (used by Fleming) and individual welfares is ignored. This does not affect our argument here since Rational Individualism insists on the use of individual welfares where the two diverge.
7. If *WE* and *EW* always yield the same result, we have WE = $W(\Sigma_j\theta_j U_j^1, \ldots, \Sigma_j\theta_j U_j^I)$ = EW= $\Sigma_j\theta_j W(U_j^1, \ldots, U_j^I)$. Differentiation with respect to U_j^i gives $\partial W/\partial EU^i = \partial W/\partial U_j^i$ at any given situation. Such an equality cannot hold through for every set of θ's unless W is a sum (unweighted or weighted with uniform individual weights) of its arguments.

Chapter 6

1. In my 1979/83 treatment, I did not discuss the big differences between willingness to pay and willingness to accept due to the unwillingness of many people to actually pay for something they believe they are 'entitled' to or other similar problems. (See, for example, Mitchell and Carson, 1989; Milgrom, 1993.) For such cases, there are added practical difficulties to discover people's real willingness to pay as a reflection of their preferences for the items as such untainted by the objections or ill-feelings associated with payment. This difficulty of the intertwining of two different types of preferences/dispreferences is similar to the intrusion of factors such as regret, anxiety, excitement, etc. into the process or outcomes of choices involving risk, making the application of the expected utility theory difficult in those cases. However, in both cases, the principles involved are not invalidated.
2. As real tax liabilities depend on non-income characteristics such as age, marital status, home-ownership, etc. the evaluation of effective income tax progressivity may not be simple. However, see Hayes *et al.* (1995) for an algorithm to evaluate effective income tax progression.
3. Second-best taxation-pricing rules are typically very complicated, even if only the efficiency consideration is taken into account. For the literature on optimal taxation, see Mirrlees (1976, 1981) and Sandmo (1976). Conditions making second-best considerations ineffective are rather stringent, for example, separability in the utility function (see Atkinson and Stiglitz, 1976; compare Bergstrom and Cornes, 1983).

4. For example, consider the argument of William Baumol and Dietrich Fischer (1979) that the use of discrimination in wage rate is much more efficient (less output foregone) than non-discriminatory taxation in achieving equality. This is based on the detailed knowledge of individual input supply functions that they recognise to be unavailable. But they suggest that some rough discrimination between broad groups of income earners such as doctors versus ditch diggers may yet be feasible. But if a discrimination, such as supplementing 'wage rates for the one and limit[ing] wages for the other' (p.522), is feasible, there is little reason to expect that it is not feasible to have higher income tax rates for doctors and lower for ditch diggers.

5. Borghans and Groot (1998) attribute the discrepancy/inefficiency to some form of monopolistic power. However, I regard the insignificant losses of the replacement of the superstars by their runners up as more important, making the discrepancy/inefficiency non-existent or insignificant for superstars in say science and technology or the generation of real knowledge in general. Here, in fact, the superstars earn far less than their marginal contributions due to the global public-good and long-term nature of knowledge.

Chapter 9

1. Political-economy issues like rent-seeking and tax policy in accordance to political instead of distortionary costs (on which see, e.g. Brennan, 1984; Buchanan, 1993; Hettich and Winer, 1997; Holcombe, 1998 and Winer and Hettich, 1998), while relevant, are not considered here.

2. Batina (1990) in fact allows for heterogeneous individuals and hence identifies a distributional term but does not relate it to the offsetting of the disincentive effects.

3. Combined with this consideration is the point that, while the existence and size of excess burdens or distortions depend on the net substitution effects, the marginal cost of fund depends on the gross substitution effect (disincentive effect when related to the income/leisure choice). See Ng, forthcoming b, (second half of its Appendix A in particular); cf. Browning and Liu (1998).

4. Gross of the income effect, a higher tax may not cause disincentive effects.

Appendix B

1. It is true that Rawls would argue that freedom to rape is not a basic liberty while the right to non-violation of body is. However, how do we determine what are basic liberties? Either it is based on the utilitarian (or at least welfarist) principle or it is open to the objection of possibly sanctioning a disastrous outcome. For the unacceptability of rights-based ethics, see Ng (1990a, Sec. IIIB).

2. Including holding the degree of altruism/malice the same across individuals; for differences in this, see the text below.

Appendix C

1. If η^{EA} is large, then the optimality condition for the division between abatement and other public goods (from the equating of the RHS of Equation C14

to zero) dictates a large η^{Ug}, making the third term of the RHS of (C15) dominating.

2. It may also be noted that the term associated with σ^{xt} in (C13) contains an expression (reflecting the indirect effects) of ambiguous sign whose parts are likely to change in offsetting directions with W. Hence, even if σ^{xt} is not assumed negligible, the qualification to our conclusion below is likely to be small.

References

Ackerman, F., Kiron, D., Goodwin, N. R., Harris, J. M. and Gallagher, K. (1997), *Human Well-being and Economic Goals* (Washington, DC: Island Press).

Adler, Matthew D. and Posner, Eric A. (1999), 'Rethinking Cost–Benefit Analysis', Chicago Law & Economics Working Paper No. 72 (2D series).

Aghion, Philippe and Williamson, Jeffrey (1999), *Growth, Inequality and Globalization: Theory, History and Policy* (Cambridge: Cambridge University Press).

Aiken, William and La Follette, Hugh (eds) (1977), *World Hunger and Moral Obligation* (Englewood Cliffs, NJ: Prentice-Hall).

Ake, Christopher (1975), 'Justice as equality', *Philosophy and Public Affairs*, 1, 69–89.

Altonji, J. G., Hayashi, F. and Kotlikoff, L. J. (1997), 'Parental altruism and inter vivos transfers: theory and evidence', *Journal of Political Economy*, 105, 1121–66.

Arneson, Richard J. (1989/1995), 'Equality and equal opportunity for welfare', *Philosophical Studies*, 56, 77–93; reprinted with a postscript (1995) in Pojman and Westmoreland (eds), (1999). pp.229–42.

Arrow, Kenneth J. (1951/1963), *Social Choice and Individual Values* (New York: John Wiley).

Arrow, Kenneth J. and Intriligator, Michael D. (1986), *Handbook of Mathematical Economics*, Vol. III (Amsterdam: North-Holland).

Arrow, Kenneth J. and Scitovsky, Tibor (eds) (1969), *Readings in Welfare Economics* (London: Allen & Unwin).

Ashenfelter, Orley C. and Layard, Richard (eds) (1986), *Handbook of Labor Economics*, Vol. 1 (Amsterdam: North-Holland).

Atkinson, Anthony B. and Stiglitz, Joseph E. (1976), 'The design of tax structure: direct versus indirect taxation', *Journal of Public Economics*, 6, 55–75.

Atkinson, Anthony B. and Stiglitz, Joseph E. (1980), *Lectures on Public Economics*, (New York: McGraw-Hill).

Auten, Gerald and Carroll, Robert (1994), 'Taxpayer behavior and the 1986 Tax Reform Act', Office of Tax Analysis Working Paper (Washington, DC, US Department of the Treasury).

Backhouse, Roger E. (1998), 'If mathematics is informal, then perhaps we should accept that economics must be informal too', *Economic Journal*, 108, 1848–58.

Bagwell, L. S. and Bernheim, B. D. (1996), 'Veblen effects in a theory of conspicuous consumption', *American Economic Review*, 86, 349–73.

Baland, Jean-Marie and Platteau, Jean-Philippe (1997), 'Wealth inequality and efficiency in the commons', Part I, *Oxford Economic Papers*, 49, 451–82.

Ballard, Charles L. and Medema, Steven G. (1993), 'The marginal efficiency effect of taxes and subsidies in the presence of externalities: a computational general equilibrium approach', *Journal of Public Economics*, 52, 199–216.

Ballard, Charles, Shoven, John and Whalley, John (1985), 'General equilibrium computations of the marginal welfare cost of taxes in the United States', *American Economic Review*, 75 (1), 128–38.

Barry, Brian M. (1995), *Justice as Impartiality* (Oxford, England: Clarendon Press; New York: Oxford University Press).

Batina, Raymond G. (1990), 'On the interpretation of the modified Samuelson rule for public goods in static models with heterogeneity', *Journal of Public Economics*, 42, 125–33.

Baumol, William J. (1967), 'Macroeconomics of unbalanced growth: the anatomy of urban crisis', *The American Economic Review*, 57, 415–26.

Baumol, William J. and Fischer, Dietrich (1979), 'The output distribution frontier: alternatives to income taxes and transfers for strong equality goals', *American Economic Review*, Sept., 69, 514–25.

Behrman, J. and Srinivasan, T. N. (eds) (1995), *Handbook of Development Economics*, Vol. 3A (Amsterdam: North-Holland).

Bénabou, Roland (1996), 'Inequality and growth', *NBER Macroeconomics Annual*, No. 1996, pp.11–92.

Bergson (Burk), A. (1938), 'A reformulation of certain aspects of welfare economics', *Quarterly Journal of Economics*, 52, 310–34.

Bergstrom, Theodore C. and Cornes, Richard C. (1983), 'Independence of allocative efficiency from distribution in the theory of public goods', *Econometrica*, 51, 753–66.

Berridge, K. C. (1996), 'Food reward: brain substrates of wanting and liking', *Neuroscience and Biobehavioral Reviews*, 20, 1–25.

Binswanger, Hans, Deininger, Klaus and Feder, Gershon (1995), 'Power, distortions, revolt and reform in agriculture land revolutions', in Behrman and Srinivasan, Vol. 3, chapter 42, pp.2659–772.

Birdsall, Nancy, Ross, David and Sabot, Richard (1995), 'Inequality and growth reconsidered', *World Bank Economics Review*, 9, 477–508.

Bishop, M. P., Elder, S. Thomas and Heath, Robert G. (1964), 'Attempted control of operant behaviour in man with intracranial self-stimulation', in Heath (1964), pp.55–81.

Blackorby, Charles and Donaldson, David (1990), 'A review article: the case against the use of the sum of compensating variations in cost–benefit analysis', *Canadian Journal of Economics*, 23 (3), 471–94.

Blaug, Mark (1998), 'Disturbing currents in modern economics', *Challenge*, 41 (3), 11–45. (Followed by an interview).

Boadway, Robin W. (1974), 'The welfare foundations of cost–benefit analysis', *Economic Journal*, 84, 926–39.

Boadway, Robin W. and Keen, Michael (1993), 'Public goods, self-selection and optimal income taxation', *International Economic Review*, 34 (3), 463–78.

Bohl, M. T. (1996), 'Some international evidence on Wagner's Law', *Public Finance*, 51 (2), 185–200.

Borghans, Lex and Groot, Loek (1998), 'Superstardom and monopolistic power: why media stars earn more than their marginal contribution to welfare', *Journal of Institutional and Theoretical Economics*, 154, 546–71.

Bowles, Samuel (1998), 'Endogenous preferences: the cultural consequences of markets and other economic institutions', *Journal of Economic Literature*, 36, 75–111.

Bowles, Samuel and Gintis, Herbert (1996), 'Efficient redistribution: new rules for markets, states and communities', *Politics and Society*, 24, 307–42.

Breen, Richard (1997), 'Inequality, economic growth and social mobility', *British Journal of Sociology*, 48, 429–49.

Brennan, Geoffrey (1984), 'Elements of a fiscal politics: public choice and public finance', *Australian Economic Review*, 3rd quarter, 67, 62–72.

Brickman, Phillip, Coates, Dan and Janoff-Bulman, Ronnie (1978), 'Lottery winners and accident victims: is happiness relative?', *Journal of Personality and Social Psychology*, 36, 917–27.

Broome, John (1991), *Weighing Goods: Equality, Uncertainty and Time* (Oxford: Blackwell).

Brown, Donald and Heal, Geoffrey (1979), 'Equity, efficiency and increasing returns', *Review of Economic Studies*, 571–86.

Browning, Edgar K. (1987), 'On the marginal welfare cost of taxation', *American Economic Review*, 77 (1), 11–23.

Browning, Edgar K. and Liu, Ligun (1998), 'The optimal supply of public goods and the distortionary cost of taxation: Comment', *National Tax Journal*, 51 (1), 103–16.

Buchanan, James A. (1993), 'The political efficiency of general taxation', *National Tax Journal*, 46 (4), 401–10.

Chang, Ming Chung (1997), 'Optimal public good provision – cases with complementarities between the public good and the taxed commodities', Typescript.

Chick, Victoria (1998), 'On knowing one's place: the role of formalism in economics', *Economic Journal*, 108, 1859–69.

Christiansen, Vidar (1981), 'Evaluation of public projects under optimal taxation', *Review of Economic Studies*, XLVIII, 447–57.

Clark, J. (1998), 'Fairness preferences and optimization skills: are they substitutes? An experimental investigation', *Journal of Economic Behavior and Organization*, 34 (4), 541–57.

Cohen, G. A. (1989), 'On the currency of egalitarian justice', *Ethics*, 99, 906–44.

Cole, Harold L., Mailath, George J. and Postlewaite, Andrew (1992), 'Social norms, savings behavior, and growth', *Journal of Political Economy*, 100 (6), 1092–125.

Congleton, R. D. (1997), 'Political efficiency and equal protection of the law', *Kyklos*, 50, 485–505.

Corden, W. M. (1974), *Trade Policy and Economic Welfare* (London: Oxford University Press).

Creedy, John (1996), 'Comparing tax and transfer systems: poverty, inequality and target efficiency', *Economica*, 63, S163–S174.

Creedy, John and McDonald, Ian M. (1990), 'A tax package to reduce the marginal rate of income tax and wage demands of trade unions', *Economic Review*, 66, 195–202.

Cremer, Helmuth and Gahvari, Firouz (1995), 'Uncertainty, optimal taxation and the direct versus indirect tax controversy', *Economic Journal*, 105, 1165–79.

Cummins, Robert A. (1998), 'The second approximation to an international standard for life satisfaction', *Social Indicators Research*, 43, 307–44.

D'Aspremont, Claude and Gevers, Louis (1977), 'Equity and the informational basis of collective choice', *Review of Economic Studies*, 44, 199–209.

David, P. A. and Reder, M. W. (eds) (1974), *Nations and Households in Economic Growth: Essays in Honour of Moses Abramowitz* (New York: Academic Press).

de Bartolome, Charles A. M. (1995), 'Which tax rate do people use: average or marginal?', *Journal of Public Economics*, 56, 79–96.

Delbrück, Max (1986), *Mind from Matter? An Essay on Evolutionary Epistemology*, edited by Gunther S. Stent, Ernst Peter Fischer, Solomon W. Golomb, David Presti, Hansjakob Seiler (Palo Alto, California: Blackwell Scientific Publications).

Delgado, J. M. R. (1976), 'New orientations in brain stimulation in man', in Wauquier and Rolls (1976).

DeMeyer, Frank and Plott, Charles R. (1971), 'A welfare function using "relative intensity" of preference', *Quarterly Journal of Economics*, 85, 179–86.

Devins, Neal and Douglas, Davison M. (1998), *Redefining Equality* (New York and Oxford: Oxford University Press).

Devinsky, O., Berić, A. and Dogali, M. (1993), *Electrical and Magnetic Stimulation of the Brain and Spinal Cord* (New York: Raven Press).

Diamond, Peter A. (1967), 'Cardinal welfare, individualistic ethics, and interpersonal comparison of utility: comment', *Journal of Political Economy*, 75, 765–6.

Diener, Ed and Suh, Eunkook (1997), 'Measuring quality of life: economic, social and subjective indicators', *Social Indicators Research*, 40, 189–216.

Dowrick, Steve (1993), 'Government consumption: its effects on productivity, growth, and investment', in Gemmell (1993), pp.136–152.

Duesenberry, James S. (1949), *Income, Saving and the Theory of Consumer Behaviour* (Cambridge, MA: Harvard University Press).

Dworkin, R. (1977), *Taking Rights Seriously* (Cambridge, Mass.: Harvard University Press).

Dworkin, Ronald (1981), 'What is equality?' *Philosophy and Public Affairs*, 10: 185–246, 283–345.

Easterlin, R. A. (1974), 'Does economic growth improve the human lot? Some empirical evidence', in David and Reder, pp.89–125.

Easterly, William (1997), 'Life during growth'. World Bank typescript. Revised (1999) version on web page http//www.worldbank.org/html/prdmg/grthweb/growth_t.htm.

Eaton, B. Curtis and White, William (1991), 'The distribution of wealth and the efficiency of institutions', *Economic Inquiry*, 29, 336–50.

Eatwell, John, Milgate, Murray and Newman, Peter (eds) (1987), *The New Palgrave: A Dictionary of Economics*, Vol. 1 (London: Macmillan).

Edgeworth, F. Y. (1881), *Mathematical Psychics* (London: Kegan Paul).

Eisenstein, Louis (1961), *The Ideologies of Taxation* (New York: Ronald).

Elster, Jon (1998), 'Emotions and economic theory', *Journal of Economic Literature*, 36, 47–74.

Elster, Jon and Roemer, John E. (eds) (1991), *Interpersonal Comparisons of Well-Being* (London: Cambridge University Press).

Eshel, I., Samuelson, L. and Shaked, A. (1998), 'Altruists, egoists, and hooligans in a local interaction model', *American Economic Review*, 88 (1), 157–79.

Farina, Francesco, Hahn, Frank and Vannucci, Stefano (eds) (1996), *Ethics, Rationality, and Economic Behaviour* (New York: Clarendon Press).

Feiwel. G. R. (ed.) (1985), *Issues in Contemporary Microeconomics and Welfare* (London: Macmillan).

Feldstein, Martin (1974), 'Distributional preferences in public expenditure analysis', in Hochman and Peterson, pp.136–61.

Feldstein, Martin (1995a), 'The effect of marginal tax rates on taxable income: a panel study of the 1986 Tax Reform Act', *Journal of Political Economy*, 103 (3), 551–72.

Feldstein, Martin (1995b), 'Tax avoidance and the deadweight loss of the income tax', NBER Working Paper No.5055 (Cambridge, MA: National Bureau of Economic Research).

Feldstein, Martin (1997), 'How big should government be?', *National Tax Journal*, 50 (2), 197–213.

Feldstein, Martin and Feenberg, Daniel (1996), 'The effect of increased tax rates on taxable income and economic efficiency: a preliminary analysis of the 1993 tax rate increases', in *Tax Policy and the Economy*, Vol. 10, pp.89–117.

Ferris, Stephen J. and West, Edwin G. (1996), 'Testing theories of real government size: U.S. experience, 1959–89', *Southern Economic Journal*, 62 (3), 537–53.

Fleming, Marcus (1952), 'A cardinal concept of welfare', *Quarterly Journal of Economics*, 66, 366–84.

Fortin, Bernard and Lacroix, Guy (1994), 'Labour supply, tax evasion and the marginal cost of public funds: an empirical investigation', *Journal of Public Economics*, 55, 407–31.

Frank, Robert H. (1985), *Choosing the Right Pond: Human Behaviour and the Quest for Status* (New York: Oxford University Press).

Frank, Robert H. (1987), 'If *homo* economicus could choose his own utility function, would he want one with a conscience?', *American Economic Review*, 77, 593–604.

Frank, Robert H. (1999), *Luxury Fever: Why Money Fails to Satisfy in an Era of Excess* (New York, NY: Free Press).

Gemmell, Norman (1993), *The Growth of the Public Sector: Theories and International Evidence* (Aldershot, England: Edward Elgar).

Goodin, Robert E. (1995), *Utilitarianism as a Public Philosophy* (Cambridge, New York: Cambridge University Press).

Grossman, Herschel (1994), 'Production, appropriation and land reform', *American Economic Review*, 84 (3), 705–12.

Hamilton, W. D. (1964), 'The genetical evolution of social behaviour. I and II', *Journal of Theoretical Biology*, 7, 1–52.

Hammond, Peter J. (1976), 'Why ethical measures of inequality need interpersonal comparisons', *Theory and Decision*, 7, 262–274.

Hammond, Peter J. (1987/1995), 'Altruism', in Eatwell *et al.*, Vol. 1, pp.85–7, reprinted in Stefano Zamagni (1995), pp.165–7.

Hammond, Peter J. (1991), 'Interpersonal comparisons of utility: why and how they are and should be made', in Elster and Roemer, (eds), pp.200–54.

Hammond, Peter J. (1996), 'Consequentialist decision theory and utilitarian ethics', in Farina, Hahn and Vannucci (eds).

Harbaugh, W. T. (1998), 'What do donations buy? a model of philanthropy based on prestige and warm glow', *Journal of Public Economics*, 67 (2), 269–84.

Hardy, J. D., Wolff, Harold G. and Goodell, Helen (1952), *Pain Sensations and Reactions* (Baltimore: The Williams and Wilkins Co.).

Hare, R. M. (1976), 'Ethical theory and utilitarianism', in Lewis (ed.), pp.113–31.

Hare, R. M. (1997), 'Justice and equality', in Pojman and Westmoreland's pp.218–28.

Harris, Richard and Olewiler, Nancy (1979), 'The welfare economics of *ex post* optimality', *Economica*, 46, 137–47.

Harrod, R. F. (1948), *Towards a Dynamic Economics* (London: Macmillan).

Harsanyi, John C. (1953), 'Cardinal utility in welfare economics and in the theory of risk-taking', *Journal of Political Economy*, 61, 434–5.

Harsanyi, John C. (1955), 'Cardinal welfare, individualistic ethics, and inter-personal comparison of utility', *Journal of Political Economy*, 63, 309–21.

Harsanyi, John C. (1995), 'A theory of prudential values and a rule utilitarian theory of morality', *Social Choice and Welfare*, 12, 319–33.

Harsanyi, John C. (1997), 'Utilities, preferences, and substantive goods', *Social Choice and Welfare*, 14, 129–45.

Hausman, Jerry A. (ed.) (1993), *Contingent Valuation: A Critical Assessment* (Amsterdam: North-Holland).

Haveman, Robert H. (1988), *Starting Even: An Equal Opportunity Program to Combat the Nation's New Poverty* (New York: Simon and Schuster).

Hayes, Kathy J., Lambert, Peter J. and Slottje, Daniel J. (1995), 'Evaluating effective income tax progression', *Journal of Public Economics*, 56, 461–74.

Headley, Bruce and Wearing, Alexander (1991), 'Subjective well-being: a stocks and flows framework', in Strack, Argyle and Schwarz, pp.49–73.

Heath, R. G. (ed.) (1964), *The Role of Pleasure in Behavior* (New York: Harper and Row).

Heath, R. G., John, S. B. and Fontana, C. J. (1968), 'The pleasure response: studies by stereotaxic technics in patients', in Kline and Laska, pp.178–89.

Herrnstein, Richard J. and Prelec, Drazen (1992), 'Melioration' in Loewenstein, George and Elster, Jon, pp.235–63.

Hersoug, Tor (1984), 'Union wage responses to tax changes', *Oxford Economic Paper*, 36, 37–51.

Hettich, Walter and Winer, Stanley L. (1997), 'The political economy of taxation', in Dennis Mueller (1989), pp.481–505.

Hirsch, F. (1976), *Social Limits to Economic Growth* (Cambridge, MA: Harvard University Press).

Hochman, Harold M. and Peterson, George E. (eds) (1974), *Redistribution Through Public Choice* (New York: Columbia University Press).

Hoff, Karla (1996), 'Market failures and the distribution of wealth: a perspective from the economics of information', *Politics & Society*, 24, 411–32.

Hoff, Karla and Lyon, Andrew (1995). 'Non-leaky buckets: optimal redistributive taxation and agency costs', *Journal of Public Economics*, 58, 365–90.

Hoffman, Martin L. (1981), 'Is altruism part of human nature?', *Journal of Personality and Social Psychology*, 40, 121–37.

Holcombe, Randall G. (1997), 'Absence of envy does not imply fairness', *Southern Economic Journal*, 797–802.

Holcombe, Randall G. (1998), 'Tax policy from a public choice perspective', *National Tax Journal*, 51 (2), 359–71.

Hook, S. (ed.) (1967), *Human Values and Economic Policy: a Symposium* (New York: New York University Press).

Ireland, Norman J. (1994), 'On limiting the market for status signals', *Journal of Public Economics*, 53, 91–110.

Jackson, Peter M. (ed.) (1993), *Current Issues in Public Sector Economics* (London: Macmillan).

Jiang, F. Racine, R. and Turnbull, J. (1997), 'Electrical stimulation of the septal region of aged rates improves performance in open-field maze', *Physiology and Behavior*, 62, 1279–82.

Joseph, Stephen and Lewis, Christopher A. (1998), 'The depression–happiness scale: reliability and validity of a bipolar self-report scale', *Journal of Clinical Psychology*, 54, 537–44.

Kahneman, Daniel, Wakker, Peter P. and Sarin, Rakesh (1997), 'Back to Bentham? explorations of experienced utility', *Quarterly Journal of Economics*, May, 375–405.

Kaplow, Louis (1996), 'The optimal supply of public goods and the distortionary cost of taxation', *National Tax Journal*, 49 (4), 513–33.

Kaplow, Louis (1998), 'Tax and non-tax distortion', *Journal of Public Economics*, 68, 303–6.

Kappel, Klemens (1997), 'Equality, priority, and time', *Utilitas*, 9, 203–25.

Kapteyn, A. and Wansbeek, T. J. (1985), 'The individual welfare function', *Journal of Economic Psychology*, 6, 333–63.

Karras, Georgios (1996), 'The optimal government size: further international evidence on the productivity of government services', *Economic Inquiry*, 34, 193–203.

Kau, J. B. and Rubin, P. H. (1981), 'The size of government', *Public Choice*, 37 (2), 261–74.

Kekes, John (1997), 'A question for egalitarians', *Ethics*, 107, 658–69.

Kelsey, David (1988), 'Policies to achieve a better distribution of income: or is a dollar a dollar?', *Oxford Economic Papers*, 40, 577–83.

Kemp, Murray C. and Ng, Yew-Kwang (1976), 'On the existence of social welfare functions, social orderings, and social decisions functions', *Economica*, 45, 59–66.

Kenny, Charles (1999), 'Does growth cause happiness, or does happiness cause growth?', *Kyklos*, 52, 3–26.

King, Mervyn A. (1986), 'A Pigovian rule for the optimum provision of public goods', *Journal of Public Economics*, 30, 273–91.

Kline N. S. and Laska, E. (eds) (1968), *Computer and Electronic Devices in Psychiatry* (New York: Grune and Stratton).

Kolm, Serge-Christophe (1993), 'The impossibility of utilitarianism', in P. Koslowski and Y. Shionoya, pp.30–66.

Kolm, Serge-Christophe (1996), *Modern Theories of Justice* (MIT Press).

Kolm, Serge-Christophe (1998), 'Chance and justice: social policies and the Harsanyi–Vickrey–Rawls problem', *European Economic Review*, 42, 1393–416.

Konishi, Hideo (1995), 'A Pareto-improving commodity tax reform under a smooth nonlinear income tax', *Journal of Public Economics*, 56, 413–46.

Koslowski, P. and Shionoya, Y. (eds) (1993), *The Good and the Economical: Ethical Choices in Economics and Management* (Berlin: Springer-Verlag).

Krugman, Paul (1998), 'Two Cheers for Formalism', *Economic Journal*, 108, 1829–36.

Krupitskii, E. M., Burakov, A. M., Karandashova, G. F. and Lebedev, V. B. (1993), 'A method of treating affective disorders in alcoholics', *Journal of Russian and East European Psychiatry*, 26 (3), 26–37.

Laitner, John and Juster, F. T. (1996), 'New evidence on altruism: a study of TIAA–CREF retirees', *American Economic Review*, 86, 893–908.

Le Grand, Julian (1997), 'Knights, knaves or pawns?: human behaviour and social policy', *Journal of Social Policy*, 26, 149–69.

Lee, Woojin and Roemer, John E. (1999), 'Income distribution, redistributive politics, and economic growth', *Journal of Economic Growth*, 3, 217–40.

Leontief, W. (1966), *Essays in Economics: Theories and Theorizing* (New York: Oxford University Press).

Lerner, Abba P. (1944), *The Economics of Control* (New York: Macmillan).

Levitt, M. S. and Joyce, M. A. S. (1987), *The Growth and Efficiency of Public Spending* (Cambridge: Cambridge University Press).

Lewis, H. D. (ed.) (1976), *Contemporary British Philosophy* (London: Allen and Unwin).

Linbeck, Assar, Nyberg, Stern and Weibull, Jörgen W. (1999), 'Social norma and economic incentives in the welfare state', *Quarterly Journal of Economics*, 116, 1–36.

Little, Ian M. D. (1949), 'The foundations of welfare economics', *Oxford Economic Papers*, 1, 227–46.

Little, Ian M. D. (1951), 'Direct versus indirect taxes', *Economic Journal*, 61, 577–84.

Little, Ian M. D. (1952), 'Social Choice and Individual Values', *Journal of Political Economy*, 60, 422–32.

Little, Ian M. D. (1957), *A Critique of Welfare Economics*, 2nd edn (London: Oxford University Press).

Little, Ian M. D. and Mirrlees, James A. (1974), *Profit Appraisal and Planning for Developing Countries* (London: Heinemann).

Livingston, Arthur (ed.) (1935), *Mind and Society*, Vol. 4 (London: Jonathan Cape).

Lockwood, Ben and Manning, Alan (1993), 'Wage setting and the tax system: theory and evidence for the united kingdom values', *Journal of Public Economics*, 52, 1–29.

Loewenstein, George and Elster, Jon (eds) (1992), *Choice Over Time* (New York: Sage).

Lunati, M. Teresa (1997), *Ethical Issues in Economics: From Altruism to Cooperation to Equity* (New York: St. Martin's Press; London: Macmillan Press).

Lybeck, J. A. and Henrekson, M. (1988), *Explaining the Growth of Government* (Amsterdam: North-Holland).

Marmola, Elisabetta (1999), 'A constitutional theory of public goods', *Journal of Economic Behaviour and Organization*, 38, 27–42.

Marr, W. and Raj, B. (eds) (1983), *How Economists Explain – A Reader in Methodology* (Washington: University Press of America).

Marschak, J. (1950), 'Rational behaviour, uncertain prospects and measurable utility', *Econometrica*, 18, 111–141; also 'Errata', 312.

Maskin, Eric (1978), 'A theorem on utilitarianism', *Review of Economic Studies*, 45, 93–6.

Meltzer, A. H. and Richard, Scott F. (1981), 'A rational theory of the size of government', *Journal of Political Economy*, 89, 914–27.

Michael, Mark A. (1997), 'Redistributive taxation, self-ownership and the fruit of labour', *Journal of Applied Philosophy*, 14, 137–46.

Milgrom, Paul (1993), 'Is sympathy an economic value?: philosophy, economics, and the contingent valuation method', in Hausman, pp.417–35.

Mirrlees, James A. (1971), 'An exploration in the theory of optimal income taxation', *Review of Economic Studies*, 38, 174–208.

Mirrlees, James A. (1976), 'Optimal tax theory: a synthesis', *Journal of Public Economics*, 6, 327–58.

Mirrlees, James A. (1981), 'The theory of optimal taxation', in Arrow and Intriligator (1986), pp.1197–1249.

Mirrlees, James A. (1982), 'The economic uses of utilitarianism', in Sen and Williams, pp.63–84.

Mitchell, Robert C, and Carson, Richard T. (1989), 'Using surveys to value public goods: the contingent valuation method', Washington, DC: Resources for the Future (Baltimore: Johns Hopkins University Press).

Mongin, Philippe (1988), 'A comment on J. Harsanyi's "Assessing other people's utilities"', in Munier, (ed.), 139–44.

Mongin, Philippe (1994), 'Harsanyi's aggregation theorem: multi-profile version and unsettled questions', *Social Choice and Welfare*, 11, 331–54.

Monroe, Kristen R. (1996), *The Heart of Altruism* (Princeton University Press).

Mueller, Dennis (1989), *Public Choice II* (Cambridge: Cambridge University Press).

Mueller, Dennis (ed.) (1997), *Perspectives on Public Choice: a Handbook* (Cambridge: Cambridge University Press).

Munier, Bertrand R. (ed.) (1988), *Risk, Decision and Rationality* (Dordrecht: Reidel).

Mulligan, Casey B. (1997), *Parental Priorities and Economic Inequality* (Chicago and London: University of Chicago Press).

Murphy, K., Shleifer, A. and Vishny, R. (1989), 'Income distribution, market size, and industrialization', *Quarterly Journal of Economics*, 537–64.

Myers, David (1996), *Social Psychology* (New York: Macmillan).

Nagel, Stuart S. (ed.) (1998), *Applications of Super-Optimizing Policy Analysis, Research in Public Policy Analysis and Management*, Vol. 8 (Greenwich, Conn. and London: JAI Press).

Nath, S. K. (1969), *A Reappraisal of Welfare Economics* (London: Routledge & Kegan Paul).

Ng, Yew-Kwang (1971), 'The possibility of a Paretian liberal: impossibility theorems and cardinal utility', *Journal of Political Economy*, 79 (6), 1397–402.

Ng, Yew-Kwang (1972), 'Value judgements and economists' role in policy recommendation', *Economic Journal*, Sept., 1014–18; reprinted in Marr and Raj, (1983).

Ng, Yew-Kwang (1975a), 'Bentham or Bergson?: finite sensibility, utility functions and social welfare functions', *Review of Economic Studies*, 42, 545–70.

Ng, Yew-Kwang (1975b), 'Non-economic activities, indirect externalities and third-best policies', *Kyklos*, 28, 507–25; reprinted in Ng (1990b).

Ng, Yew-Kwang (1977), 'Towards a theory of third-best', *Public Finance*, 1–15.

Ng, Yew-Kwang (1979/1983), *Welfare Economics: Introduction and Development of Basic Concepts* (London: Macmillan).

Ng, Yew-Kwang (1980), 'Toward eudaimonology: notes on a quantitative framework for the study of happiness', *Mathematical Social Sciences*, 1, 51–68.

Ng, Yew-Kwang (1981a), 'Welfarism: a defence against Sen's attack', *Economic Journal*, 91, June, 527–30.

Ng, Yew-Kwang (1981b), 'Bentham or Nash?: on the acceptable form of social welfare functions', *Economic Record*, 57 Sept., 238–50; reprinted in Ng (1990b).

Ng, Yew-Kwang (1982), 'Beyond Pareto optimality: the necessity of interpersonal cardinal utilities in distributional judgements and social choice', *Zeitschrift für Nationalökonomie (Journal of Economics)*, 42 (3), 207–33.

Ng, Yew-Kwang (1983), 'Some broader issues of social choice', in P. K. Pattanaik and M. Salles, pp.151–73.

Ng, Yew-Kwang (1984a), 'Expected subjective utility: is the Neumann–Morgenstern utility the same as the neoclassical's?', *Social Choice and Welfare*, 177–86; reprinted in Ng (1990b).

Ng, Yew-Kwang (1984b), 'Quasi-Pareto social improvements', *American Economic Review*, Dec., 74 (5), 1033–50; reprinted in Ng (1990b).

Ng, Yew-Kwang (1985), 'Some fundamental issues in social welfare', in Feiwel, pp.435–69; reprinted in Ng (1990b).

Ng, Yew-Kwang (1987a), 'Diamonds are a government's best friend: burden-free taxes on goods valued for their values', *American Economic Review*, 77, 186–91.

Ng, Yew-Kwang (1987b), 'Relative-income effects and the appropriate level of public expenditure', *Oxford Economic Papers*, 293–300.

Ng, Yew-Kwang (1988), 'Economic efficiency versus egalitarian rights', *Kyklos*, 215–37.

Ng, Yew-Kwang (1989a), 'What should we do about future generations?: the impossibility of Parfit's Theory X', *Economics and Philosophy*, 5, 135–253.

Ng, Yew-Kwang (1989b), 'Individual irrationality and social welfare', *Social Choice and Welfare*, 6, 87–101.

Ng, Yew-Kwang (1990a), 'Welfarism and utilitarianism: a rehabilitation', *Utilitas*, 2 (2), 171–93.

Ng, Yew-Kwang (1990b), *Social Welfare and Economic Policy* (Hemel Hempstead, Hertfordshire: Harvester Wheatsheaf).

Ng, Yew-Kwang (1992a), 'Do individuals optimize in intertemporal consumption/saving decisions?: a liberal method to encourage savings', *Journal of Economic Behaviour and Organization*, 17, 101–14.

Ng, Yew-Kwang (1992b), 'Utilitarianism and interpersonal comparison: some implications of a materialist solution to the world knot', *Social Choice and Welfare*, 9 (1), 1–15.

Ng, Yew-Kwang (1993), 'Mixed diamond goods and anomalies in consumer theory: upward-sloping compensated demand curves with unchanged diamondness', *Mathematical Social Sciences*, 25, 287–93.

Ng, Yew-Kwang (1995), 'Towards welfare biology: evolutionary economics of animal consciousness and suffering', *Biology and Philosophy*, 10 (3), 255–85.

Ng, Yew-Kwang (1996a), 'Happiness surveys: some comparability issues and an exploratory survey based on just perceivable increments', *Social Indicators Research*, 38 (1), 1–29.

Ng, Yew-Kwang (1996b), 'Complex niches favour rational species', *Journal of Theoretical Biology*, 179, 303–11.

Ng, Yew-Kwang (1997), 'A case for happiness, cardinal utility, and interpersonal comparability', *Economic Journal*, 107 (445), 1848–58.

Ng, Yew-Kwang (1999), 'Utility, informed preference, or happiness?', *Social Choice and Welfare*, 16 (2), 197–216.

Ng, Yew-Kwang (forthcoming a), 'From separability to unweighted sum: a case for utilitarianism', *Theory and Decision*.

Ng, Yew-Kwang (forthcoming b), 'The optimal size of public spending and the distortionary cost of taxation', revision under consideration by *National Tax Journal*.

Ng, Yew-Kwang and Wang, Jianguo (1993), 'Relative income, aspiration, environmental quality, individual and political myopia: why may the rat-race for material growth be welfare-reducing?', *Mathematical Social Sciences*, 26, 3–23.

Nielsen, Kai (1985), *Equality and Liberty: a Defence of Radical Egalitarianism* (Totowa, NJ: Rowman & Allanheld).

Nozick, Robert (1974), *Anarchy, State, and Utopia* (New York: Basic Books).

Okun, Arthur M. (1975), *Equality and Efficiency: The Big Tradeoff* (Washington: Brookings Institution).

Olds, J. and Milner, P. (1954), 'Positive reinforcement produced by electrical stimulation of septal area and other regions of the rat brain', *Journal of Comparative Physiological Psychology*, 47, 419–27.

Osborne, D. K. (1976), 'Irrelevant alternatives and social welfare', *Econometrica*, 44, 1001–15.

Oswald, Andrew J. (1997), 'Happiness and economic performance', *Economic Journal*, 107, 1815–31.

Pareto, V. (1935), *The Mind and Society*, trans. Livingston (London: Cape).

Parks, Robert P. (1976), 'An Impossibility theorem for fixed preferences: a dictatorial Bergson–Samuelson welfare function', *Review of Economic Studies*, 43, 447–50.

Pattanaik, Prasanta K. (1971), *Voting and Collective Choice* (Cambridge: Cambridge University Press).

Pattanaik, Prasanta K. and Salles, Maurice (eds) (1983), *Social Choice and Welfare* (Amsterdam: North-Holland).

Patterson, M. M. and Kesner, R. P. (1981), *Electrical Stimulation Research Techniques* (New York: Academic Press).

Patterson, M., Krupitsky, E., Flood, N. and Baker, D. (1994), 'Amelioration of stress in chemical dependency detoxification by transcranial electrostimulation', *Stress Medicine*, Apr., 10 (2), 115–26.

Payne, J. E. and Ewing, B. T. (1996), 'International evidence on Wagner's hypothesis: a cointegration analysis', *Public Finance*, 51 (2), 258–74.

Peltzman, S. (1980), 'The growth of government', *Journal of Law and Economics*, 23, 209–87.

Pencavel, John (1986), 'Labor supply of man: a survey', in Ashenfelter and Layard pp.3–102.

Perotti, Roberto (1996), 'Growth, income distribution, and democracy: what the data say', *Journal of Economics Growth*, 1, 149–87.

Persson, Torsten and Tabellini, Guido (1994), 'Is inequality harmful for growth?', *American Economic Review*, 84, 600–21.

Phelps, Edmund S. and Zoega, Gylfi (1998), 'Natural-rate theory and OECD unemployment', *Economic Journal*, 108, May, 782–801.

Pigou, Arthur C. (1912/1929/1932), *Wealth and Welfare*. Later editions (1920, 1924, 1929, 1932) assume the title *The Economics of Welfare* (London: Macmillan).

Pigou, Arthur C. (1928), *Public Finance* (London: Macmillan).

Pojman, Louis P. and Westmoreland, Robert, (eds) (1997), *Equality: Selected Readings* (Oxford: Oxford University Press).

Pollak, Robert A. (1979), 'Bergson–Samuelson social welfare functions and the theory of social choice', *Quarterly Journal of Economics*, 93, 73–90.

Portney, Paul R. (1990), 'Economics and the Clean Air Act', *Journal of Economic Perspectives*, 4 (4), 173–81.

Posner, Richard (1981), *The Economics of Justice* (Cambridge, MA: Harvard University Press).

Putterman, Louis, Roemer, John E. and Silvestre, Joaquim (1998). 'Does egalitarianism have a future?', *Journal of Economic Literature*, 36, 861–902.

Qizilbash, Mazaffar (1998), 'The concept of well-being', *Economics and Philosophy*, 14, 51–73.

Radford, C. (1988), 'Utilitarianism and the noble art', *Philosophy*, ixiii, 63–81.

Rae, John (1834), *New Principles of Political Economy*, reprinted as *The Sociological Theory of Capital*, edited by Charles W. Mixter (1990), (New York: Macmillan).

Ramsey, F. P. (1928), 'A mathematical theory of saving', *Economic Journal*, 38, 543–59; reprinted in Arrow and Scitovsky (1969).

Rawls, John (1971), *A Theory of Justice* (Cambridge, MA: Harvard University Press).

Rawls, John (1982), 'Social unity and primary goods', in Sen and Williams, pp.159–85.

Robbins, Lionel (1938), 'Interpersonal Comparison of Utility: a Comment', *Economic Journal*, 48, 635–41.

Roberts, Kevin W. S. (1980), 'Social choice theory: the single-profile and multi-profile approaches', *Review of Economic Studies*, 47, 441–50.

Rodrik, Dani (1998), 'Why do more open economies have bigger governments?', *Journal of Political Economy*, 106, 997–1032.

Roemer, John E. (1986), 'Equality of resources implies equality of welfare', *Quarterly Journal of Economics*, 101, 751–84.

Roemer, John E. (1996), *Theories of Distributive Justice* (Cambridge, MA: Harvard University Press).

Roemer, John E. (1998), *Equality of Opportunity* (Cambridge, MA and London: Harvard University Press).

Rose-Ackerman, Susan (1996), 'Altruism, nonprofits, and economic theory', *Journal of Economic Literature*, 34, 701–28.

Ryan, Richard M., Chirkov, Valery I., Little, Todd D., Sheldon, Kennon M., Timoshina, Elena and Deci, Edward L. (forthcoming), 'The American dream in Russia: aspirations and well-being in two cultures', *Personality and Social Psychology Bulletin*.

Samuelson, Paul A. (1967), 'Arrow's mathematical politics', in S. Hook.

Samuelson, Paul A. (1977), 'Reaffirming the existence of reasonable Bergson–Samuelson social welfare functions', *Economica*, 44, 81–8.

Sandmo, Agnar (1976), 'Optimal taxation: an introduction to the literature', *Journal of Public Economics*, 6, 37–54.

Saunders, Peter (1993), 'Recent trends in the size and growth of government in OECD countries', in Gemmell.

Schmid, G. (1993), 'Equality and efficiency in the labor market', *Journal of Socio-Economics*, 22, 31–67.

Schyns, Peggy (1998), 'Crossnational differences in happiness', *Social Indicators Research*, 43, 3–26.

Sen, Amartya K. (1967), 'The nature and classes of prescriptive judgments', *Philosophical Quarterly*, 17, 46–62.

Sen, Amartya K. (1969), 'Quasi-transitivity, rational choice, and collective decisions', *Review of Economic Studies*, 36, 381–93.

Sen, Amartya K. (1970a), *Collective Choice and Social Welfare* (Amsterdam: North-Holland).

Sen, Amartya K. (1970b), 'The impossibility of a Paretian liberal', *Journal of Political Economy*, 78, 152–7.

Sen, Amartya K. (1973a), *On Economic Inequality* (Oxford: Clarendon).

Sen, Amartya K. (1973b), 'On ignorance and equal distribution', *American Economic Review*, 63, Dec., 1022–4; reprinted in Sen (1982).

Sen, Amartya K. (1979), 'Personal utilities and public judgments: Or what's wrong with welfare economics?', *Economic Journal*, 89, 537–58; reprinted in Sen (1982).

Sen, Amartya K. (1981), 'A reply to "Welfarism: a defence against Sen's attack"', *Economic Journal*, 89, 537–58; reprinted in Sen (1982).

Sen, Amartya K. (1982), *Choice, Welfare and Measurement* (Oxford: Basil Blackwell).

Sen, Amartya K. (1985), *Commodities and Capabilities* (Amsterdam: North-Holland).

Sen, Amartya K. (1986), 'Social choice theory', in Arrow and Intriligator, pp.1073–181.

Sen, Amartya K. (1992), *Inequality Reexamined* (Oxford: Clarendon).

Sen, Amartya K. (1997), 'Quality of life and economic evaluation', *Academia Economic Papers*, 25, 269–316.

Sen, A. and Williams, B. (eds) (1982), *Utilitarianism and Beyond* (Cambridge: Cambridge University Press).

Skolnik, M. L. (1970), 'A comment on Professor Musgrave's separation of distribution from allocation', *Journal of Economic Literature*, June, 8, 440–2.

Slemrod, Joel and Yitzhaki, Shlomo (1996), 'The costs of taxation and the marginal cost of funds', *International Monetary Fund Staff Papers*, 43 (1), 172–98.

Smart, J. J. C. and Williams, B. A. O. (1973), *Utilitariansim: For and Against*, (Cambridge: Cambridge University Press).

Snow, Arthur and Warren, Ronald S. Jr. (1996), 'The marginal welfare cost of public funds: Theory and estimates', *Journal of Public Economics*, 61 (2), 289–305.

Stiglitz, Joseph J. (1988), *Economics of the Public Sector* (New York: Norton).

Stiglitz, Joseph J. (1999), 'Public policy for a knowledge economy', reported in *The Age*, 27 Mar. 1999.

Strack, Fritz, Argyle, Michael and Schwarz, Norbert (eds) (1991), *Subjective Well-Being: An Interdisciplinary Perspective* (Oxford: Pergamon Press).

Strauss, John and Thomas, Duncan. (1995), 'Human resources: Empirical modeling of household and family decisions', in Behrman and Srinivasan pp.1883–2023.

Stuart, Charles (1984), 'Welfare cost per dollar of additional tax revenue in the United States', *American Economic Review*, 74 (3), 352–62.

Sugden, Robert and Weale, Albert (1979), 'A contractual reformulation of certain aspects of welfare economics', *Economica*, 46, 111–23.

Summers, R. and Heston, A. (1991), 'Penn World Table (Mark 5): an expanded set of international comparisons, 1950–1988', *Quarterly Journal of Economics*, 106, 327–68.

Sumner, L. W. (1996), *Welfare, Happiness, and Ethics* (Oxford: Clarendon Press; New York: Oxford University Press).

Suzumura, Kotaro (1997), 'Partial welfare judgements as preliminaries for rational social choice', Institute for Social and Economic Research Working Paper, Osaka University.

Suzumura, Kotaro (1999), 'Consequences, opportunities, and procedures', *Social Choice and Welfare*, 16 (1), 17–40.

Temkin, L. S. (1987), 'Intransitivity and the mere addition paradox', *Philosophy and Public Affairs*, 16 (2), pp.138–87.

Trivers, R. L. (1971), 'The evolution of reciprocal altruism', *Quarterly Review of Biology*, 46, 35–57.

Turnbull, Geoffrey K. and Chang, Chinkun (1998), 'The median voter according to GARP', *Southern Economic Journal*, 64, 1001–10.

Valenstein, E. S. (ed.) (1973), *Brain Stimulation and Motivation* (Glenview, Illinois: Scott, Foresman).

van Praag, Bernard M. S. (1968), *Individual Welfare Functions and Consumer Behaviour* (Amsterdam: North Holland).

van Praag, Bernard M. S. (1991), 'Ordinal and cardinal utility: an integration of the two dimensions of the welfare concept', *Journal of Econometrics*, 50, 69–89.

Varian, Hal R. (1993), *Intermediate Microeconomics: A Modern Approach* (New York: Norton).

Veblen, Thorstein (1929), *The Theory of the Leisure Class,* reprinted in 1970, by (London: Unwin).

Veenhoven, Ruut (1984), *Conditions of Happiness* (Dordrecht: Kluwer Academic).

Veenhoven, Ruut (1993), *Happiness in Nations: Subjective Appreciation of Life in 56 Nations 1946–1992* (Rotterdam: RISBO).

Watson, R. (1977), 'Reason and Morality in a World of Limited Food', in Aiken and LaFollette, pp.115–23.

Wauquier, A. and Rolls, E. T. (eds) (1976), *Brain-Stimulation Reward* (Amsterdam: North-Holland).

Weintraub, E. Roy (1998), 'Controversy: Axiomatisches Mißverständnis', *Economic Journal*, 108, 1837–47.

West, Edwin G. (1991), 'Secular cost changes and the size of government', *Journal of Public Economics*, 45, 363–81.

Weymark, J. A. (1991), 'A reconsideration of the Harsanyi–Sen debate on utilitarianism', in Elster and Roemer, pp.255–320.

Wicksteed, Philip H. (1933), *The Common Sense of Political Economy*, edited by Lionel Robbins (London: Routledge).

Wilkinson, Richard G. (1997), 'Health inequalities: relative or absolute material standards?' *British Medical Journal*, 314, 22 Feb., 591–5.

Wilson, E. O. (1975), *Sociobiology: the New Synthesis* (Cambridge, MA: Harvard University Press).

Wilson, John D. (1991), 'Optimal public good provision with limited lump-sum taxation', *American Economic Review*, 81 (1), 153–66.

Winer, Stanley L. and Hettich, Walter (1998), 'What is missed if we leave out collective choice in the analysis of taxation?', *National Tax Journal*, 51 (2), 373–89.

Winkelmann, Liliana and Winkelmann, Rainer (1998), 'Why are the unemployed so unhappy?', *Economica*, 65, 1–15.

Yadin, E. and Thomas, E. (1996), 'Stimulation of the lateral septum attenuates immobilisation-induced stress ulcers', *Physiology and Behavior*, 59, 883–6.

Zamagni, Stefano (ed.) (1995), *The Economics of Altruism* (Aldershot, Brookfield, Vt, USA: Edward Elgar).

Name Index

Subject Index